The Real AA

Behind the Myth of 12-Step Recovery

by

Ken Ragge

See Sharp Press ◆ Tucson, Arizona ◆ 1998

Ragge, Ken.
    The Real AA : behind the myth of 12-step recovery / Ken Ragge. --
Tucson, AZ : See Sharp Press, 1998.
    256 p. ; 23 cm.
    Includes bibliographical references and Index.
    ISBN 1-884365-14-0

    1. Alcoholics Anonymous. 2. Alcoholics - Rehabilitation.
3. Alcoholism - Treatment. 4. Twelve-step programs. 5. Oxford Group. I.
Title.
                        362.29286

Cover design by Clifford Harper, interior design by Chaz Bufe. Printed on acid-
free paper with soy-based ink by Thomson-Shore, Inc., Dexter, Michigan.

In memory of Al Clem and Carlos Grado,
true friends

Contents

Introduction

[Stanton Peele has worked for decades to bring sanity to America's addiction treatment system, and is almost certainly this country's best known and most articulate critic of the disease theory of alcoholism. He has tirelessly advocated treatment based on scientific research (letting research findings determine treatment) rather than, as at present, treatment based on religious ideology (letting ideology determine treatment, scientific evidence be damned). In addition to being a Ph.D. and attorney, he is also a best-selling author. His works include Love and Addiction, Diseasing of America, *and (with Archie Brodsky)* The Truth About Addiction and Recovery.*]*

Ken Ragge has produced a remarkable document in *The Real AA*. At a time when AA and its 12-Step philosophy are a national religion, Ken has the guts, the knowledge, and the insight to show the dark side of this moon.

He does so in a low-key, but interesting and well-reasoned way. Starting with the heretofore unacknowledged synthesis of AA with the evangelical Protestant Oxford Group Movement (for years after the 1935 date officially given for Bob Smith and Bill Wilson's founding of AA, it was still an Oxford Group chapter), Ken details AA's religious genesis and nature. This analysis alone would qualify *The Real AA* as a major contribution to the field of alcoholism.

But Ken does more, much more. He analyzes the role of avoidance and plain old obtuseness in the lives of alcoholics, who generally mask through drinking unpleasant feelings that others face and cope with. He shows how the structure and beliefs of AA serve to provide an alternative focus and explanation for alcoholics' lives, given their continuing inability—supported by AA—to come to grips with what is truly on their minds (or in their subconscious).

Ken has a unique style. He gives detailed descriptions of research studies that reveal that AA's claims are hogwash (for example, the famous study by Marlatt et al. showing that alcoholics who drink disguised amounts of alcohol drink less than those who think they are drinking alcohol but are not). He spends equal time detailing the psychological backdrop to alcoholism and the case histories of alcoholics (some, like Bob Smith and Bill Wilson, central figures in the field).

On top of this, Ken gives an intimate portrait of the AA meeting and its philosophy (as embodied in its 12 Steps), and of how this process is actually enacted within the working AA group. Ken gives as good an exegesis as we are likely to see of the way AA groups and their senior members direct and indoctrinate new members (that is, the mere 5 to 10% who continue to attend) into a strange self-abnegation and sense of guilt and powerlessness built on the promise that eventually they too can reign supreme over newer AA members! AA is a power trip for the psychologically debilitated, as Ken makes exceedingly clear.

In this book, Ken supports many of the contentions from David Rudy's anthropological study of AA entitled, *Becoming Alcoholic* (just as Ken gives a ground's eye view of Jay Hull's "Self-Awareness Model," by which alcoholics welcome alcohol's consciousness-obliterating effect). I might add that Ken also follows many of my own arguments in *Diseasing of America*.

But Ken has a gut feeling for these research findings that can only be hard-earned through direct experience. He has seen and lived through things that others of us only write about.

In doing so, Ken answers the critical question about AA. Given its limited success, why do AAers love it so well? Like the addicted lover who clings to a destructive mate (and Ken analyzes the range of addictions in this book), the AA member who eventually succeeds in quitting drinking often accepts the devil's bargain of giving up the core part of him or herself.

Consider that Bill Wilson entered an extended depression lasting more than a decade following his formation of AA, while he and others argued that AA was the path to emotional purity and contentment. (Other early AA members simply drank themselves to death, some while serving as effective spokespeople for the group.)

Or take Ken's chapter on Kitty Dukakis, who entered addiction treatment first for taking one diet pill daily, only to embark on an extended depression followed by a brief interlude of intense alcoholism. Ken details the countless futile 12-step treatments Kitty endured which first convinced her (with near-fatal results) that she was a lifelong alcoholic (even though she had only recently acquired a drinking problem), and which then convinced her that she was a manic-depressive requiring around-the-clock medication. And to think, Kitty once thought that taking a single diet pill daily for 26 years was a big problem!

But, Kitty, like Bill W., was not deterred from spreading the gospel of AA. Like so many other tortured souls (the parallel with Heaven's Gate is inevitable), the AAer responds to internal torment and self-doubt with renewed enthusiasm and efforts to convert the uninitiated.

At the same time, Ken shows how researcher/academics like Harvard psychiatrist George Vaillant respond to their own data showing that AA treatment is useless or worse by committing large parts of their clinical and academic work to expounding the AA philosophy—as though by simply showing that they accept AA and that AA accepts them, they have made some unique contribution to the alcoholism field!

The result of this "scientific" and clinical madness is an America (and next the world) gone mad, where—as more and more people embrace helplessness and a pervasive loss of control—more and more join AA or other 12-Step groups.

The result is not an empowered, self-controlled America (which would be explicitly against AA's philosophy). The result is an America preoccupied in a confused way with its depressed emotions and addicted actions, seeking vainly for explanations in the wrong places (God and genes) for a destructive way of life that AA does not remedy, but rather exacerbates and embodies.

—Stanton Peele

REFERENCES

Hull, J. 1987. Self-awareness model. In: Blane, H.T., and Leonard, K.E. (eds.). *Psychological Theories of Drinking and Alcoholism* (pp. 272-304). New York: Guilford.

Marlatt, G.A.; Demming, B.; and Reid, J.B. 1973. Loss of control drinking in alcoholics: An experimental analogue. *Journal of Abnormal Psychology* 81:223-241.

Peele, S. 1995. *Diseasing of America* (2nd ed.; 1st ed., 1989). New York: Free Press.

Rudy, D. 1986. *Becoming Alcoholic: Alcoholics Anonymous and the Reality of Alcoholism.* Carbondale, IL: Southern Illinois University.

Foreword

[Jack Trimpey is the founder and president of Rational Recovery (RR), the largest and most well known of the "alternative" self-help approaches to alcohol abuse. Jack has been one of the most insightful and acerbic critics of AA for over a decade now. RR, virtually alone among the "alternative" groups and approaches, has had the courage to consistently expose the damage done to individuals and society by 12 steppism, has consistently exposed the dishonesty and hypocrisy of many 12-step advocates, and is actively seeking legal redress for those coerced into 12-step "treatment." For more information, contact RR at the address listed in Appendix B.]

I am honored to welcome you to a wonderful book, *The Real AA*. I first read this book under the title *More Revealed* in 1991, during a time when my wife, Lois, and I were building the foundation for Rational Recovery. I was delighted, as I think you will be, to read the first book identifying Alcoholics Anonymous as a wolf in sheep's clothing. In fact, the past editions of *More Revealed* sported a cartoon on the cover, showing Sherlock Holmes yanking the sheep costume off a very surprised and disgruntled wolf.

I knew immediately, judging the book by its cover, that Ken Ragge was a kindred spirit, one of millions of people who, like myself, had experienced the recovery cult first hand. But when I read the pages inside, I knew that I was reading a very important book, one that would eventually help change America's perception of its most revered social institution, AA.

Unable to find a publisher insightful enough, or a bookseller brave enough, Ragge self-published his book, and ended up giving away copies for free. He was portrayed as a radical, an angry man, and he absorbed invective usually reserved for public enemies. But now he has linked up with See Sharp Press, a publisher that has played a vital role in exposing the American addiction tragedy (the recovery group movement). *More Revealed* was a book before its time, for not enough had happened by then to alert the public that something *terrible* has happened to America on its way to a better future.

While societies historically have applied common sense to the eternal enigma of substance abuse, America has embraced a radically different approach, the *disease* concept of addiction, and now boasts the greatest crisis of mass addiction in human history. Few were ready, when this book was first published, to think that by accepting the disease model of addiction, and accepting AA's recovery group concept as *the* standard approach to deterring addiction, America had taken one of the worst turns in its history. But a lot has happened in the last five or six years, and it appears the timing for this See Sharp Press publication of *The Real AA* is perfect.

Together, the War on Drugs, and its flip side, the 12-step addiction treatment industry, have threatened to transform America from the land of the free into a therapeutic state. Ragge was among the first to understand the grave threat to American freedoms posed by the recovery group movement. He does not dance around the academic question of whether or not AA is a cult; he simply credits you with the native intuition to see that it is one, and through the eyes of a former insider, he illustrates "how it works," to use a 12-step insider cult-expression.

I have met Ken Ragge and corresponded with him extensively. He is a gentle, bright man, most unlike the his opponents' depictions, and he very clearly loves America. He is afraid of what's in store for us if we do not wake up and put down the insanity that has overtaken common sense in our public institutions. Every age has its own visionaries, the ones whose eyes adjust to the darkness so that they can see what others do not. Many remain silent, fearing ridicule and reprisal, but some, like Ken Ragge, stand up and shout out loud about what they see, so that everyone can hear. Every society owes a debt to its self-appointed sentinels who see danger and reflexively attack wolves in sheep's clothing. Ken Ragge's *The Real AA* is a pivotal work, and already has brought the beginning of change.

The Real AA is an exposé which will stir many people to raise their voices and use their precious freedom of speech, people who have suspected that something is wrong in the addictions field, but could not quite identify what that something is. I think that Ken Ragge correctly sees a gathering storm which will shake America to the core (and we hope back to her senses). The Weimar Republic of pre-Nazi Germany was a society, which, seeing only the friendly side of tyranny, embraced a beastly mentality that brought national and world catastrophe. Ominous parallels exist which suggest a new "AAmerica" emerging from the recovery group movement, one nation under God-as-you-understand-Him, with serenity and treatment for all. (To help prevent this, we've formed the Rational Recovery Political and Legal Action Network [RR-PLAN], a small group of activists who challenge the involvement of AA in state and local governments.) Change will come only when people raise their voices and use their precious freedom of speech.

Perhaps it is my duty here to prepare you for what you will shortly read by stating my opinion that AA is the most insidious and pernicious cult in world history. If this seems overstated, then let me tell you why I believe this is so.

Over the years, Rational Recovery has received tens of thousands of calls from people who have not been helped, and in fact have been harmed, abused, or discriminated against by the recovery group movement and its business arm, the addiction treatment industry. We hear from people fleeing from AA thugs, i.e., "interventionists," intent on apprehending and incarcerating people in treatment centers (for their own good, of course) for no other reason than that they drink too much. We hear from others inside 12-step gulags (treatment centers where residents are browbeaten into submission to AA while cut off from contact with the outside world, all reading material removed from their possession except for a copy of "The Big Book," aka *Alcoholics Anonymous*). Some of them learned about RR from housekeeping staff or from counselors in back rooms who secretly (to save their jobs) gave them the RR number. One woman got the RR number from tiny graffiti in the lavatory, exactly in the fashion described in Margaret Atwood's *The Handmaid's Tale*. Another woman in an Arizona prison for drunk driving (she had injured no one) was denied early release solely because she refused to attend AA, and she served an additional year behind bars because of her refusal. Recently, a man writing under the pseudonym, "Dr. X-Ray," in *The Journal of Rational Recovery*, revealed that he would have been denied a liver transplant if he hadn't agreed to participate extensively in AA. Facing death, he complied with AA's humble program of coercion.

But by far the most frequent calls we receive are from the walking wounded, the ones who could not accept the 12-step program after many meetings, treatment centers, and much sincere effort, but who could not yet discern that they were "unsuccessful" simply because they were still in their right minds. They now suffer from new problems, however (problems in addition to their original drinking or drugging problems). They are very often depressed, feeling like failures, their self-confidence seriously undermined by the bludgeon of "denial" accusations that pathologize the questioning attitude and that create reflexive distrust of one's own thought processes. They come to believe that there is something fundamentally wrong with themselves, and that they are somehow "marked" to continue drinking or using and eventually to self-destruct. They drink or use more than they did before AA/the treatment industry, and they drink or use more unpredictably and more self-destructively. They mistrust the good, believing that if they momentarily feel well, they are only dry drunks incapable of true happiness, or just on a "pink cloud" of undeserved comfort. They feel like walking time bombs, waiting to inexplicably explode into a frenzy of drunkenness and self-destruction. Tragically, they are *grateful* to their captors, unable to turn on their tormentors and say, "It is all of you, and not I, who are crazy." They are afraid—afraid of themselves, afraid to think, afraid they will "slip," and afraid of AA. They say, "Now, don't get me wrong. I don't want to say anything bad about AA, but I haven't gotten much out of it." Even after a decade of meetings, depressed and "relapsing" all the while, they insist, "It's really a good program. It's just me. AA has helped more people than any other program, uh, ever." Asked to name one such person, most cannot, and if they do, we simply ask, "Are you sure that is a good example of being helped?" And for the first time, some people laugh. If they laugh deeply, it could mark the beginning of their recovery. Indeed, one of the most common comments made by callers to RR is, "This means I'm not crazy!"

When Lois and I began hearing these same stories over and over around 1988, we identified a syndrome—a common picture with a common thread tying all the stories together—and we called it the *recovery group disorder;* later we added the term *addiction treatment disorder* to differentiate the setting in which the offending indoctrination occurred.

Services called "addiction treatment" are invariably designed for other unrelated conditions, and rarely result in the end of an addiction. Addiction treatment was created by rivers of federal cash released by politicians who know nothing of addiction and by members of AA in public positions. One nonprofit organization, AA, has spawned a great school of little fish, the thousands of nonprofit organizations that swim in the river of cash. Each little nonprofit is a spinoff of AA, each part of a complex web of prevention, treatment, "education," networking, public relations, and lobbying functions that comprise the infrastructure of the addiction treatment industry, which, of course, extends into the nation's hospitals, places of employment, traffic courts, civil courts, drug courts, and swelling prisons.

The recovery group movement is the greatest religious movement in American history, considering the number of people involved, the money expended, and its impact on public affairs. AA has become a "cultocracy" whose more charming members have gained elected office, as in the case of former Texas Governor, Ann Richards, and who have built huge AA empires. They have gained employment in public institutions, including your own state Department of Drug and Alcohol Programs, and your own county alcohol and drug services agencies, which are virtually all AA-based and administered by members of AA. Recovery group movement members are loyal to AA first, and other loyalties come second. Today, AA has 80,000 community cell-groups and 1.2 million active members in the U.S. and Canada, and its step-creed is the main ingredient in virtually all of the nation's 18,000 or so treatment centers. Thousands of treatment units in prisons have AA as the central ingredient, and new "treatment on demand" (whose demand?) facilities are being built at a rapid pace. One must wonder how such an enormous government complex has come to be, considering the obvious religiosity of its catalyst, the 12-step program.

We know that Bill W., a stockbroker who was incapable of staying sober without acting like a missionary, has been exalted by his following and held up as an ideal to the world. But there were two physicians involved in early AA, Drs. Bob Smith and Wm. Silkworth. From its beginning, AA's success has depended upon the *medicalization* of substance addictions, even if the treatment amounts proponent, Enoch Gordis, M.D., Director of the National Institute for Alcohol Abuse and Alcoholism, has admitted, "The treatment field is based on a hunch. There is no science in the treatment industry." But later, Dr. Gordis cited studies his agency funded as evidence that "Treatment works!"—a drumbeat motto of the recovery group movement. How did the highest executive in the alcoholism movement conclude this? By citing a $27 million study, Project MATCH, which had no measure of "no-treatment," and only compared AA with pop psychology methods, showing no significant difference between them. Then, he cited the notorious CALDATA study (some call it the "cooked data" study) which measured the success of addiction treatment by crimes that didn't happen, fewer emergency room calls, program compliance, and other soft measures of social benefit—not individual abstinent outcome.

Politicians and bureaucrats now pitch treatment with, "Every dollar spent on addiction treatment saves the taxpayer seven dollars!" Goodness, we all ought to be rich by now, and the streets safe as a nursery. Although treatment clearly doesn't work, hucksterism does, but only as long as it is uncontested. At a recent public meeting, a representative of RR-PLAN challenged a spokesman for the California Department of Drug and Alcohol Programs on CALDATA's lack of abstinent outcome data. The AA-bureaucrat impatiently answered, "Abstinence just isn't going to happen! We know that addiction is a chronic, lifelong disease, and they will never really quit using." This, of course, amounts to a death sentence for addicted Californians, but as long as the dying go to meetings and work a good Program, "Treatment works!"

AA has gained awesome power from the medical profession, allowing it to leap, as if on steroids, over the U.S. Constitution's wall of separation between church and state, and land on its feet as our *de facto* state religion. Here is how it works. Suppose you are a doctor and you either steal some morphine from the formulary or show up drunk in the operating room. A nurse will report you, but not to the medical licensing board, who really ought to know, or to the police, who arrest people behaving dangerously or criminally, but to a hospital diversion committee. That committee may then report you, not to the medical licensing board or to the police, but to a state diversion committee. Both committees will offer you a draconian contract that requires you, not to abstain from alcohol or drugs, but hospital diversion committee. That committee may then report you, not to the medical licensing board or to the police, but to a state diversion committee. Both committees will offer you a draconian contract that requires you, not to abstain from alcohol or drugs, but to enter an addiction treatment program immediately, report all "relapses," i.e., drinking or using to the committee, and be monitored through the spiritual fellowship of AA for at least several years. Guess who sits on the diversion committees? Good guess; all of them (except for a few token "normies") will be grateful/zealous members of AA, grateful that they were not reported years ago to the licensing board or to the police for similar misbehavior, and grateful that they are still in practice. If you object to the 12-step program in any way or object to their demand that you attend numerous AA meetings after your lengthy treatment, you will cease to be a physician.

The medical profession is at the top of the professional pecking order, so that today there is no alternative to AA for impaired professionals in any state. By active, explicit discrimination, the only professionals who survive the crisis of addiction-related job impairment are the ones who become active, grateful members of Alcoholics Anonymous. Having had a spiritual awakening—and a very important political rehabilitation—these missionaries take their newfound message of disease victimhood to others in their practices, to their colleagues, and to others in the professional community. One physician's assistant from a Western state said that when he challenged the 12-stepping diversion committee with his belief that he is securely and permanently abstinent, the committee replied that abstinence is not the goal of the committee—it is the *surrender of control* they are interested in. Of course, anyone who suggests that you surrender control *wants control.*

No doctor who wishes peace of mind can openly challenge the fraud of addiction treatment. For example, former Surgeon General, C. Everett Koop, M.D., insists that addiction is a disease, despite there being no evidence for this claim. He strongly recommends addiction treatment, in spite of the fact that no specific treatment for the hypothetical diseases, alcoholism and addiction, has ever been identified. Dr. Koop knows that the abstinence outcome of addiction treatment is still unchanged from about 5% during the 1950s, which was an educated guess of AA's success rate by Bill Wilson himself. But the medical and counseling professions have gone too far into the woods, have supervised their own malpractice for too long, and they will not find the way out of the ethical catastrophe of addiction treatment until common people declare Emperor-AA naked.

The nature of the problem may be political, but the real reason AA has emerged in control is that the step program is a highly sophisticated cult indoctrination program that specifically targets vulnerable, *disabled* people—not disabled in the ordinary sense, but disabled by hopelessness, toxicity, and despair. Desperate newcomers to the recovery group movement are in the grip of pleasure and don't know how to get loose. The world is usually coming down on them, bad things are happening, and they are extremely vulnerable to suggestion and exploitation; any solution to what appears to be a hopeless situation appears worth trying. They are in no position to argue much of anything, because they have struck out any number of times—hence their search for help.

Clearly, every single person who has looked at the 12-step program the first time has noticed its apparent religiosity. So, when they are told, "Oh, it's not religious, silly; it's just spiritual," most people give in. They surrender their own judgment in favor of the group's. It is a betrayal of self, but just a little betrayal, to go with the flow and see where we go. This is actually the "first step," which prepares groupers for acceptance of progressively more bizarre self-betrayals, until finally they snap and give up trying to think altogether. By then they are convinced that they have a disease and that God performs miracles on demand for none other than Alcoholics Anonymous. A few stop drinking, tentatively, but most leave, seriously disoriented in their thinking about substance abuse and about themselves. They now carry the curse of AA, i.e., the prediction that they will fail to remain sober, and fail in conducting independent lives. The 12-step program of AA, I believe, is by far the most significant cause of mass addiction in America. Spreading the seeds of addiction before itself, AA claims it is the solution to an ever growing menace to society.

The Real AA contains excellent passages showing the anti-family nature of AA, not only with the disease concept as a wedge between family members, but with attention to the "codependency" ruse, which shifts responsibility for addiction onto others and draws them into expensive and damaging treatment experiences. Groupers (as steppers) have extraordinary confidence that their program is meant for everyone, and that the end, which is surrender of personal autonomy to AA, justifies any means.

When I first read *The Real AA* (then *More Revealed*) six years ago, I was surprised at Ragge's assertions that AA makes a distinct claim to be superior to Christianity or any other organized religion, but history has shown him right. Folklore has it that the Steps were transmitted from God to Bill Wilson via automatic handwriting during a spiritualist, channeling-type trance. This would make him at least a prophet of a new social order based on AA, but newer authors such as John Mellon (*Mark as Recovery Story*, University of Illinois Press, 1996) take this a bit further by asserting that Bill W's ministry was really the Second Coming, that the Holy Bible has been completely misunderstood all along, and that Jesus of Nazareth, an alcoholic, was the actual founder of AA 2000 years ago.

Amoeba-like, AA swallows everything in its path, subtly converting grand theories like medicine, psychoanalysis, and cognitive-behavioral therapy into mere vehicles for its recovery group agenda. From its beginnings, as set forth in Twelve Steps and Twelve Traditions, AA has coveted medicine and religion. Having swallowed medicine, the counseling professions, and government, AA's quest for Christianity is well under way.

If you feel disturbed at what Ken Ragge will say, or with what I say here, be sure that you know why you feel that way. Perhaps is it because you will re-live a most painful experience from your experience in the 12-step program. Or is it because you cannot afford for us to be right? If Ken and I wrong, you have little to fear, for others will certainly see through our ruse just as you do, and the truth as you understand it will eventually be known.

There is a grand illusion at work in the recovery group movement—that it is wise for addicted people to congregate, that people drink or use for hidden reasons, that recovery results from a process of self-discovery or religious experience, and that it is remedial to belong to a herd of others who share the common passion and memory of intoxicated pleasure. It is tempting to believe that the government can create a new social order by mandating 12-step participation, but only you can decide, "Where will we go from here?"

—Jack Trimpey, Founder, Rational Recovery

Preface

This edition of *The Real AA,* published by See Sharp Press, is a somewhat revised version of my self-published book, *More Revealed,* which went through two printings in 1991 and 1992.

The bulk of the sources used in describing AA and its forerunner, the Oxford Group, are from AA and Oxford Group literature. In my analysis of the dynamics of AA, I have made every effort to be fair. There is great variation by geographic region in meeting format, readings, language, and cliches. Every effort has been made to stay as close as possible to the original, universal sources of AA doctrine: the official literature, most particularly the "Big Book" and *Twelve Steps and Twelve Traditions.*

Since this is not a scientific work *per se,* I've usually used only one study, or occasionally two, to back up a point. Other sources of documentation, and more thorough works on the various areas covered in the text, are listed in Appendix D. The ones cited here are generally the most methodologically sound, the first published, and/or the most frequently cited.

In the chapter, "What Is Addiction?," although I've used the word "definition," I attempted to be expository rather than definitive.

In some of the sections on the origin of addictions, I cite few sources. The models I've used are purely to provide a context for addiction, and I've therefore made no distinction between, for example, over-learned behavior and other learning, and between emotions and feelings. While distinctions in language are extremely important in the laboratory and in academic publications, "a sense of self-efficacy" translates most easily as "self-confidence" or a "can-do attitude" to those of us who are nonacademics. I hope that throughout the book I've presented an easily understandable and enlightening view of addiction.

The people to whom I owe a debt of gratitude for their direct assistance is almost endless, but I would first like to thank someone who wasn't directly involved with this book, my college English teacher, Margaret Starker. She taught me, in contradiction to everything I already knew, that I had an ability to communicate ideas through writing.

I cannot sufficiently express the gratitude that I feel toward friends and family for their encouragement and assistance. Too numerous to mention them all, I would like to single out my sister Claire. She gave me great encouragement and spent countless hours reading and helping me revise the manuscript. I would also like to thank the many people who read earlier copies of the manuscript and offered criticism and encouragement.

Finally, I want to thank Kathy Espin for her kind patience in wielding the editor's knife on the first edition of this book, and Chaz Bufe for his editing help with the second edition.

As in any nonfiction work, the ideas expressed are, at the very least, based on the ideas of others. In this respect, I must express gratitude to the people whose names are found in Appendix D, most particularly Alice Miller and Stanton Peele. Many of their ideas, although perhaps in a different context than in the original texts, will be found within this book.

—Ken Ragge

1: In the Beginning

"The worst of madmen is a saint run mad."
—Alexander Pope[1]

In 1939, shortly after its founding, Alcoholics Anonymous was in debt and its membership broke. Hope for the organization's financial stability was pinned to the sale of their newly published book; *Alcoholics Anonymous*. A small group of early AA members, including co-founder Bill Wilson, were discussing what to do. Morgan, a new member, had an idea. He had connections in the media from his days as an advertising man. He could arrange for an interview on a popular nationwide radio program. As the AA literature tells it:

> Somebody sounded a note of caution: What if the lately released asylum inmate Morgan should be drunk the day of the broadcast! Hard experience told us this was a real possibility. How could such a calamity be averted?
>
> Very gently we suggested to a resentful Morgan that he would have to be locked up somewhere until the night of the broadcast. It took all of salesman Henry's wiles to put this one over, but he did. How and where we would lock him up was the only remaining question. Henry, with full faith now restored, solemnly declared that 'God would provide.' . . . Grumbling loudly, Morgan was conducted into captivity. For several days we took turns staying with him right around the clock, never letting him get out of our sight. . . .
>
> Sighs of relief went up in every New York member's home when Morgan's voice was heard. He had hit the deadline without getting drunk. It was a heart-stirring three minutes.[2]

Morgan told a tale of alcoholic ruin and of the recovery he and others had found in AA.[3]

What went on there? The group was so afraid that Morgan would go on a binge that they locked him up so that he could go on the air to tell how the group helped him recover from his drinking problem. If hard experience told the group's members that he was likely to get drunk, how good was his "recovery"? If they didn't have faith in his sobriety, how much faith did they have in their program?

To understand their behavior it is first necessary to have some knowledge of the history of Alcoholics Anonymous and the workings of its parent, the Oxford Group.

The AA story begins with Frank Buchman, a Lutheran minister from Pennsylvania. In China in 1918 he began holding a series of meetings called "house parties." A house party was defined as "an informal gathering of friends in a hotel or college . . .where countless people who would never have darkened the door of a church found a practical, working faith in surroundings where they felt at home."[4] Buchman was attempting to bring about a revival of what he perceived to be first-century Christianity, hence his group's first name: First Century Christian Fellowship. Later, Buchman and his loose-knit "fellowship" capitalized on perceived but nonexistent ties to internationally prestigious Oxford University after the name "Oxford Group" was reportedly coined by a South African baggage handler and adopted by the group in 1921.[5]

World Peace through "God-Control"

Literature from the 1930s, when AA and the Oxford Group were one, describes their major goals. From one of leader Frank Buchman's speeches:

> The secret is God-control. The only sane people in an insane world are those controlled by God. God-controlled personalities make God-controlled nationalities. This is the aim of the Oxford Group.
>
> The true patriot gives his life to bring his nation under God's control. Those who oppose that control are public enemies. . . .
>
> World peace will only come through nations which have achieved God-control. And everybody can listen to God. You can. I can. Everybody can have a part.[6]

Thus the Oxford Group was the bearer of the secret of sanity. Members, being sane people, had the power to make others sane. This was the "patriotic" duty to which members were supposed to dedicate their lives. All who opposed their plans for "world peace" (Oxford Group world domination) were public enemies. Everyone was welcome to join in the great, moral crusade.

For those who were *too insane* to join on their own, the Oxford Group had special methods to help them, called "the five Cs." Once "helped" through the five Cs, one could live life sanely, meaning in accordance with "the four absolutes" and "the five procedures."

The Four Absolutes: The Yardstick of Sanity

The four absolutes were absolute purity (which refers predominately to sex), absolute honesty, absolute unselfishness and absolute love. The absolutes were the measuring sticks by which one's actions and thoughts were to be judged. At first glance, they seem to be a worthy ideal. Attempts to live up to the absolutes, however, could hardly have served other than to make Oxford Groupers feel guilty.

To understand this, imagine a man with only one dollar in his pocket. He is waiting to take the bus to work, and the fare is exactly one dollar. An obviously poorly fed panhandler asks for some change for food. To be absolutely unselfish, the man would have to give up the dollar. But what about his obligation to his employer and his family? Would it be absolutely loving to miss work, possibly lose his job and not be able to provide for his family? But wouldn't it be a violation of absolute unselfishness to be concerned only with his family? The panhandler is very obviously in need. In terms of the absolutes, there is no rational, logical, *guilt-free* solution. One's ability to reason is worthless, as there is no "spiritual" solution through logic. Any logical solution would leave the man a guilty sinner. He would be doomed to fall short of the ideal.

Such lose/lose situations presented no problem for groupers. They held the intellect in scorn anyway. In their belief system, people were stymied in their spiritual growth to the degree that they ran their lives through following their own wills.

Reason suspended, the groupers had a "spiritual" way of dealing with all of life's problems, no matter how huge or how trivial. Groupers had Guidance.

The Five Procedures of the Sane

The first of the five procedures, Guidance, was to listen for messages from God. Members were to spend an hour in the morning in meditation, pen in hand, and write all thoughts that came to mind. The next procedure, checking guidance, was to determine whether the thoughts were from the subconscious, from the evil one, or from God Himself. They were first checked against the four absolutes, and then checked by other group members.* Elders were particularly important in this because they were further along the Spiritual Path and therefore better able to determine what was really from God.

Guidance was also considered available all through the day. Not only was Guidance relied upon if a problem arose, but it also determined (at least in theory) what a member should do with his time and what to prepare for dinner.[7] The third procedure, of "giving in to God," complete "surrender" to Guidance, was complete surrender to "God-control." It was sanity.

The fourth procedure was Restitution. Amends were to be made for past shortcomings. These shortcomings were predominately the sins committed before having "surrendered to God," or "giving in to God," as measured against the four absolutes.

The fifth procedure, "sharing," had two parts: sharing for witness and sharing for confession. Sharing for witness was also known as "The Fifth Gospel" and "The Gospel of Personal Experience." These names are particularly appropriate because Oxford Groupers considered sharing for witness the equivalent of the handing down of the New Testament gospels.[8] In other words, an elder grouper's sermon was considered as wise, true and as spiritually inspired as the words of Matthew, Mark, Luke and John.

Sharing for confession meant the confession of sins. Unlike in most Christian churches, this wasn't done between oneself and God, with a priest in private, or, to a limited extent, at a service. Open

---

*This is a common practice in religious cults. The member is told to ask for "Divine Guidance," and then to subject it to other members' interpretation. Imagine if a member believed that God had told him that the group's doctrine was wrong in some respect, or perhaps even that the sect was evil and he should leave. The group, of course, would make every effort to help him to understand that he was mistaken. It wasn't God, but rather Satan or whatever other evil force the particular cult utilized, suggesting such things.

confession, along with "sharing for witness," formed the core of the meeting experience.

The Oxford Group's meetings were rather informal. Everyone was on a first-name basis. They had no "clerical class," relying instead on the elders as preachers. The preacher, or leader, was any elder who was thought to have a particularly relevant "message" or "story" for that evening. For instance, if a newcomer was expected to be present, someone with a similar background or who suffered from similar sins prior to being saved might be chosen by the members to lead.

After the reading of selected Bible passages, the leader would speak. His sharing would begin with the confession of sins of the past and end with the rewards of "surrender" to God-control through the Oxford Group. After the sermon, members would give confessions and witness from the floor. According to numerous participants and observers, the meetings were extremely emotional and hypnotic; there was often a great deal of good-natured laughter, as well.

The Five Cs

The most important duty of Oxford Group members was to win souls for Christ. Since most targets for recruitment were already members of Christian churches, it is more accurate to say that they worked to win souls for the Oxford Group. The five Cs were the "scientific" method of "life-changing," or making the insane sane, and were presented in an Oxford Group manual called *Soul Surgery*.[9] The five Cs are Confidence, Confession, Conviction, Conversion and Continuance.[10]

Non-groupers, in spite of being members of Christian churches, were characterized as "hungry sheep who are dependent upon us, whether or not they or we realize it, for finding the way to the great spiritual Shepherd of men's souls."[11] In order to reach the target of scientific conversion, Guidance was used. After "God" told him who to go after, the grouper would "lay siege with all the powers, seen and unseen, that he could muster to his support."[12]

The first step in working with others, or "laying siege," was to come "so wholly into the confidence of the one we seek to help along the avenue of personal friendship that we know his verdict on his own case, see him through his own eyes."[13]

In winning the confidence of the "lost sheep," the grouper is advised to "avoid argument" and to "adapt the truth to the hearer's need."[14] While "adapting the truth" might seem to fall short on the yardstick of absolute honesty, it must be remembered that, having adopted the absolutes, the grouper's reason was suspended and the inconsistency would not be noticed. It also would be unreasonable to expect a sane person (a person under God-control) to question the morality of any action necessary to make the insane (those not under God-control) sane. After all, he would be following direct orders from God as communicated through Guidance. It is easy to imagine that the Oxford Groupers must have seen themselves as "serving a Higher Purpose."

The second C, Confession, was used as a means of manipulation. Whereas in Christianity, as in other major religions, confession is a method of clearing the conscience, of removing a sense of separateness from God, in the Oxford Group, as in other cults, confession ultimately served quite different purposes:

Through the avenue of confidence we win a man's friendship. Through confession we may win his soul. . .[15]

If we are honest and humble and truthful, God will keep us human and sympathetic, and we may be able to use our very weaknesses and temptations . . .[16]

Honesty, humility and truth are, of course, admirable qualities. However, it is somewhat less than absolutely honest to feign friendship and, with ulterior motives and absolute absence of real penitence, go through the act of confession. It is also arrogant to assume that anyone who isn't a fellow grouper is a lost sheep who needs to be "helped."

Confession had another use for the Oxford Group soul surgeon: "To go with a confession of unworthiness . . . tends to disarm criticism . . ."[17]

The second C, the extraction of Confession, was considered of ultimate importance and great effort was made to get it: "When he is certain that the need for confession exists, the soul surgeon must be lovingly relentless in insisting that the confession be made . . ."[18]

This "loving relentlessness" takes on a rather sinister air when one considers the group's "hospital work." An alcoholic patient, locked away in a hospital, would be given only a Bible to read and was allowed only groupers for visitors during the "Oxfordizing" period."* The poor victim was under steady pressure, perhaps for days, weeks or months, to accept Oxford Group interpretations of the Bible and to accept the Oxford Group's will as God's will. Even outside of hospitals, the groupers' techniques sometimes led to severe emotional damage, including nervous and mental breakdowns.[19]

The third of the five Cs, Conviction, was defined as "a vision of the hideousness of his own personal guilt . . ."[20] If the lost sheep didn't seem to feel guilt intensely enough, an effort was made to increase and intensify his guilt.[21]

Sincere confession, confession for what one feels a genuine sense of guilt and shame, was used by the Oxford Group member, as in other cults, for further manipulation. Having "befriended" the lost sheep, gotten a confession of guilt and intensified that guilt, the grouper now had the lost sinner in an extremely vulnerable position. Overwhelmed by *"the hideousness of his own personal guilt,"* The lost sheep needed resolution. His grouper "friend" had already prepared a way out. The soul surgeon had described, in *humble* confession, how he was saved by "the programme of His Kingdom."

The lost sheep was almost found. All he needed for Conversion, the fourth C, was to have faith. This meant to be *obedient* to "the programme of His Kingdom," since faith, for the Oxford Group, was defined as obedience.[22]

For the soul surgeon, the work was not yet done. One final C, Continuance, remained. The most important element in Continuance was to get the new convert working to convert others. The convert was told, "As we have freely received, so we must freely give." This was because it was ". . . one of the surest safeguards against its [the conversion experience] soon becoming unreal."[23] *In order for a grouper to maintain his unusual beliefs, he had to convince others of their truth.*

The degree to which one's life is changed by this process is great: "The central pivot around which his life revolves must now be not self but others, not serving his own interests or development but serving and winning others . . ."[24] Anything interfering with full

---

* All cults use some method to separate their target from outside sources of information.

dedication to "winning others was considered selfish at best. Some of
the reasons given for weak dedication to practicing soul surgery were
spiritual laziness, spiritual cowardice and "Satan's active interference."[25] Needless to say, such admonitions would intensify a
slacker's feelings of guilt, leading to an even greater dependence on
Guidance and a greater need to win converts.*

The Oxford Group was most concerned with bringing rich, famous
and powerful public figures under God-control so their influence
could be used to sway the public. One apparent success, the son of
rubber baron Harvey Firestone, was to play an important part in the
birth of Alcoholics Anonymous and was to have a great influence on
its development:

> . . . Events were taking place independently in two American cities
> which were to lead to his [Buchman's] principles being applied to
> such hospital cases by [Alcoholics Anonymous], first throughout
> America and then all over the world.
>
> In Akron, Ohio, Jim Newton . . . found that one of Firestone's sons
> was a serious alcoholic. He . . . took him first to a drying-out clinic
> . . . and then on to an Oxford Group conference in Denver. The young
> man gave his life to God, and thereafter enjoyed extended periods of
> sobriety. The family doctor called it a "medical miracle."
>
> Firestone Senior was so grateful that, in January 1933, he invited
> Buchman and a team of sixty to conduct a ten-day campaign in
> Akron. They left behind them a strong functioning group which met
> each week in the house of T. Henry Williams . . . Among them were
> an Akron surgeon, Bob Smith, and his wife Anne. Bob was a secret
> drinker . . .[26]

Dr. Bob Smith was to become revered as one of the two
co-founders of Alcoholics Anonymous.

The Oxford Group, through the Firestone publicity, presented itself
as having a "program" explicitly for drunks in addition to sinners in
general. The meeting left behind at T. Henry Williams' in 1933 was
an Oxford Group meeting and was to stay that way for several more
years.

Meanwhile, in New York, the other co-founder-to-be was on a

---

* Robert J. Lifton, the world's foremost authority on "totalitarian organizations," refers to
the psychological need of the converted to convert others as "the psychology of the pawn."

downhill slide with his drinking problem. Bill Wilson was hospitalized several times at Towns Hospital in New York City. During his first two stays, his doctor, William Silkworth, impressed on him the hopelessness of alcoholism. Silkworth's theory on alcoholism was that it was "an allergy combined with a mental obsession," and that abstinence was the only remedy. Once a drink was taken, the allergy would take over and an "alcoholic" could not stop.

Armed with the knowledge that he was "powerless over alcohol and that just one drink would cause him to lose control," Wilson's condition got decidedly worse. While previously he might go months without a drinking binge, after "treatment" Wilson would "work through hangover after hangover, only to last four or five days, or maybe one or two."[27]

Wilson, perhaps with direct coaching from Silkworth, came to the conclusion that "nothing could keep him from what he would later call the 'insidious insanity' of taking the first drink."[28]

His mental state became so bad after "treatment" that "Terror, self-hatred, and suicidal thoughts became his constant companions. . . . He contemplated suicide—by poison, by jumping out the window."[29]

Meanwhile, unknown to Wilson, an old drinking buddy he hadn't seen in five years was getting a message directly from God. In Guidance with other groupers, "God" told Wilson's friend, Ebby, to visit him. Ebby's visit was in November 1934.

They talked for several hours. One of the things that impressed Wilson most during the visit was that "Ebby looked different; there was a new way about him . . ."[30] When asked what happened, Ebby answered, "I've got religion."[31] Wilson was also impressed that Ebby didn't preach. As noted previously, in Oxford Group conversion techniques the method wasn't to preach but to first confess to win confidence. Apparently this is what Ebby did. To quote AA literature, "Ebby had told his story simply, without hint of evangelism."[32] An integral part of his story was salvation from drinking through the Oxford Group, which he described as more spiritual than religious.

During the ensuing days, Wilson remained impressed with the fact that while he was drinking, Ebby was sober.* This led Wilson to set out for Calvary Mission where the Oxford Group held meetings. He arrived drunk.

At its American headquarters, the Oxford Group dealt particularly with drunks. As Wilson later described it:

> I could smell sweat and alcohol. What the suffering was, I pretty well knew. . . . Penitents started marching forward to the rail. Unaccountably impelled, I started too. . . Soon, I knelt among the sweating, stinking penitents. . . . Afterward, Ebby. . .told me with relief that I had done all right and had given my life to God.[33]

After the meeting, Wilson was told to go to Towns Hospital where Ebby and other group members could see him. Two or three days later, Wilson checked in. At Towns, he was given the standard treatment, barbiturates and several hallucinogens, including belladonna and henbane, until "the face becomes flushed, the throat dry, and the pupils of the eyes dilated."[34]

After several days, Ebby came to see him. While there is no record of what was said, it is recorded that after Ebby left, "Bill [Wilson] slid into a very deep melancholy. He was filled with guilt and remorse over the way he had treated Lois [his wife] . . ."[35] Evidently, Ebby had done something to provoke this emotional state and, knowing the five Cs, it's easy to put together what happened.

Ebby was sent to Wilson by Guidance. He won Wilson's "Confidence" through "humble confession," eliciting a confession from Wilson. Apparently Wilson confessed to something he had tremendous guilt over: the way he had treated Lois. Ebby was able to use this to give Wilson a "vision of the hideousness of his own personal guilt."

Now the time of Conversion was upon Wilson. In what appears to have been a drug-and-stress-induced hallucinatory breakdown, Wilson found "the programme of His Kingdom." From that day forward, Bill Wilson never drank again.

By 1935, Wilson and his wife were both regular attendees at Oxford Group meetings. He was very impressed with what he saw and heard. As he described it:

---

* Ebby later died from drinking. See Pittman (1988):157

On the platform and off, men and women, old and young, told how their lives had been transformed. . . . Little was heard of theology, but we heard plenty of [the absolutes] . . . Confession, restitution, and direct guidance of God underlined every conversation. They were talking about morality and spirituality, about God-centeredness versus self-centeredness.[36]

Knowing that "If he did not work, he would surely drink again, and if he drank, he would surely die,"[37] Wilson set out to "work with others." This was the fifth C, Continuance. Rather than go to work to support himself and his wife, over whom he had felt such guilt, he dedicated himself, full-time, with a "burning confidence and enthusiasm," to "give freely that which was so freely given."

After six months, Wilson was a total failure, not having saved one drunk. The groupers were reportedly "cool" to his "drunk-fixing." Whether they were upset because of his failure or because he concentrated only on drunks is not clear.*

Part of Wilson's "vision" was to create a "chain" of alcoholics, one bringing others who brought still others under God-control. The Oxford Group Movement was after everyone, not just drunks. Independent of AA literature, a writer on Frank Buchman's life quotes someone telling Wilson, "You're preaching at these fellows, Bill. No one ever preached at you. Turn your strategy round."[38]

This seems to indicate that Wilson's early problem with the Oxford Group's coolness towards him was essentially a matter of incompetence at "soul surgery."

In mid-1935, Dr. Silkworth came to Wilson's rescue. He gave Wilson some advice that was to have a profound impact and lead him to great success winning souls in a different fashion. It also was to lead, over the next few years, to schism from the Oxford Group for him and his soon-to-be-gathered flock of lost sheep.

Silkworth advised him to not talk about the absolutes and his spiritual (conversion) experience at first with potential converts. Silkworth told him:

---

* It is interesting to note that while at this time he was, according to AA literature, under criticism for being concerned exclusively with drunks, he would be later described in the Big Book (*Alcoholics Anonymous*) as planning to save the entire world.

You've got to deflate these people first. So give them the medical business, and give it to them hard. Pour it right into them about the obsession that condemns them to drink and the physical sensitivity . . . that condemns them to go mad or die . . . coming from another alcoholic . . . maybe that will crack those tough egos deep down. Only then can you begin to try out your other medicine, the ethical principles you have picked up from the Oxford Groups.[39]

This advice, to use fear to make indoctrinees amenable to conversion through guilt, was new to the Oxford Group. It wasn't long before Wilson had the opportunity to try out the new techniques, but first, one more missing piece was to be put in place.

In May 1935, Wilson made a business trip to Akron, Ohio. Alone in a strange city, he was tempted to enter a bar. He was afraid he would drink. He realized he needed a drunk to work on. Although he hadn't yet saved anyone, trying to seemed to have kept him from drinking. It was at this point that he realized what is considered by present-day groupers to be a milestone in the birth of AA, that, "You need another alcoholic just as much as he needs you!"[40]

Armed with the knowledge that "working with another" would provide protection from drinking and the inevitable insanity or death of alcoholism, he set out to find his subject. After contacting an Akron grouper, he was put in touch with Dr. Bob Smith, the "secret" drinker in T. Henry Williams' group. Smith had been a grouper for years, but had admitted his drinking problem just weeks before Wilson's arrival. AA literature describes the encounter:

> [Wilson] went very slowly on the fireworks of "religious experience." First, he talked about his own case until Bob "got a good identification with me." Then, as Dr. William D. Silkworth had argued, Bill hammered home the physical aspects of the disease, "the verdict of inevitable annihilation."[41]

After one more drinking spree, Smith stopped drinking permanently. Bill Wilson and Dr. Bob were soon at work bringing new souls into the Oxford Group and under God-control. Before Wilson returned to New York, they had formed "that first frightened little group of Akron alcoholics, each wondering who might slip next."[42]

While this "frightened little group" held beliefs almost identical to the Oxford Group, the difference which would lead inevitably to schism already existed. It was the difference in conversion techniques. Oxford Group soul surgery techniques called for augmentation of *guilt* leading to the conversion experience. The alcoholics had learned, through their own conversion, a different method: augmentation of *fear* with an *initial* diminution of guilt. "It's not you're fault, it's a disease. There is nothing you can do about it. You'll die unless you believe."

When a person was properly convinced and had reached a point of proper desperation, guilt was then applied to bring about conversion to God-control. These new groupers were motivated, not primarily by guilt, but by fear.

Other groupers, being God-controlled through guilt, were accustomed to using guilt to manipulate others. This evidently irritated the growing number of alcoholics in the Oxford Group. Wilson attributed this friction to the particular nature of alcoholics,

> Drinkers would not take pressure in any form, excepting from John Barleycorn himself. They always had to be led, not pushed . . .When first contacted, most alcoholics just wanted to find sobriety, nothing else . . . .They simply did not want to get "too good too soon."[43]

Wilson's statement illustrates the early genesis of AA's belief in the uniqueness of alcoholics and also the need for a new, slower conversion process to complete God-control.

Another cause of irritation on both sides was that the alcoholics' sins were so much worse than those of many of the other groupers. One of the early alcoholics in the Oxford Group, responding to a non-alcoholic grouper saying that smoking was his worst sin, thought "Oh yeah? Well, that pipe will never take you to the gutter."[44] While alcoholic groupers took pride in their sins and scorned the triviality of the sins of the non-alcoholic groupers, the non-alcoholics saw the alcoholics as lowering their prestige.[45]

The Oxford Group in New York apparently wasn't as tolerant of the fear-converted alcoholics as the group in Akron. Wilson, who had formed a group in the fall of 1935, was soon to learn that the Calvary Mission groupers were told not to go to his meeting. According to AA literature, it was thought that Wilson's group was not "maximum,"[46] meaning that they were less than totally dedicated. Wilson's guidance was considered "off."[47] He didn't give all the credit to the

Oxford Group.[48] (Perhaps that's how they knew his guidance was off.) And the alcoholics limited themselves to saving other alcoholics.[49] Another major issue was that the alcoholics preferred to remain anonymous, which was contrary to Oxford Group methods of public witness. Rather than breaking away from the Oxford Group, as Wilson's wife Lois described it, the Oxford Group "kind of kicked us out."[50] New York AA was on its own in 1937.

In 1938, Wilson set to work writing the Big Book, a sacred text for alcoholics. The purposes of the book were to "[set] forth a clear statement of the recovery program," "prevent distortion of the message," "publicize the movement," and, hopefully, "make money."[51]

It was in the writing of the Big Book that the core of AA's "program of recovery" was first formalized as "The Twelve Steps." While the first and last step mentioned alcohol, they were, for all other practical purposes, the Oxford Group *"programme."* AA literature describes the writing of the Steps:

> As he started to write, he asked for guidance. And he relaxed. The words began tumbling out with astonishing speed. He completed the first draft in about half an hour, then kept on writing until he felt he should stop and review what he had written. Numbering the new steps, he found that they added up to twelve—a symbolic number; he thought of the Twelve Apostles, and soon became convinced the Society should have twelve steps.[52]

To this day, when an AA member is questioned about the origin of the steps, his response will probably include the phrase "spiritually inspired," meaning that the steps came directly from God to Bill Wilson's pen. And, of course, being "spiritually inspired," the Twelve Steps are beyond reproach.

The first edition of the Big Book was published in April 1939.[53] It contributed to the break with the Oxford Group in Ohio, where there were problems keeping alcoholic Catholics in the Akron group. The Oxford Group used the King James version of the Bible and engaged in open confession. Both practices clashed with Catholic teaching.[54]

It was a difficult situation, since the alcoholics felt that they owed their lives to the Oxford Group. Some members decided, presumably with God's Guidance, to start their own separate meeting in Cleveland. Free from Oxford Group control, they could obey God.

Apparently, one of His earliest instructions was to throw out the Bible. The Big Book could be used at meetings instead. The Bible was found to be unnecessary, *irrelevant*. It is interesting to note that the Oxford Group's "Fifth Gospel" put personal testimony *on a par* with the New Testament. Alcoholics Anonymous, at its founding, put it *above* the Bible.

The Cleveland group was the first to report the effectiveness of the Big Book, rather than the Bible, in converting hospitalized patients.[55]

The Big Book had been carefully worded to avoid offending Catholics, so they could now describe themselves as spiritual (they were concerned with "fitting themselves into God's plan"), not religious (they didn't use the Bible as their ultimate authority). Being "spiritual, not religious," confession didn't exist. It was sharing.

In the latter part of the '30s, it became important to AA to disassociate itself, at least in the public eye, from the Oxford Group because of the growing distrust and contempt the American public held for the Group. In August 1936, Oxford Group founder Frank Buchman was quoted by a major New York newspaper as follows:

I thank heaven for a man like Adolf Hitler, who built a front line of defense against the anti-Christ of Communism . . . Of course, I don't condone everything the Nazis do. Anti-Semitism? Bad, naturally. I suppose Hitler sees a Karl Marx in every Jew. But think what it would mean if Hitler surrendered to the control of God. . . . The world needs a dictatorship of the living spirit of God. . . . Human problems aren't economic. They're moral, and they can't be solved by immoral measures. They could be solved within a God-controlled democracy, or perhaps I should say a theocracy, and they could be solved through a God-controlled Fascist dictatorship.[56] *

---

* *The Open Secret of MRA*, a defense of Buchman and Buchmanism, includes the complete text of the *New York World-Telegram* interview. It is interesting to note the differences in the original from 1936 and AA's abbreviated version published in 1984 on pages 170-171 of *Pass It On*. AA quoted in a fashion that put Buchman in a much better light than even the Buchmanites had attempted to. Most of what is quoted here was left out of the AA version. Perhaps most interesting is that, in the AA version, "the control of" is dropped out of mid-sentence, changing "surrender to the control of God" to "surrender to God." Apparently, Oxford Group language was still considered too hot to print in AA literature, even when quoting the Oxford Group's leader *fifty years later*.

These remarks and charges of Nazi sympathies didn't sit well with the American people. Frank Buchman and his organization's Guidance were in serious question.* Buchman's statements served notice to the American people how misguided and dangerous it can be to believe that one's thoughts are the Word of God.

Though they pale against the charges of Nazi sympathies, other criticisms were leveled against the Oxford Group. Most involved arrogance due to the Oxford Group's belief that its members alone were sane and getting direct messages from God and that others, even members of Christian churches, were lost sheep. These charges included blindness to thinking, undercutting churches, hypocrisy, self-congratulatory sanctimoniousness, and an inability to tolerate criticism.

Just as the Oxford Group hit its crest of popularity, public awareness of its true nature hit its zenith causing the Oxford Group's popularity to nosedive. The Oxford Group became so unpopular that it disassociated itself *from itself* in the public eye. In 1938 Frank Buchman renamed the group Moral Re-Armament.

While these events had their effects on the development of Alcoholics Anonymous, probably none affected their doctrine so greatly as the continued public drunkenness of the Firestone heir converted to God-control. One of the Oxford Group's biggest public relations coups had become, if not for the Oxford Group as a whole, an embarrassment to its contingent of ex-drunks.

To prevent this embarrassing situation from recurring, AA's public relations were built upon the "spiritual principle" of "anonymity." While "God" had told the Oxford Group it was everyone's duty to give public testimony, God seems to have told the early AAs, very pragmatically, that if people were one night swayed by testimony on the radio, and the next heard how the speaker had gotten drunk, it would hurt His program.

---

* The Buchmanites claimed complete innocence. After the war, they announced the matter settled with what they said was a copy of a document found by the Allies after the fall of Nazi Germany. *Time* magazine, with all the resources at its disposal, made a search for, but, apparently, could never find any such document in the Allied records. Tom Driberg, in *The Mystery of Moral Re-Armament*, quotes a story that *was found* in the Nazi secret police records that an ex-AA member might find amusing. A Swedish woman who had been angrily denouncing the Nazis, after attending an Oxford Group meeting, felt *guilty* and proceeded to "make amends," writing a letter of apology to the Nazi leader.

The idea of "anonymity at the media level" sprang from Wilson's vision of a chain of alcoholics. AA literature tells of how the founder of AA in Boston drank himself to death, but during periods on the wagon managed to carry the message to others. As they tell it:

> Its founder could never get sober himself and he finally died of alcoholism. Paddy was just too sick to make it. Slip followed slip, but he came back each time to carry AA's message, at which he was amazingly successful. . . . Then came the last bender, and that was it.[57]

Evidently, if people don't know that the bearer of yesterday's message is drinking himself to death today, it doesn't matter. The messenger can do God's work, bring others under God-control and "give to others that which has been so freely given." This is what the early AA members were doing with the radio interview cited at the beginning of this chapter. There was no question of honesty. They were doing what God told them to do. And they were afraid not to. If they didn't have faith in (that is, weren't obedient to) God and didn't work to bring others into the Program, they would be in serious danger of drinking. To avoid that danger, individual Alcoholics Anonymous members, and AA as a whole, have been very obedient ever since.

When the Big Book was published in 1939, AA membership was about 100. As of 1997, AA reports more than 1.8 million members in over 120 countries.[58]

Articles in medical, psychological and alcoholism journals still frequently describe AA in terms such as "undoubtedly the most successful," and "far and away the largest membership."

But the question remains . . .

---

1. Horace, book I, Ep. VI, cited from Harrison (1934)
2. AA (1957):174-175
3. AA (1984):209-210
4. Buchman (1961):xvii
5. Driberg (1964):52
6. Buchman (1961):24-25
7. Driberg (1964):193
8. MacMillan (1933):139-151

9. Walter (1932)
10. Walter (1932):30
11. Walter (1932):38
12. Walter (1932):33
13. Walter (1932):30
14. "Ten Suggestions for Personal Work" cited from Walter (1932):44
15. Walter (1932): 42
16. Walter (1932):61
17. Walter (1932):59
18. Walter (1932):52
19. Driberg (1964):62
20. Walter (1932):64
21. Walter (1932):64-78
22. MacMillan (1933):24
23. Walter (1932):92
24. Walter (1932) 93
25. Walter (1932):18
26. Lean (1985):151-152
27. AA (1984):108
28. AA(1984):106
29. AA (1984):106
30. AA (1984):111
31. AA (1984):111
32. AA (1984):115
33. AA (1984):118
34. Pittman (1988):164
35. AA (1984):120
36. AA (1984):127
37. AA (1938):15
38. Lean (1985):152
39. AA (1957):68
40. AA (1984):136
41. AA (1980):68
42. AA (1984):146
43. AA (1957):74-75
44. AA (1980):140
45. AA (1980):158
46. AA (1980):174
47. AA (1984):174
48. AA (1984):174
49. AA (1984):174
50. AA (1984):174
51. AA (1984):190

52. AA (1984):198
53. AA (1957):viii
54. AA (1980):162
55. AA (1980):168
56. Birnie (1936)
57. AA (1957):96
58. From AA's web site: http://www.alcoholics-anonymous.org/factfile/doc07.html

2: Does it Really Work?

Keep-coming-back-it-really-works!
—AA Chant

Without a doubt, the general consensus in this country is that Alcoholics Anonymous is an effective remedy for alcoholism and is the treatment of choice. Virtually all treatment centers in the United States funnel their clientele into Alcoholics Anonymous or sister groups such as Cocaine Anonymous.

Rarely, if ever, does the mass media carry anything except the highest praise for AA and treatment facilities. In newspaper articles, television news features and radio interviews, politicians, movie stars, famous athletes and even an ex-first lady carry the message that they had faced alcoholic ruin, but "being in recovery"[*] saved their lives.

The multi-billion-dollar treatment industry advertises the need for "treatment," costs of which can run into the tens of thousands of dollars for a standard 28-day stay. Each business sells its own treatment as the best available for those suffering from what they claim is an incurable, progressive disease. And they report success rates as high as 90 percent.

Though not all advertisements explicitly offer "medical treatment," it is usually implied. While often set in hospitals, treatment is not usually "medical," although a small number of alcoholics, perhaps 10 or 15 percent, do need medical assistance for a few days of detoxification. However, any medical attention generally stops there; and

_____

[*] Use of the phrase "in recovery" is an excellent indication of Twelve Step membership. Other indications are use of the word "sober" to mean abstinent and references to amount of time "sober."

a large majority of "alcoholics" need no medical treatment what-soever. The stress is, instead, on AA indoctrination.

AA members in the early 1940s, according to Jack Alexander in *Life* magazine, claimed 100 percent success with "non-psychotic drinkers who sincerely want to quit."[1]

While the 100 percent claim was questioned, a 75 percent claim was accepted without question; and it has often been cited in the scientific literature and praised as a "remarkable" rate of recovery. The Big Book claims 50 percent at once, 25 percent after some relapses, and improvement in the others. They do, however, have a qualifier: these are the rates for those who "really tried."

It seems that almost no one subjected these numbers to rigorous examination. The first report of anyone actually conducting such an examination appeared on the other side of the world in an Australian medical journal in 1948.

The author, while extolling the virtues of AA, reported that, from his observations, "Only about 10 percent of patients give up drinking at once. The majority of the others may remain sober for weeks or months and then relapse."[2]

Many people have such faith they see no need to actually keep count and perhaps even look upon the idea of tracking results, of questioning the effectiveness of their "spiritual principles," as offensive. It would be putting science over personal experience (the Fifth Gospel from the Oxford Group).

In medicine, however, the normal method of determining the effectiveness of a treatment is to compare it against other treatments and/or no treatment at all.

There have been two controlled studies of the effectiveness of Alcoholics Anonymous independent of any other type of treatment. Since they deal with persons required by the court to attend AA, they demonstrate the relative effectiveness of AA in a coercive context. Since a significant number of AAs are first indoctrinated in this way, both studies are relevant.

The first experiment was done in San Diego, California. Chronic offenders, averaging twelve prior drunk arrests each, were given a 30-day suspended sentence and one-year's probation. A requirement of probation was that they remain abstinent for one year.

A court judge randomly assigned 301 people to one of three categories: no treatment; a psychiatrically oriented community alcoholism clinic; and Alcoholics Anonymous. Complete data for a minimum of one year was available on 241 cases. In the no-treatment group, 56 percent were rearrested. The AA group fared the worst: 69 percent of the AA group was rearrested, while 68% percent of the clinic group was rearrested. An interesting question, one that was not answered in the research paper, is whether the clinic, as is customary, also sent its clients to AA.

In the first month, all groups did equally as well (or poorly, depending on how one chooses to look at it). After the first month, presumably when AA or clinic attendance should have begun showing its effect, both groups lost ground against the no-treatment group. Also, while only 11 of the 241 persons credited AA with their longest period of abstinence, nine of these eleven, or a full 80 percent, were rearrested. *Those who credited AA the most were rearrested the most.* The authors of the report stated:

> Some of the present writers [3 of 5] were quite optimistic about the possibilities of enforced referral to treatment, but the early encouraging anecdotal reports are not borne out by present data.[3]

In another study of court-referred treatment, done in Lexington, Kentucky, 197 alcoholic patients took part.[4] They were randomly divided into five groups: professional "insight" therapy; professional behavior therapy; lay-led behavior therapy; AA; and a no-treatment control group. Of the 197 patients who began therapy, 104 were still available for the one-year final outcome study.

Of the subjective measures, perhaps the most telling is the number of respondents who reported improvement for the final three months. AA tied with the no-treatment control group for the smallest percentage of those who could report improvement. One of the professional groups and the lay group fared remarkably better. All groups had some members who attended AA but the lay-led group, which reported the best results on this measure, had the *least* intense AA involvement.

Compounding this pathetic outcome for AA is that the 12 who stuck with AA for the year scored progressively worse on two important MMPI (Minnesota Multiphasic Personality Inventory) scales. One of these, the Finney Addiction Scale, is used to identify people who have trouble with narcotics by measuring the personality qualities such people tend to have. The AA members became more like the kind of people who have narcotics problems.

The other measure, called the Hysteria Scale, is related to people who have somatic complaints and to the denial of difficulties. *The AA group, the group that reported the least success, was also the one most inclined to hide its difficulties.*

The main criticism of these two studies is that they deal only or predominately with people coerced into treatment by the legal system. This, of course, is true. It is also true, however, that they make an excellent case against court-mandated AA attendance.

There have been no controlled studies done of AA versus other treatments in a noncoercive environment. The effectiveness of AA has been so unquestioned that most studies comparing treatments compare different versions of AA-based treatment. "Successful outcomes" are often defined, not in moderation or abstinence, but *in rates of AA attendance.* However, some revealing studies have been conducted.

A most revealing study of the overall success of AA was done by Harvard psychiatrist and prominent authority on the "disease" of alcoholism, George Vaillant. In one of the longest studies of its size and type, Vaillant followed 100 men for eight years. The men selected were the first 100 consecutive admissions for detoxification at an alcoholism clinic. They were followed up annually. Praised for his candidness, Vaillant wrote of his project in his book, *The Natural History of Alcoholism:*

> It seemed perfectly clear . . . by turning to recovering alcoholics [AA members] rather than to Ph.D.s for lessons in breaking self-detrimental and more or less involuntary habits, and by inexorably moving patients . . . into the treatment system of AA, I was working for the most exciting alcohol program in the world.
>
> But then came the rub. We tried to prove our efficacy . . .
>
> After initial discharge, only 5 patients in the Clinic sample *never* relapsed to alcoholic drinking, and there is compelling evidence that the results of our treatment were no better than the natural history of the disease. . . . Not only had we failed to alter the natural history of alcoholism, but our death rate of three percent a year was appalling.[5]

Stanton Peele, an independent investigator of Vaillant's study, after examining some of Vaillant's unpublished data, concluded:

> Of those who quit drinking on their own, none of the twenty-one men followed up since the end of the study were abusing alcohol. . . . *Relapse was more common for the AA group:* 81 percent of those who quit on their own either had abstained for ten or more years or drank infrequently, compared with the 32 percent of those who relied on AA who fall in these categories.[6]

Despite the fact his own data shows people do worse with AA than without it, in the same book where he presents the failure of "inexorably moving patients . . . into the treatment system of AA," Vaillant goes into detail telling *how* AA works. Perhaps even odder, he states, ". . . if we have not cured all the alcoholics who were first detoxified over 8 years ago, the likelihood of members of the Clinic sample attending AA has been significantly increased."[7]

Odd indeed, for a doctor to discount not having cured or ameliorated the symptoms of an illness, but to instead boast of getting the patients to join AA. How can this be?

One possibility is that George Vaillant is "God-controlled." He gives indications that this may be so. In attempting to explain the division between those (like himself) who believe that AA works and those who don't, he offers, "for AA to work, one must be a believer."[8]

Perhaps the problem with Vaillant's alcoholic patients dying at an "appalling" rate wasn't because of a failure of AA but because of a failure on the part of his patients to believe in AA. This was in spite of the fact that those who didn't believe, and wouldn't go, did better.

Another indication that he's a present-day grouper is that he advises that "Clinicians and relatives alike need to take the first 'step' of Al-Anon seriously: they must admit their own 'powerlessness' over alcohol."*[9]

It seems that Vaillant himself takes the first step seriously and has admitted his powerlessness. Has he taken the second? The third? Whether he has or not, he certainly seems to be "working the

---

* This is the same as AA's first step. Al-Anon was originally formed to give the wives of the early AAs an opportunity to "work a spiritual program." It is now available to those who work with, or are friends of, alcoholics.

twelfth." The Twelfth Step is "to carry the message," meaning to work to bring new people into "the program." To this end, George Vaillant, as a *medical* expert on alcoholism, advised in the prestigious *Harvard Medical School Health Letter*, "Sooner or later, and preferably sooner, the alcoholic should be induced to attend meetings of Alcoholics Anonymous."[10]

One study, of many, which indicates *how* AA works in hospitalized patients brings to mind "Oxfordizing" and the five Cs. In a Texas hospital, 35 men with varying lengths of hospitalization in an AA-based program underwent psychological testing.[11] It was found that the longer a patient was in the program, the higher he scored on responses indicating defeat, guilt, and fear. Perhaps most important, as the patients became more indoctrinated into AA, their self-concepts became progressively more negative than when they first sought help for their drinking problems. As with the Oxford Group before it, Alcoholics Anonymous uses guilt to bring about conversion to membership. Alcoholics Anonymous has the added benefit of manipulation through fear. With these tools at its disposal, indoctrination proceeds. This is all done to get a person with a drinking problem to join what has been called—and AA's own statistics back up—"a society of slippers."[12]

The "medical" justification for AA indoctrination used by treatment enterprises and by AA itself is the disease theory of alcoholism. Many of us have accepted this theory for humanitarian reasons. But careful examination of the disease theory shows that its effects have been far from humanitarian.

1. Alexander, J. *Saturday Evening Post*, March 1, 1941, cited from AA reprint, "The Jack Alexander Article . . . about A.A."
2. Minogue (1948)
3. Ditman et al (1967)
4. Brandsma, Maultsby and Welsh (1980)
5. Vaillant (1983a):283-285
6. Peele (1989):194
7. Vaillant (1983a):292
8. Vaillant (1983a):298
9. Vaillant (1983a):303
10.Vaillant (1983)
11. White and Porter (1966)
12. AA (1987)

3: The Disease Theory

The idea that habitually drinking to excess is a disease originated with Dr. Benjamin Rush in the early 1800s.[1] Rush considered intemperance, lying, murder, and political dissent, to all be diseases,[2] and he held that being a black person was a disease symptom.[3] He believed that "desire overpowered the will" in habitual drunkards, meaning, in 20th-century terms, that they "lost control." His cure was abstinence from distilled spirits.

Rush's ideas were adopted by the growing Temperance Movement. By the 1840s, hundreds of thousands of members of the Washingtonians, a society of reformed drunks pledged to abstinence, were preaching about their personal experience of loss of control and religious cure.

It's of great significance that, apparently, through the first two centuries of colonial America, until 1795, no one ever reported loss of control. Prior to that date, when people drank too much, it was *because they wanted to.*

The Washingtonians soon disappeared, but Rush's ideas, enmeshed in strong currents of Protestant Revivalism, were influential through the late 1800s and into the early part of this century. With the collapse of the Washingtonians, secret societies of abstainers formed, such as the Most Worthy Scribe of the Sons of Temperance and the Independent Order of Good Templars. The Good Templars alone claimed 300,000 members. These groups virtually disappeared in the early 1900s with the development of the prohibition movement. However, the idea that alcoholism is a disease didn't disappear.

Central to today's alcoholism movement are Alcoholics Anonymous and the disease theory of alcoholism. Modern disease theory is based on the results of one 1945 survey.[4] The survey consisted of 36 questions thought important by AA members, and it was distributed to AA members through an AA magazine, *The Grapevine*. The AA editors chose E.M. Jellinek to compile the results. Although Jellinek had some misgivings due to the obvious methodological deficiencies of the survey, he felt that there was also a great advantage: "All subjects were members of Alcoholics Anonymous. . . . It is difficult to get truthful data on inebriate habits, but there need be no doubt as to the truthfulness of the replies given by an A.A. . . ."[5]

It seems that AA made an excellent choice in Jellinek. He already held their positions as "truthful" and he considered AA's members the only credible source of information about alcoholics.

Out of the 158 questionnaires received, 60 were thrown out either for being incomplete, from women, or for having multiple responses on one questionnaire. Even though non-AA members were never queried, and even though the results were never checked experimentally, the 98 responses from AA members to an AA survey, compiled by an admirer of AA, form the "factual" basis for the disease concept of alcoholism. This point is so important that it bears reiteration: Jellinek's small, after-the-fact, terribly flawed survey is the "scientific" evidence for the disease theory of alcoholism as espoused by the alcoholism treatment industry and (unofficially) by Alcoholics Anonymous.*

The seven major beliefs of the disease concept of alcoholism and their Big Book origins are:

1) **An intense, physically based craving is responsible for an alcoholic's "loss of control" of drinking behavior**. The cliché, "one drink, one drunk," comes from the Big Book. Dr. Silkworth's introduction also stresses this concept. And there are dozens of personal stories in the Big Book that stress the loss of control supposedly suffered by alcoholics.

---

* Some AA members have stated that the disease concept was foreign to early AA, since it was a spiritual, not medical, program. However, much reference is made to alcoholism being a disease by the earliest members of AA in the Big Book. In telling of her own conversion process, one of the "pioneers of AA" says, "I was suffering from an actual disease that had a name and symptoms like diabetes or cancer . . ." (p.227) Other early Big Book references by the earliest members to alcoholism as a disease can be found on pages 187, 191, 307 and 308.

2) **An alcoholic cannot be responsible for his behavior when either drinking or in pursuit of alcohol.** The craving takes over normal mental function. The Big Book refers to "the subtle insanity which precedes the first drink"[6] and states that "we were alcoholic and could not manage our own lives."[7] Frequent mention is made of Dr. Jekyll/Mr. Hyde transformations when alcoholics are seized by the obsession to drink or when they're under the influence.

3) **The disease is progressive and incurable**, with "jails, institutions, and death" the only possible fates unless *lifetime abstinence* is observed. Also from the Big Book: "Over any considerable period we get worse, never better."[8]

4) **Abstinence is unlikely to be maintained without special assistance.** From the Big Book:

> [We must] make clear three pertinent ideas:
>
> a) That we were alcoholic and could not manage our own lives.
>
> b) That probably no human power could have relieved our alcoholism.
>
> c) That God could and would if He were sought.[9]

In personal story after personal story in the Big Book, AA members say that no matter how hard they tried, until they "surrendered" they couldn't maintain abstinence. The Big Book also heavily stresses that "Alcoholics rarely recover on their own."

5) **The underlying disease gets worse even during periods of abstinence**, meaning that even if one is abstinent, a return to drinking will be to progressively worse drinking, as if one had been drinking all along. The Big Book tells of the case of a 30-year-old man who was drinking to excess. It was affecting his business so he stopped. Twenty-five years later he retired, began drinking again and died within four years.[10] The phrases "Once an alcoholic, always an alcoholic"[11] and "no real alcoholic *ever* recovers control"[12] are among Big Book references to this concept.

6) **The disease is independent of everything else in a person's life and has a life of its own.** This means that people don't abuse themselves with alcohol because of problems in their lives; they have problems in their lives because alcoholism or alcohol has taken control of them. AA's first step, "We admitted we were powerless over alcohol—that our lives had become unmanageable," shows the assumed relationship. Because of this force more powerful than themselves, alcoholics' lives are disordered. Fixing the alcohol problem is assumed to be a prerequisite to fixing any other area of a person's life.

7) **"Denial" is both a major symptom of alcoholism and major impediment to successful recovery.** Persons afflicted with alcoholism deny their problems as a result of "disease processes." Intervention by others, especially those "in recovery," is often necessary for the alcoholic to understand his situation. This element of the disease of alcoholism is not mentioned in the Big Book, at least not directly. Some present-day writers have suggested that early AA didn't consider denial an element of alcoholism.

Certainly the word as used today wasn't in the Big Book. It is, however, implied in the first step. Religious conversion techniques have always called for confession. Without *denial* of sin, admission (confession) would be unnecessary.

The most important "medical" reason for considering alcoholism a disease is that people do sicken and die from habitual over-consumption of alcohol. When one points out to believers in "the disease" that patterns of alcoholism much more closely resemble habits and compulsions such as nail biting and compulsive gambling than actual diseases, the invariable response is that it is a disease because it is fatal. But does this make sense? Car accidents, war and the failure of parachutes to open during free-fall are all fatal too. Are they diseases because they are fatal? Calling something a disease implies the need to seek medical treatment; and, of course, medicine does have a proper role in treating all these things. After car accidents, during wars, and, in rare instances, after parachutists hit the ground, medical experts are the ones who take x-rays, give transfusions, set broken bones, and carry out other tasks for which they have special training. They also treat people who have poisoned themselves with alcohol—that is, they treat the *results* of drinking behavior. But there is no more medical treatment for *the behavior* of excessive drinking than there is medical treatment for careless driving, over-ambitious world leaders, or improperly folded parachutes.

The general public accepted the disease theory more out of compassion than an understanding of the semantics of "disease" definitions. Proponents of the disease theory argued that people with drinking problems should be helped, not jailed. It made sense and still does. The problem has been the nature of the "help."

Medicine's Answer to the Disease

Once alcoholism was defined as a disease, the problem was laid on the doorstep of medicine. AA has been shown to be ineffective. But can medicine help?

Many studies have tested this. One particularly simple study done in London[13] assigned married male alcoholics to one of two groups. One group received the full gamut of medical treatment: psychiatric care, doctors, hospitalization, whatever seemed appropriate during the one-year course of the study. The medical services offered were comparable to those available in America. The other group received one hour of common sense advice on how to deal with everyday problems. They were told they were alcoholic, needed to quit drinking and that it was up to them to do so. Both groups had equal AA involvement.* At the end of the year, there was no significant difference between the two groups.

Closer to home, the disease theory has been a tremendous boon to the American treatment industry. Millions of potential clients now have insurance to cover medical treatment. With billions of dollars available, the industry works to convince potential clients of the need for treatment. To capture and maintain market share, individual corporations work to convince potential clients to choose their particular brand of treatment.

Since ads rarely or never mention AA, it is likely that those in charge of marketing know that if the nature of their "therapy" and "aftercare" were known, it would cost market share. Instead, each

---

* The presence of AA in treatment is not so widespread or intense in England as it is here.

business concentrates on the need for treatment and boasts of special expertise, an exceptionally understanding, caring environment and, most of all, exceptional treatment success.

The boasted efficiency of for-profit treatment centers is, at best, misleading media hype. When the data these claims are based on is examined, it becomes clear that the question "Who is in treatment?" is more important than "What is the treatment?" These "scientifically proven" treatment programs are "proven" using biased samples, and in the conspicuous absence of control groups. When the demographics of the test subjects are examined it is found that:

1) they are married
2) they are employed
3) they have relatively high social and economic status
4) they are relatively young

All of these factors are indicative of a successful outcome with or without treatment (of any sort).

Other biasing factors are that those who drop out are not included and that short-term follow-ups are routinely used. Results from three-, six- or twelve-month follow-ups may *look* remarkable but, when all factors are accounted for, the amazing 80 or 90 percent success rates become equal to those of every other commonly used treatment and to the "success rate" of no treatment at all.

The commonly used treatment methods for alcoholism have *never* been proven effective. The only evidence for success are the pronouncements of those who have been given the "Keys to the Kingdom"* and the promotional sales work of the multi-billion dollar treatment industry.

Finally, there is little support for the disease theory among alcoholism researchers. Even "experts" like George Vaillant have major disagreements with many of its elements. It seems that AA supporters are much less concerned with defending untenable

---

* Of course, this language would never be used in public or with a prospective new member. As the Big Book advises on page 93, ". . . you had better use everyday language to describe spiritual principles. There is no use arousing any prejudice he may have against certain theological terms and conceptions about which he may already be confused. Don't raise such issues . . ."

positions than with defending the funneling of patients into AA-based treatment programs and on to AA. All of the basic assumptions of the disease theory have been proven untrue.

Loss of Control

One of the most carefully researched elements of the disease theory is the concept of loss of control. While it may be a common *subjective* experience, it is not physically based, as a wealth of research has shown.

The most often-cited experiment, due to its methodological soundness, was reported in 1973.[14] It involved 32 alcoholics and 32 social drinkers as controls. Both groups were treated identically. The 32 alcoholics were divided into two groups. Under the guise of a taste test, both groups were told that they would be rating a new product that had not yet reached the market. One group was told they were taste-testing Brand X vodka, the other, Brand X tonic water. In the group told they were taste-testing alcohol, the drinks were mixed in front of them. The catch, however, was that only half actually received alcohol. The other half were poured drinks from vodka bottles which had been filled with decarbonated tonic water. So, half the group that thought it was testing plain tonic water was actually given vodka. For those given vodka in both test and control groups, the concentration was one part vodka to five parts water. It was an amount that would evade detection after use of a mouthwash.

All participants were given two ounces of each of the three different brands as an "introductory sample." This was the priming dose that, according to the disease theory, would cause loss of control. Twenty minutes later, the actual "taste testing" began. Each participant was given three 24-ounce decanters, each decanter labeled as a different brand. They were told to drink as much as they needed to in order to rate it.

No one lost control. No one drank all the liquid. The most important result of the experiment was that the amount drunk was determined not by whether there was alcohol in the drink, but by whether the subjects thought there was alcohol in the drink. The ones who thought they were drinking plain tonic water, whether they were really drinking alcohol or not, drank about ten ounces. Those who thought they were drinking alcohol drank more than twice as much, whether or not they were in fact drinking alcohol. It made no difference whether they were really drinking alcohol or not. *What made the difference was what they believed and what they expected based on that belief.*

The loss of control hypothesis has been tested many times. In another type of experiment, alcoholics who had to have suffered the DTs* in order to participate were allowed to drink all they wanted until a certain cut-off date.[15] Before the cut-off date, *they tapered off on their own* in order to avoid severe withdrawal. Researchers gave subjects boring and tedious tasks to perform in order to earn "credits" for drinks. *Even when the subjects were going through withdrawal from prior earned drinking bouts, they saved drink credits for later use.*

Loss of control has never been proven and, time and again, has been shown not to exist.

AA-oriented people like to point out that all experimentation has been done under hospital and laboratory conditions. It has not been done "in the real world." But they miss the point. The point, regarding loss of control, is that belief and environmental effects are more important than the chemical effects of alcohol.

Another premise of disease theory is loss of control of behavior due to alcoholism. "Bad behavior," like fighting with the wife, missing work, getting into fights, skipping school, and committing crimes, is considered a disease symptom. The possibility that those who, for whatever reason, are inclined to break such societal rules and conventions would also be likely to behave badly in their drinking behavior is completely discounted. The use of unacceptable behavior as a diagnostic factor in alcoholism has expanded to such an extent that self-destructive consumption is no longer necessary for diagnosis. Now, as little as one drink a day may qualify one for the label "alcoholic."

The belief that alcoholism is progressive and incurable also has a firm hold on popular consciousness, even though it has been successfully challenged time and again. One of the first studies to report a return to social drinking by alcoholics was published by Davies in 1961.[16] He used extremely stringent requirements in order

---

* DT's, or *delirium tremens*, is the most severe symptom of chronic alcohol poisoning and occurs in only the worst cases of alcohol over consumption.

to avoid error and criticism. The 93 alcoholics in the study had to meet the World Health Organization's criteria for alcoholism. To qualify as having become a moderate drinker, the subject must have *never* been drunk in the years after hospital release. The shortest time period allowed was seven years. Davies found that seven of the 93 who qualified as alcoholics had returned to moderate drinking, according to his extremely restrictive criteria.

The announcement created a storm. Everyone knew that alcoholics *couldn't* return to social drinking. There was something wrong with the study. Two of the criticisms were particularly amusing in the light of the careful restriction used in the categories. One was that the test subjects had never really been alcoholics, *because they drank too much*, meaning they drank too much to have ever been alcoholics.[17] The other was that the subjects' moderation in drinking didn't count because it was *too moderate*.[18]

Other studies have followed. The largest was by the prestigious Rand Corporation.[19] In a follow-up of 548 alcoholics at eight different AA-based treatment centers, the Rand researchers found that 18 percent of subjects had moderated their drinking and had become non-problem drinkers after treatment. Only 7 percent managed to abstain for the four-year follow-up period. And those who had some or complete success remaining abstinent, *as a group*, ended up with twice as many drinking-related problems as those who had moderated their consumption. Overall, the "abstainers" did almost as poorly as those who were still problem drinkers at the four-year point. The Rand Report also pointed out that those who came to believe the "traditional alcoholism ideology" and had successfully adopted the AA self-image of "alcoholic" were the ones most likely to continue heavy, problematic drinking.

Long-term studies of the drinking habits of young people also contradict the idea of the inevitable progression and incurability of alcoholism. A 20-year follow-up of college students found it rare for a student who drank until blackout to be doing so 20 years later.[20] Another study followed high school sophomores for 13 years.[21] The data showed that levels of alcohol consumption in the teen years were only *mildly* predictive of later consumption. Teenage abstinence was also found to be mildly predictive of later heavy drinking. In other words, in this study and others, *abstinence has been found to "progress" to alcoholism almost as often as teenage alcohol abuse.*

The concepts of inevitable progression and incurability have great value—great dollar value—to the multi-billion dollar treatment industry and, as Dr. Silkworth taught Bill Wilson, great indoctrination value.

Another characteristic of the "disease" of alcoholism, one which is increasingly stressed by the treatment industry in its struggle to fill beds, is the symptom of denial. Obviously, those who engage in self-destructive behavior of any type usually have a strong tendency to discount the damage they inflict upon themselves. Denial as defined under the disease theory of alcoholism, however, has a much broader and more sinister meaning.

Refusing to turn oneself over to the treatment authorities is denial. One cannot abstain on one's own, they say, so anyone who believes that he can is displaying the symptom of denial. Anyone caught in the webs of the treatment/AA system who believes that he can moderate his drinking is guilty of denial. Failure to take the full first step of Alcoholics Anonymous, admitting that one is "powerless" and can't manage one's own life, is denial. Either you begin accepting their doctrine or you are suffering a symptom of alcoholism. Stopping drinking is insufficient. One still must accept having the disease and submit to the treatment authorities.

Prior to alcoholism as defined by AA, the only other "social ill" for which denial was considered a symptom occurred in the Middle Ages. In the "diagnosis" of witchcraft, a sure sign that a woman was a witch was her denial of being one. Her subsequent death by dunking was the final proof of her guilt. It must have been as difficult for someone accused of witchcraft to argue her way out of it as for someone today who, once accused, can't help but "prove" his alcoholism by denying it.

It is important to point out that AA members really believe that alcoholism is a disease with the specific characteristics mentioned here. Much of the reason for this is entirely semantic. By defining alcoholism as a disease and attaching each of the elements of the disease theory to that definition, the theory ends up proving itself, much as the basic assumptions about witchcraft *proved* the existence of witchcraft to almost everyone's satisfaction in the Middle Ages.[22]

Imagine, for instance, that the flu was redefined as an always-fatal disease. If it isn't fatal, it isn't the flu. Now imagine a doctor with a patient who is running a fever, coughing and headachy. If the patient should die, he can be held up as an example of the inevitable fatality of the flu. But what if the patient lives, as is to be expected? He didn't have the flu. How could he have? The flu, by definition, is always fatal. Using such a circular definition makes it impossible to prove that the flu isn't always fatal. The presence of the same virus and symptoms in those who live and those who die is irrelevant. If it isn't fatal, it isn't the flu.

The definition of alcoholism accepted by AA members and presented by them to the public operates in the same way. It doesn't matter how many alcoholics have moderated their drinking behaviors. Using the disease definition, it can't be proven that alcoholism isn't irreversible and progressive. If it is reversed and doesn't progress, it isn't alcoholism.

AA has a semantic method of dealing with the many people who don't fit their model. They aren't "true alcoholics." Whenever anyone returns to "social drinking," the first response of the groupers is that sooner or later "the disease" will get them. They will either return to AA with proper penitence or they will die. Of course these things don't always happen. When they do, it proves the nature of the disease and the wisdom of AA. When they don't, it is obvious that the persons in question never were "true alcoholics."

As with people experiencing other of life's problems, people with drinking problems sometimes feel as if their lives are out of control. At vulnerable times, it is always helpful to find support until one regains one's bearings. The support can be from friends, family, one's minister, a psychologist, or any of innumerable other sources. Unfortunately, due to the dominance of the AA-and-treatment-industry-serving disease theory, when someone with drinking problems looks for help, all that they usually find are expensive treatment centers and AA indoctrination.

The heart of the disease theory is the idea that people are helpless to change themselves, to manage their own lives. The disease theory denies, in the face of all available evidence, the God-given human potential for growth and change. Convincing someone that they are incompetent to deal with an unwanted habit or dependence has never been shown to help them change it.

However, the AA/disease theory of powerlessness through physi-cal/genetic/allergic susceptibility to alcohol does serve to create an additional dependency, *a dependency on AA and expensive treatment* *centers.* One walks in with what is usually a transitory problem and, if treatment is "successful," one spends the rest of one's life under the weight of the belief that, as a defective person, one must faithfully follow most of the Oxford Group precepts or die.*

Much has been said in this chapter about what alcoholism *isn't.* If it isn't a disease, what is it?

---

1. Levine (1978)
2. Peele (1989):54
3. Szasz (1977):154
4. Jellinek (1946)
5. Jellinek (1946):6-7
6. AA (1938):40
7. AA (1938):60
8. AA (1938):30
9. AA (1938):60
10. AA (1938):32-33
11. AA (1938):33
12. AA (1938):30
13. Edwards et al (1977)
14. Marlatt et al (1973)
15. Bigelow and Liebson (1972)
16. Davies (1962)
17. Maidman (1963)
18. Kjolstad (1963)
19. Polich (1980). See also Armor et al (1978)
20. Fillmore (1975)
21. Temple and Fillmore (1986)
22. Szasz (1977)

---

* This may seem like a strong statement. The particular threats of death implicit and explicit in AA doctrine will be dealt with later.

4: What is Addiction?

The Merriam-Webster dictionary defines alcoholism as "continued excessive and usually uncontrollable use of alcoholic drinks." The definition is quite valid if "uncontrollable" refers to uncontrollable by *others*. The evidence is clear, however, that alcoholics can and do control their drinking when they want to.

Even AA-based treatment centers usually expect alcoholics and addicts to voluntarily stop drinking and using. Publicly funded treatment centers often demand that an alcoholic or addict stop using *before* being allowed to enter treatment. The discrepancy between how alcoholism has been defined and real-life patterns of alcohol abuse has led one leading alcoholism researcher to say that alcoholism exists "in our language and in our minds, but not in the objective world around us."[1]

Of course, the phenomenon of long-term drinking of alcohol to excess does indeed exist. The problem with the dictionary definition of alcoholism, and virtually all others, is that they are loaded with implied or explicit reasons for, or characteristics of, the behavior they describe.

To keep things in the broadest perspective, *addiction* will be defined here as *the continual repetition of a normally non-problematical behavior to self-destructive excess*. This definition leaves room for a broad range of behaviors including, but not limited to, alcohol and drug addictions, "love" addiction, sex addiction, religious addiction, work addiction, compulsive exercise, television addiction, overeating, bulimia, and compulsive gambling. This definition also assumes no origin, lifetime course, or resolution for these behaviors. Although no physical cause is implied, there is room for one or more presumed cause(s). This definition is also free of the circular trap inherent in definitions such as "the flu is an always fatal disease." Such definitions impart little real information; they are loaded, biased, and include much *misinformation*.

The addictions listed above seem extremely varied.* At first glance, they seem to have little in common except their harmfulness—it seems to defy logic that some people would engage in these behaviors to such excess that they cause themselves, and sometimes those about them, great harm. But most commonly recognized addictions involve chemicals, and the use of a chemical is at the center of many addictive behaviors. Derivation of an inordinate amount of pleasure from alcohol or a drug seems to be the *cause* of these addictions.

It is often assumed that people derive euphoria, or an inordinate amount of pleasure, from their addictions. In fact, all activities to which people become addicted can be rewarding to almost anyone at one time or another.

Many people enjoy the euphoria attached to a drink or two. People enjoy sex. People are thankful for the pain-killing relief associated with being "high" on narcotics in surgical wards. People find great rewards in prayer or reading religious literature. Many people enjoy exercise, a brisk walk, jogging or working out. A lot of people occasionally enjoy playing cards or slot machines. Almost everyone engages in these behaviors at one time or another, and most of these behaviors are considered good for people. This is one strange twist in addiction: behavior, which in and of itself is harmless, and perhaps even essential to life, is carried to excess.

Another strange twist is that people in the throes of their addictions are not happy people. They do not enjoy their addictions. We are all familiar with the images of the woman who turns to prostitution to support her heroin habit, the alcoholic who loses his job and family, the gambler who loses his paycheck, and the love addict who could be happy if only . . .

It has long been a mystery why people are so compelled. For centuries, labeling such people weak or immoral was thought to explain it. Today, with impetus from the groupers, many people have come to see these behaviors as diseases, but this explanation requires

---

* Ironically, the strongest support for describing such a broad range of behaviors as addictions is likely to come from present-day groupers. Not only do they consider most of the listed behaviors addictions, but they also consider most of them diseases.

"faith," since every bit of independent evidence contradicts it.

Many modern-day beliefs about addictions are derived from beliefs about the opiates, drugs like heroin and morphine. It has been inferred from laboratory studies with animals and the behavior of many addicts that these drugs cause certain bodily changes which set up particular reactions. If a user were to stop, he would soon be in a temporary, but excruciatingly horrible, physical and emotional state. This state, thought to be entirely derived from the chemical, is called withdrawal. Under the duress, or fear, of withdrawal, addicts were thought to be driven to seek out more of the drug. We have held this view for decades.

Without doubt, some people go through severe physical withdrawals, and some people will do anything for a "fix." Research results, while not contradicting these details, paint quite a different overall picture of addiction/withdrawal than that of the disease model. One study which contradicts the assertion of the inevitable addictive power of morphine was done in 1982.[2] Fifty patients who had just completed surgery were allowed to self-administer morphine for their pain around the clock. Even though they used higher doses than street addicts use, some for as long as six days, they didn't become addicted. They didn't suffer withdrawal. *In every case they decreased use of the morphine as their pain from surgery decreased.*

During the Vietnam War, many U.S. soldiers became addicted to heroin. The problem was so widespread that many government officials feared what would happen when the troops returned home. There were visions of drug addicts running wild in the streets committing crimes to feed their habits. That didn't happen. After returning home, only about one-eighth became readdicted.[3] It was also found that, of those who didn't quit upon return, 63 percent had been using narcotics before going to Vietnam.

Rather than looking at heroin addiction as merely a pharmacological effect of using heroin, it is more productive to look at the many other factors that come into play. For instance, what is the effect of the environment?

By comparing the Vietnam Vets with troops stationed in other areas, it becomes clear that being in the war zone, and presumably the associated stress, had a lot to do with whether or not a soldier would become addicted. Soldiers stationed in other areas, like Thailand and Korea, where heroin was available, but which were away from the war zone, had a much lower rate of addiction. It is also noteworthy that even *after* addiction, a change of environment, specifically going home, usually "cured" the soldiers stationed in Vietnam.

Another interesting fact about heroin addiction is that an injection of saline solution will stop the withdrawal.[4] This, of course, only works if the addict receiving the injection doesn't know it is just saline. Also, the severity of withdrawal symptoms depends on the environment. Someone who withdraws in jail may have dramatic symptoms similar to those portrayed in television dramas. However, in other places, such as certain treatment communities or hospital surgical wards, withdrawal is either mild or doesn't exist at all.[5]

Even in non-chemical addictions, like gambling, withdrawal symptoms often appear.[6] Gambling behavior spans a range of intensity from tourists who lose a few nickels in a slot machine to the most compulsive gamblers who lose their homes, families and even their lives rather than *not* gamble. Of course, with non-chemical addictions, it is difficult to attribute the extremes in behavior to a physical cause, such as chemical action or bad genes.

The supposed physical nature of alcohol and drug addiction is belied by the techniques used to determine its existence. There is no test for it. No one can test a blood sample and tell whether a person has a physiological characteristic that defines him or her as addicted. There is no genetic test, or even proven cause-and-effect connection between any addiction and a physiological propensity to addiction. The way addiction is determined is by *asking about* behavior and *asking about* the results of that behavior.

An almost endless series of animal experiments was thought to have proven that addiction is caused solely by the consumption of alcohol or drugs. Typically in animal research, great effort is needed to get animals to consume drugs or alcohol. One way this is done is to add alcohol or another drug to the available water. The animals must drink the laced water or die of thirst. Once they become habituated, they continue to drink the laced water even when plain water is added to the cage. This was thought to prove the addictive properties of the drug itself. However, not all the variables were considered.

The severe deprivation needed to induce addiction, and the unnatural conditions needed to maintain it, were not taken into account. For example, for addicted rats housed in groups, which is natural for rats, the consumption of drugs decreased when they had a choice. Those alone in a cage, in solitary confinement, continued to increase their intake even if they had the choice to cut down.[7] Rather than the rats being slaves to the chemical, *their chemical consumption was directly related to their environment.*

In some of the cruelest experiments, monkeys were "wired up" so that they could press a lever and inject themselves with a drug. The monkeys, isolated from others of their kind and restricted from normal monkey behavior, sometimes even strapped to the wall of a cage, will inject themselves until death. These studies have been used to demonstrate the addictive nature of *the drug itself.*

A more sophisticated method of getting animals to drink or drug themselves heavily is called intermittent reinforcement.[8] In this method, a rat is fed just enough to keep it always hungry. The hungry rat is placed in a cage where it can get only a tiny pellet of food about every minute. Under these conditions, if alcohol is available, the rat will quickly begin to "drink alcoholically." If an opiate solution should be available instead, it will become a "drug addict." In either case the rat is apt to be aggressive and to behave bizarrely in other ways, such as eating its litter.*

This appears to be an excellent demonstration of the power of the drugs. Any substance considered addictive can be used and the results will be similar. The only weakness in this model of addiction (which is also its strength) is that *the conditions create excessive behavior.* The behavior isn't caused by the particular chemical available.

Water can be substituted for the alcohol or drug. Rats will consume as much as one-half of their body weight in water in just three hours. They will become aggressive and behave bizarrely. They become just as "addicted to water" as they do to alcohol and opiates. Of course, the root of the excessive behavior in rats is not in the alcohol, the opiate or in the water. It is in the environment and in the rats.

Rats aren't the only animals that respond this way under intermittent reinforcement. Excessive behavior has been induced in a long list of animals including squirrels, pigeons, monkeys, and even humans. Nor is food the only item which can be manipulated to bring

---

*The eating of litter referred to here is a condition called "pica." It is not a response to starvation but to stress. The rats were always *hungry*, not starving.

on excessive behavior. *Anything needed* by any mammal, including humans, can be used. Water, sex, space or status can all be used to bring about the same effect.

Very little is needed to bring about the excessive behavior characteristic of addiction. All that is necessary is for the animal or person to be in a *frustrated state.* Something must be needed which is not available in sufficient quantity but available enough so that continued effort will partly fill the need. Giving up must appear to be the worst option. For instance, if rats are given the same amount of food at once instead of a little at a time, they will eat it and give up on finding more. Their behavior doesn't become excessive. It is only in the frustrating gap between enough reward to keep trying and not enough to fill the need that excessive behavior occurs. It can be stated that chronic frustration causes excessive behavior. While overly simplistic, it can be stated that *chronic frustration causes addiction.*

It might seem difficult to translate laboratory experience into the human experience of addiction outside the laboratory. Humans are different from animals in that, relatively speaking, we live by reason rather than instinct. We learn much faster. Our behavior is much more complex. With our greater abilities, we have an almost unlimited range of possible responses in any given situation. While we are not so obviously restricted in choice as laboratory subjects, there are parallels.

For all of our greater skills at reasoning, we have a matching greater set of needs to fill. A rat may be relatively content with some food, water, companionship from fellow rats, and an exercise wheel. People, however, need much more.

Outside of the laboratory, addiction strikes hardest at those who are chronically frustrated in attempts to fill their needs due to an environment which limits choice. Alcoholism, heroin addiction, smoking, and overeating are all much more frequent among the poor. The recent crack epidemic is almost entirely an urban poor phenomenon. Poverty is a powerful restricter of choice and a powerful source of chronic frustration. By the same token, the high rate of addiction among U.S. soldiers in Vietnam occurred in an environment of intermittent reinforcement.

The most important thing for any organism is survival. In Vietnam, it must have been almost impossible to feel safe, to feel that survival was not threatened. In a war, particularly in a guerrilla war where the whole country is a war zone, there are few, if any, safe choices. Many troops must have been chronically in a state where no choice was a safe choice but where things weren't so hopelessly threatening as to give up. They were, in terms of addiction, much like the rats in an experimenter's cage. Instead of food being in short supply, safety was. Like the rats, they had no good choice. The rats had no good choice because there literally wasn't enough food available, and what was available was made so under intermittent reinforcement conditions. The humans most needed safety. It was at best only sporadically available.

Of course, for the servicemen, safety was just one factor. Physical hardship, being isolated from their loved ones, and being at the whim of forces beyond their control were others. These factors tend to breed excessive behavior. Once the environment changed, once they were removed from these no-good-choice situations, the soldiers' addictions faded away.

The hospital patients receiving self-administered morphine were in an entirely different situation. They were *removed from* everyday sources of frustration; they were in a temporary situation. Anything of importance *outside* the hospital simply had to wait. Their biggest need was to deal with the post-surgical pain, and the solution to the pain problem was self-administered morphine. Although the drug is considered highly addictive, no one became addicted. There were no powerful forces of intermittent reinforcement at work; there was no high level of frustration. Self-administering the drug was an ideal solution to the overriding problem of pain. As the pain diminished, the morphine lost its purpose.

It's interesting to speculate what might have happened if the patients had been suffering severe chronic pain. Given a choice, would they have maintained the level of self-administration as needed for the pain? Would they have had a severe reaction to removal of the drug if they had still perceived it as needed? Would they have "craved" it?

Environmental conditions alone fall far short of explaining addiction in humans. Poor people are more likely to suffer from addictions, but not every poor person becomes an addict, alcoholic, smoker or overeater; and only some American soldiers became addicted in Vietnam. Also, those with the most opportunity and choice, the rich, sometimes become addicted.

The environment is important, but the person is more important. Rats in a cage have little or no choice in how to fill their needs. Either the experimenter provides for their needs, ignores them, or purposely frustrates them. For human beings, even the most deprived environments provide opportunities to fill needs and avoid chronic frustration. Another difference between humans and caged rats is that, except for the people in prison, there are no bars holding anyone in an impoverished environment. A person has no *external* physical restraints preventing him from picking up and moving, getting an education, changing social circles, switching jobs or whatever else may seem desirable.*

Clearly social and economic hurdles do exist, but the focus here is on formidable *internal restraints* which are just as restrictive, if not more so, than prison bars. . . .

---

1. Rohan (1978)
2. Bennett et al (1982)
3. Robbins et al (1974)
4. Light and Torrance (1929)
5. Zinberg and Robertson (1972)
6. Wray and Dickerson (1981)
7. Hadaway (1979)
8. Falk (1981) and Falk and Tang (1980)

---

* Certainly, coming from a sociological or political perspective, there are serious barriers in the everyday world that we, as a people, need to address. The above is not about what our social institutions should or shouldn't be doing. It is about helplessness and hopelessness, powerlessness, at an *individual*, psychological level. When hope is lost, all is lost. "If I think I can, I may or may not be able to do it. If I *know* I can't, I won't even try."

5: Models

Internal restraints are heavily based in the *perception* of control. An excellent model of the formation and nature of some of these restraints is Seligman's concept of learned helplessness.[1]

Learned Helplessness

Lessons in which helplessness is learned are among the most damaging for any living creature. An experiment done with dogs demonstrates what happens. Dogs exposed to uncontrollable electric shocks will, after a time, give up trying to get away. They lie helplessly and make no further attempt to escape. Even when placed in a situation where they could escape, *they don't even try*. What happens with such dogs has been repeated in similar experiments with humans. The response in people is basically the same.

When a human is faced with an *uncontrollable situation*, fear, anxiety, or frustration develops depending on the intensity of the unavoidable negative stimuli. As attempts to control the situation fail, the person learns that control is impossible and depression sets in. Punishment will now be taken indefinitely, with no further attempt to escape. Once one learns he is helpless, no further effort will be *wasted* in trying to control the situation. When later confronted with other problems, there is a tendency to generalize the prior lessons of helplessness by giving up more easily. Even if he accidentally solves a problem, a person who has learned that he is helpless is unlikely to make the cause-and-effect connection. His ability to learn has been diminished.

One particularly relevant experiment was done with inner city schoolchildren.[2] The children were chosen because their teachers considered them, due to their consistent failure, incapable of learning to read English. However, in just a few hours, the experimenters taught them to read complete paragraphs of Chinese characters. They didn't know that they were learning to read. They didn't know that it was wasted effort. They thought that they were just associating symbols with words. Since they learned so rapidly it is obvious that they were intelligent enough to learn to read; but evidently they had learned that they were incompetent and powerless. As long as they didn't know that they were doing the impossible, they didn't know that their effort was wasted. They could and did learn to read.

Learned helplessness restricts choices. For instance, if a child learns that he is incapable of reading, he will give up even trying to read; and because he gives up trying, he will probably never learn to read. He will simply not choose any option in life that requires reading. Because he has learned that the reading is an unobtainable goal, pursuing that goal seems wasted effort. A child who has given up on reading will also feel inadequate around those who can read and may use his inability to read as proof of his own general incompetence.

It must be remembered that *the restriction in choice is not due to any innate incompetence; it is due to learned helplessness. It is due to past experience.*

The powerful effect of learned helplessness in *everyone* is demonstrated by hypnosis. When a subject is hypnotized, the part of the mind that knows what is possible and what is not is "asleep." In such circumstances, *everyone is capable of doing the apparently impossible.* For instance, childhood memories can be recalled in great detail, people can make their bodies rigid enough to be laid out between two chairs and then support a heavy person sitting on them, they can change their heart rate and skin temperature, and they can walk on hot coals without getting burned.

Learned helplessness clearly limits choice and, in limiting choice, sets the stage for chronic frustration.

A Model of the Human Mind

In the simple model presented here, the mind can be thought of as consisting of two parts: the conscious and the subconscious. The subconscious mind can be thought of as a library or data bank containing everything a person has learned and an automatic system for acting on that information. The conscious mind can be thought of as a control center in contact with diverse areas of the subconscious. It is in the conscious mind that analysis is done and decisions are made.

The conscious mind can deal with only a limited amount of information at a time. However, the subconscious continually processes and acts on information that is outside of conscious awareness.

A good example of the relationship and actions of the conscious and subconscious minds is the learning of complex behavior. When learning to type, a person must consciously consider each particular letter to type, its location and perhaps how hard to tap the keys. With practice, however, this process becomes subconscious. A word is seen and "automatically" entered with no conscious attention paid to the location of the keys, the amount of pressure to exert or even the particular letters making up a word. This is normal human learning, *the grouping of skill and detail together as a subconscious response pattern.* This frees the conscious mind of repetitive detail.

Just as in typing, in the normal course of life most of our action is based upon prior learning and we respond with "pre-programmed" precision to external stimuli. We hear a ringing sound and without thought we go to the door or the telephone, making the distinction without conscious comparison or trial and error. It has long since been thought through. It has long since been learned.

The subconscious has limitations. It is not capable of reasoning. It can only recall what has been learned. *It can only repeat decisions already made in the past by the conscious mind.* For example, if an experienced typist comes across a rarely or never-before-typed symbol, the subconscious can't handle it. It "notifies" the conscious mind of the situation. The conscious mind, with its attention now focused on the problem, will use its own skills to analyze and solve it. Should the rare symbol appear often, it will be learned, meaning the subconscious will begin dealing with it automatically.

As has been shown, there is communication between the two parts of the mind. In learning, information and behavior patterns are transmitted from the conscious mind to the subconscious. The subconscious, for its part, notifies the conscious mind when an automatic learned response is unavailable, when a decision must be made.

The subconscious also communicates with the conscious mind by generating emotion.

Emotion

Emotion can be considered to serve two purposes. It draws conscious attention to a situation and prepares the body for expected action. For instance, driving a car, a learned behavior, is done almost entirely automatically. When driving a familiar route, such as a daily drive to work, little conscious attention is paid to the actual driving. The subconscious handles most of the details. Little thought is given to adjusting speed, breaking or making turns. Conscious attention is likely to be focused elsewhere, perhaps planning the day or listening to the radio.

Now imagine a driver's response should a car begin swerving in front of him threatening to run him off the road. The response is a rush of adrenaline, an instantaneous increase in heart rate, an increase in blood pressure and the tensing of various muscles. The subconscious has made a judgement of danger and, in a most dramatic way, has gotten the attention of the conscious mind. It has also done much more. It has prepared the body to deal with the situation. Whatever the conscious, reasoning mind decides to do, the body is already prepared to respond quickly.

Emotions are not based in the reasoning part of the mind. They do not normally respond to direct conscious control. For instance, in the driving example, the driver uses the subconscious judgement of danger and preparation for action (fear) to focus attention on the problem and to respond efficiently, to take evasive action. When the danger is passed, the subconscious returns the body to its normal state. The heart slows, blood pressure lowers, and breathing slows down. The conscious mind's job is to analyze and act on the information provided by the subconscious. A direct attempt by the conscious mind to "get rid of" the emotion, in this case fear, would be an attempt to do away with a source of information and preparedness. It would be like closing one's eyes. *Emotions are a special form of awareness and preparation based on that awareness.*

As long as there is proper two-way communication between the conscious and subconscious, any emotional state is either "rationally" appropriate or, as new information is processed, becomes so. Take, for example, a person who is intimidated by computers. He may have learned this fear from others who are also intimidated by computers or perhaps from prior experience in a programming class he failed. Imagine that he is told by his boss that the office he works in is to be computerized and that everyone must learn word processing. As he attends class, something within the range of two extremes is likely to happen. At one extreme, he would meet with great success in learning to use a computer and wonder how he ever got by without one. At the other, he would be confronted with frustrating, embarrassing, or humiliating failure. In the first case, as it becomes clear that a computer makes things easier instead of harder, his emotional response to the thought of using a computer approaches gratitude. The fear response dissipates entirely. In the context of *his* experience, his emotional state is entirely "rational." In the second scenario, fear and intimidation increase. On the basis of *his* personal experience, the emotional response is still "rational." Emotional response has nothing to do with cold, impartial logic. There is no "what one should feel." Emotions are subconscious judgments based on one's own past experience. They are also the best conclusions that one can reach *in the context of one's past experience*.

Human adaptability is very much based on proper communication between the conscious and subconscious minds. Proper communication gives flexibility of response and allows the two separate sets of skills and resources in the subconscious and the conscious minds to work together. This allows emotional responses to automatically correspond to the demands of a current situation.

When something prevents information from being passed to the subconscious for storage, or prevents information from being retrieved, we call it a learning disorder. When someone's conscious mind is not aware of emotional states or doesn't provide accurate feedback to the subconscious, we may, depending on the severity, label that person mentally ill.

---

1. Seligman (1975)
2. Rozin, Poritsky and Sotsky (1971) cited in Seligman (1975)

6: Early Childhood Lessons

The impact of early childhood lessons can be best understood in a biological framework. Since human beings, relative to other animals, survive by intellect rather than instinct, a human child's primary biological urge is to *learn* how to survive, *to learn to be like his parents.* In this context, the parent is the supreme, unquestionable authority. Winning parental approval is, in the child's mind, equivalent to being worthy of survival (lovable, good). Parental disapproval, likewise, is equivalent to a message that something about the child is, in some way, unfit for survival (unlovable, bad). Through parental expressions of approval and disapproval, the child learns to see the world, and himself, through his parents eyes. Barring traumatic events, what a child learns by about age six remains as a framework upon which all future learning is based.

This parental authority, based in a *biological* assumption of parental fitness for both parenthood and survival, is the ultimate measuring stick for the child's perception of his own fitness for survival/goodness/lovability or unfitness/badness/unlovability.

In the "ideal" family, parents have excellent self-images, a good sense of their own self-worth, and a system of values that serves them well. They effectively pass these on to their children through modeling, mirroring, warm and loving support, and encouragement of and confidence in the child's growing ability. In the ideal family, the child learns that he is lovable by being loved. He learns that he is capable of loving by the warm response of his parents to his loving gestures. Because parents are the ultimate authority, their show of interest and concern for the child, and treatment of the child as valuable, *can't* be questioned. All this is learned. All this is the framework on which future lessons are built.

Children are aware of, and extremely sensitive to, the emotional responses of their parents; and they internalize these responses. This is an important way parents pass information on to their children. For instance, if a small toddler tries to put a key into an electrical outlet, a parent's emotional response (fear) is internalized in the child. The child learns when to be afraid. This serves the child well, since mother and father won't always be there to protect him. His recollection of his parent's fear, now his fear, will be sufficient to prevent him from trying it again.

The parent's emotional response, or lack of one, is the core of childhood lessons. If a parent would, in a cool, detached way, say "Don't do that," the child's long-term, if not also short-term, response would be entirely different. *It is the emotional context and emotional charge that give a lesson meaning, staying power and force.*

When looking at a particular childhood situation, it is important to recognize that the emotional response of a parent is much more important than, and overrides, what is said. Context is everything. "Isn't that nice," in response to a child's action, in and of itself, has little or no meaning to the child. The important message is carried in the body language, the tone of voice, and the look in the parent's eyes. "Isn't that nice," with an angry glance and tense voice, is a far different message from "Isn't that nice," eyes full of warmth and affection, a relaxed smile, soft voice and maybe a warm hug. Children internalize both the statements and the emotional content, but the emotional content is what defines the words and the event as a whole.

Lessons learned build upon previous lessons and set the stage for future lessons. To learn mathematics, for example, children first learn simple arithmetic. The knowledge of arithmetic is the basis on which algebra and geometry are learned. Any lower-level error left uncorrected will adversely affect, if not render impossible, the learning of later, more advanced lessons.

In the same way, the building blocks with which children form their view of the world and of their place in it are based on the emotional responses of early childhood authority figures, most particularly the parents. In the first six years of life, a child has basically learned "who he is" through the lessons taught at home. Later experience outside the home tends merely to confirm the lessons already learned.

Our more complex responses, activities, and attitudes, such as what kind of work we do, who we fall in love with, how we raise our children, how we feel about members of other races and the opposite sex, our religion, the foods we like to eat—nearly everything about us—are heavily based upon prior learning, little of which is ever, or ever needs to be, re-examined and changed.

In the ideal family, a child reaches adulthood with confidence in his ability, a healthy respect for and awareness of his needs, and an awareness of the surrounding opportunities to fill those needs. Should life circumstances change, he will learn new lessons. The ideal person from the ideal family is ideally adaptable.

Of course the ideal family is just that, an ideal. But even in the "average" family, the lessons learned will vary greatly—in degree, if not so much in substance—from the lessons usually learned in the family of an addicted person.

Although a connection has long been suspected, only recently has investigation begun on the connection between severe childhood abuse and the development of addictions. In two studies, abuse of illegal drugs by a largely criminal group of adolescents was found to be associated with prior physical and sexual abuse.[1] In a third study, severe childhood physical, emotional, and/or sexual abuse was found in 90 percent of the addicts and alcoholics who went through a gay treatment center.[2] While in itself inconclusive, this early evidence indicates that there is a connection between an abusive childhood environment and severe chemical addiction in adulthood.

There has also been a wealth of indirect evidence that supports the existence of a connection between child abuse and the development of addictions. Among this evidence is the fact that alcoholic parents are the most likely to produce alcoholic or drug-abusing offspring.[3] Alcoholic fathers (and one could assume alcoholic mothers) are more likely to physically and sexually abuse, inflict "cerebrocranial trauma," and create a home life for their sons of "chronic discord."[4]

Certain parental behaviors and attitudes have also been associated with later addictive behaviors in children. Parents of young adult substance abusers have been described by their children as "cold, indifferent, controlling and intrusive."[5] Independent researchers have found fathers of drug addicts to be rejecting and lacking warmth.[6] Others found that drug abusers come from families in which there was "a communication gap and either laissez faire or authoritarian discipline" and also where the "most powerful parent modeled the use of psychological crutches to cope with stress."[7]

Children at high risk of becoming substance abusers (children of alcoholics, the same group that is so frequently physically and sexually abused and has a chaotic home life) have been found to be "less emotionally controlled."[8] In one study teachers described them as "emotionally immature, unable to take frustration in stride, sensitive to criticism, moody and depressed."[9] Preadolescent sons of alcoholics have been described as having characteristics of "emotional immaturity, low frustration tolerance, and moodiness."[10]

Children who later become alcoholics have been described as having "antisocial tendencies," "a negativistic outlook"[11] and as being "marked by social nonconformity and delinquency."[12] They also have been found to be nail biters, to be shy, to suffer nightmares and phobias, to throw tantrums, to have tics, to stutter, to suck their thumbs, and to have eating problems.[13]

While many outside observers, particularly psychiatrists, often see the behavior of "pre-alcoholics" as evidence of a genetic "predisposition to alcoholism," it seems ludicrous to assume that any possible genetic personality predisposition *overrides* being physically, sexually or emotionally abused, growing up with cold, indifferent, rejecting parents, or growing up with a parent who is likely to inflict "cerebrocranial trauma" on their child.

Clearly, not all abused children grow up to be addicted, so abuse can't be said to be the only factor in producing addiction. But severe abuse is an effective way to teach certain lessons.

At the heart of addiction in humans is learning that *essential* parts of the self are bad/unlovable/unsuitable for survival. Two of the essential parts learned to be bad are the intellect and internal emotional experience. What happens to children, as may have happened to their parents before them, is that they learn *to not experience, to not be aware of,* some or all of their emotions.

For instance, if anger is one of the emotions considered bad, the child, when displaying anger, will be given the message that to be angry is bad. No distinction may be made for the child—or perhaps will even be seen by the parents—between the internal experience of anger, the proper and appropriate expression of anger, and having a temper tantrum. For instance, if a small child becomes angry and throws food, instead of simply teaching the child that throwing food is unacceptable behavior, the parent also gives the message, either implicitly or explicitly that anger is bad.

This may be reinforced by the parents' own behavior. They may be so good at "controlling" (repressing) their own anger that the only model the child sees is either total lack of expressed anger or explosions into vindictive, verbally, and/or physically abusive rage. In this situation the child only sees, and therefore learns to consider, anger as a destructive force.

The ways parents express disapproval for the child's experience of anger are as varied as the methods parents have of showing displeasure. They can vary from physical punishment to verbal disapproval to the withdrawal of affection. Perhaps the most insidious, for a small child, is the expression of hurt feelings by a particularly insecure and needy parent because the child is angry with the parent. While pre-adolescents and adolescents often respond quite differently, nothing is so frightening or reprehensible to a small child as a parent being in pain. The child comes to see experiencing anger as betraying his parents. However it may be taught, the small child sees himself as responsible and learns that to be angry is to be bad.

Anger is far from the only emotion likely to be taught as being bad. A child may be taught that sadness, fear, warmth, affection, and even happiness, are bad and must be suppressed and eliminated.

Child abuse often plays a direct role in the learning process. Imagine an alcoholic father or mother who regularly gets drunk and beats a child. The child's normal, natural, healthy responses would only serve to provoke further punishment. Under such circumstances, a child may learn not to show or to even feel anger, fear, or sadness. In the child's mind, if the parent is displeased, the child is somehow wrong and it is up to the small child, with a child's limited intellect, to figure out how.* The lesson to the child may be obvious: "I am bad because I am angry" (or sad, or afraid). Every effort is made to be

---

* There are limits to this. It has been reported that if a parent tries to kill or dismember his or her child, the child will redefine the parent as "bad." However, this evidently must be more than "moderate dismemberment." I know a man whose mother, in one of her often repeated rages expressed at him, cut his finger off when he was three years old. When questioned about his family background, he can give the details, but it is still, over twenty years later, in a framework of, "Well, if I didn't keep my room so messy . . . ," "Well, if I had behaved . . ." and "Yes, but she joined the church and quit doing it." He has never processed, and perhaps never will, that *he was just a little kid, and no little child deserves to have his finger cut off.* The last time I spoke with him he was struggling to stop snorting and injecting speed, which along with other behaviors, continues to prove to him that he is the one who is *bad.*

good. The child would learn not to be, at least in his conscious awareness, angry, afraid, or sad.

In learning to suppress emotion, a child learns to suppress his mechanisms for calling conscious attention to a problem, preparing for action on that problem, and processing information for future reference. A child learns to sabotage his mechanisms for awareness, response, and change.

A tragic example of learned self-sabotage shows that it is what is learned, not how it is learned, that is important. In this instance the lesson clearly was not a result of parental child abuse but of a brutal coincidence. Eric M. is an ex-alcoholic now approaching 40. As an 11-year-old child, he was occasionally permitted to move the family car out of the driveway. One Sunday afternoon, he did so without the proper permission of his father who became angry and scolded him. Young Eric, feeling he was being treated unjustly, was defiantly angry. The next day he went off to school still simmering about the dispute. When he returned home, his father was dead. He had suffered a heart attack.

In the boy's mind, reeling with grief and guilt, one idea in particular stuck and stuck fast—never be angry with someone you love; they will go away. This belief affected his life in two disastrous ways. First, since a major part of grieving is being angry, he carried that grief with him. Second, he *automatically* suppressed his awareness of anger towards others, especially those he loved. In his mid-30s, he was abandoned after a year-long love relationship. He didn't get angry, at least not consciously. His friends and AA sponsor also abandoned him. His AA "friends" abandoned him because he was depressed; it upset their serenity. His sponsor accused him of being willful and ungrateful. Eric still didn't get angry.

By this time he had lost 20 percent of his body weight, had not been able to sleep more than an hour or two at night for months, and thought he was going out of his mind. He wasn't angry. He just wanted to kill someone. Himself. Because he was afraid to be angry, rather than his anger serving useful purposes, such as providing information and preparing him to defend his person, it nearly destroyed him.

Other lessons assault the child's trust of his ability to reason and to use his intuition. When parents make statements about their own feelings that are directly contradictory to the child's keen perception of such things, the child becomes confused. One mistake that parents often make, perhaps in trying not to be cold and unloving as their own parents may have been, is to *always* express love toward their children even at times when they don't feel it. The child, being perceptive to the real emotional state, is thrown into confusion.

If the child doesn't question further, he will be trapped into figuring out how he is wrong. Either his perception is wrong or his parent really doesn't love him. If he believes his perception wrong, he comes to distrust his intuition. If the child comes to the conclusion that the parent doesn't love him, the parent being the measure of what is right, he has no choice but to see himself as unlovable. If he questions the parent and gets the message that his *awareness* is displeasing, he may learn to not be aware. He will learn to "automatically not notice." He will make the conscious decision to pretend not to notice and practice it until it becomes subconscious. Later in life, he may well wonder how he could have been so gullible as to fall for a woman who didn't love him or how he could be so wrong in sizing up business partners.

Assaults may be directed against the child's trust in his ability to use his reason, to think. When parents criticize their child's ability to think, the child internalizes his parents statements and their emotional context. They are internalized as the child's own thoughts and feelings toward himself. If criticism is severe enough, the child may learn he is *helpless* to think. He'll learn to automatically *not try* to think things through.

In the addictive family system, children often learn other lessons which diminish their capacity to fill their needs later in life. Some of the lessons which cause the most trouble are those directly concerning basic lovability and fitness for life. When parents are incapable of loving their young child, the child doesn't see it as the parents' problem. He is left to figure out how he is wrong. He can either think, "There is something wrong with me; I am unlovable," or "There is something wrong me; I shouldn't want to be loved," or both.

In the same way that a child learns that he is unlovable, he may learn that he is incapable of loving. If parents are incapable of being touched by their child's displays of love, again the child is in the position of figuring out how he is wrong. He can either think, "There is something wrong with me; I can't love the right way," or "There is something wrong with me; I shouldn't want to love."

Since in early childhood parental love is equivalent to a message of fitness for survival, fitness for life, children who learn that they are unlovable are in for serious problems. Just like the hungry rats in the cage who could never get quite enough food, such children often never get enough love and approval throughout their entire lives. They tend to spend their lives compensating for their "unfitness" or "unlovableness." They've already been taught that their emotions are wrong, and as long as they don't allow themselves to become aware of the emotions involved in the lessons of unlovability, the lessons can't be relearned correctly. Since the lessons are kept buried away, they can't be challenged. What the adult normally does is everything possible to prove his fitness in his parents' eyes. He can be not angry, not sad, not afraid, or not aware.

The lessons which interfere with later love and intimacy vary tremendously. If parents ignore their children, the children build their world view on the belief that they should be ignored, that they are not worthy of attention. In adulthood, they may be confused by others showing them attention. The *subconscious* judgement may be made, "Something is wrong with them; they think I'm worthy of attention," or, "I'm doing something wrong; I'm drawing attention." A parent may ridicule a child for any demonstration of a desire for, or expression of, affection. In such cases, as an adult, he may ridicule those who try to show him love and affection.

Parents who are unable to express love and affection may substitute other things for love. For example, instead of expressing love for their child by hugging, caressing, and other warm and affectionate interaction, they may, out of a sincere attempt to love their children, buy them things instead. A child who grows up under such circumstances may, as an adult, "do everything for" someone they care about and wonder why they don't get anything in return. Of course, "everything" doesn't include giving genuine warmth and affection, and the "love object" is not chosen with a consideration of his or her ability to give and appreciate warmth and affection, but for the willingness to accept material goods.

One important area is the role of God in the addictive family system. Parents, as the ultimate authority, define God for their children. The child's view of God is in large part an image of the values of the parents. In the ideal family, God plays a central role in the child's feelings of self-worth and is seen as a loving and kind protector, as an extension of parental love. In the addictive family system, God is often used by the parents to enforce discipline. Veiled and not-so-veiled threats of eternal damnation are made by the parents in order to enforce rules which can be enforced in no other way.

In families where essential parts of the natural internal experience of thought and emotion are taught to be evil, God's role may be cast as the "thought and emotion police." For example, if a child is suspected of having thoughts unacceptable to the parents, the child may be told it is displeasing to God and that the child must not think them if he wants to go to heaven. Of course the child knows the alternative to heaven is hell. In the family in which children are taught the parental belief that anger, in and of itself, is bad, religion will be selectively used to enforce the family rule. For instance, if such a family happens to be Christian, the children will likely never be told about Christ's anger when throwing the money-changers out of the temple.

To the child in such dysfunctional families, God is seen as an agent of the abusive parent and God's love is seen as parental "love." For instance, imagine the effect on a ten-year-old girl who on Saturday night is molested by her drunken father. Sunday morning she goes to Sunday school class. Imagine the message *she* gets when she hears the teacher read from the Bible, "Honor thy father and they mother, that all may be well with thee and thou mayest live long on the earth." God, in the child's mind, is on the side of a man who has just molested her and, if she doesn't honor him, God will kill her. This is hardly the message intended.

Children who have learned to disrupt their normal mental functioning may never become directly critical of their parents' actions in early childhood. They are even less likely to question the lessons learned as a result of those actions. However, they may have such a negative concept of God that, at the first opportunity, and quite understandably, they reject God and religion as terrible oppressors.

1. Dembo, Dertke et al (1988) and Dembo, Williams et al (1988)
2. Nissan and Sandoval, *Journal of Psychology and Human Sexuality*

3. Tarter (1988):189
4. Tarter (1988):193
5. Schweitzer and Lawton (1989)
6. Emmelkamp (1988)
7. Jurich et al (1985)
8. Tarter (1988):191
9. Aronson and Gilbert (1963)
10. Tarter (1988):191
11. Tarter (1988):192
12. Tarter (1988):192
13. Tarter (1988):191

7: The Adult

The adult in the addictive family system tends to have severely limited awareness. In childhood, particularly early childhood, he knowingly struggled to not be angry, sad, or afraid. In adulthood, he operates "on automatic." By then, lessons may have been so well learned that, only at times is there so much as a vague sense of anxiety, or perhaps a sense of emptiness. When "bad" emotions do manage to leak through, they aren't viewed as important information or preparation. They are more likely a source of confusion or fear; they shouldn't be there.

One reason that emotional experience continues to be seen as bad, even after adult reasoning ability has developed, is that, having a history of being suppressed, the emotions are "behind the times." Imagine, for instance, a bright child who has learned that he is intellectually incompetent. Any attempt to "be smart" in school brought humiliation from his peers.

Later in life he may feel anxious or fearful when faced with an exam. Even though circumstances are different from those in childhood, childhood feelings are apt to surface because of similarities to early experiences. He knows that his feelings are "wrong" and an "interference," so he will make every effort to suppress, ignore, and/or discount them. By suppressing his fear and anxiety, by refusing to be aware of a wealth of subconscious information, he never learns to automatically discriminate between childhood situations where he was humiliated and similar situations in adult life. The subconscious continues to act on the old lessons: "I am stupid and will be humiliated."

In normal functioning, the subconscious would generate fear and make pertinent information on similar past situations available to consciousness. The conscious mind, in response, would focus its attention on the problem. Knowing why the fear was generated, it would be able to rationally evaluate the situation. The conscious mind would have awarenesses such as, "I am well prepared. I will do fine," "These are different people. Even if I do poorly, they won't ridicule me," or "I've shown myself I'm not stupid, but smart by . . ." The subconscious, having gotten conscious attention, would be ready to listen, ready to learn. In this way, perhaps immediately, perhaps over time, the subconscious would learn to discriminate between past and present situations.

The "addictive personality" operates in quite a different fashion. The generation of emotion is seen as the problem. The real problem is seldom recognized and even more rarely dealt with. Even worse, when the feared humiliation doesn't happen, it is seen as proof of the "wrongness" of the fear. This assures that continuing action is taken which keeps the functioning and the contents of the subconscious far below potential. The "addictive personality" bypasses learning, growth, and normal human functioning.

Restricting one's ability to feel and deeming one's feelings "in-appropriate" severely limits the ability to fill needs or *even to be aware of them*. For example, if someone has been punished in childhood for being successful, has been warned against the terrible things that will happen if he succeeds, or has been taught the "futility" of trying to succeed, he may well avoid success in adult-hood. Even if he attains it, the accompanying anxiety may be so intense that success is an extremely unpleasant experience for him. In such circumstances, in order to make the anxiety go away, the success will be thrown away.

In a similar way, if a child learns that to feel good is bad, the adult will automatically avoid feeling good. While conscious effort may be focused on some goal, the subconscious will, outside of conscious awareness, act on the old lessons. It will sabotage conscious efforts to feel good, which it holds as a dangerous condition.

Perhaps the most severe internal restrictions typical of addicted people involve emotional intimacy. People who are taught, and continue to believe, that normal human emotional response is to be suppressed have severe problems with closeness. To the degree that a person is unable to experience and to express anger, sadness, fear, happiness and other feelings, he is unable to be intimate with friends and lovers.

This is at the root of the loneliness often experienced by addicted people. Even if they're in a room full of people, being unable to communicate with themselves, not being with themselves, they can't communicate, can't be with, others. *No relationship with another human being can be less superficial than the relationship one has with oneself.*

Other important restrictions are those caused by learned helplessness. Just like the perfectly capable child who learns that he is incompetent to read, the addicted person may learn that he is incompetent to succeed in important areas of his life and hence may give up trying. For instance, he may learn that he is incompetent to earn a living, make friends, be attractive to the opposite sex, love somebody, be loved, be a desirable party guest, maintain a marriage, appreciate art or music, get along with the boss, or be happy.

Once people learn helplessness, they have difficulty making the associations which prove the belief untrue. For instance, if a boy learns that he is too uncoordinated to play football, even if he should become a video game whiz, he will be unlikely to make the connection between coordination and his new skills. If he had realized that it takes coordination to play video games, he likely would never have become a skilled player. He would have given up because he would have believed that to try to excel at something that requires coordination is a wasted effort.

When attempts to fill a need do not fail often enough for helplessness to be learned, but do fall short of filling the need, a chronic state of frustration arises, just like that of the rat in the cage under intermittent reinforcement. Having learned to sabotage normal mental functioning, the person may be unable to recognize, much less fill, his needs. As a matter of fact, he may see avoiding the awareness of certain (or all) emotional states as a *primary* need. Under these conditions, somewhat less severe than total helplessness (paralyzing depression), he will engage in excessive behavior.

A generally transitory form of this often occurs after the death of a spouse or a divorce. It is not unusual for someone who has suffered such a loss to experience extended depression, to drink to excess, or to behave excessively in other ways. Normally, after a period of weeks, months, or maybe years, feelings are processed, hope is regained and efforts are made to directly fill the "empty place." The difference between someone who drinks to excess due to temporary feelings of hopelessness and frustration and those who drink due to chronic, lifelong feelings of hopelessness and frustration is the difference between transitory alcohol and drug problems and "having the disease of alcoholism."

Psychological tests indicate some important characteristics of those with severe chronic drinking and drug problems. The Minnesota Multiphasic Personality Inventory (MMPI) is one of the most widely used tests for psychological diagnosis. It is made up of 566 true/false questions. It is designed to detect attempts at both looking good and outright lying. Various scales, or subsets of the 566 questions, have been used to distinguish persons with various types of "pathology."

The MacAndrew Alcoholism Scale[1] was designed in the early 1960s to separate alcoholics and drug addicts from psychiatric patients. Due to its high rate of accuracy, it is still in use today. Drug addicts and alcoholics (from ages 18 to 70, average age 42) differ significantly in their responses to 49 of the 566 MMPI questions. They see themselves as "bad." They are more likely than others to agree with the statement, "I deserve severe punishment for my sins." Their levels of self-awareness are lower than those of psychiatric patients. They are so low, in fact, that alcoholics/addicts are either ignorant of, or discount, physical pain. While they report more coughing and vomiting blood than non-addicts/alcoholics, they also report they feel little or no pain. In terms of awareness of emotional factors underlying their behavior, they are more likely than psychiatric patients to agree with the statement, "Evil spirits possess me at times."

Probably the clearest example of diminished awareness in alcoholics is how they see themselves and their parents. One need not look far to find examples where early childhood "self as bad/parent as good" lessons are carried into adulthood with a total blindness to the extremity of childhood situations. Two of the best examples, due to their celebrity as alcoholics, are Bob Smith and Bill Wilson, the co-founders of Alcoholics Anonymous.

In the first "personal experience" story in the Big Book, Bob Smith describes his parents:

My father was a professional man of recognized ability and both my father and mother were most active in church affairs. Both father and mother were considerably above the average in intelligence.[2]

In his biography, *Dr. Bob and the Good Oldtimers*, an AA-written and officially approved book, a quite different, although not necessarily contradictory, picture emerges. Evidently, Dr. Bob's mother was a stern religious fanatic who spent her time obsessively involved in her church and who had little time for her only child:

Mrs. Smith . . . was described as a stern, tight-lipped, churchgoing lady who busied herself with the countless social and religious activities of [her church]. . . . Mrs. Smith felt that the way to success and salvation lay through strict parental supervision, no-nonsense education, and regular spiritual devotion.[3]

Contrasting with this outwardly pious attitude was a cold, indifferent woman who had little concern, much less love and affection, for her son.

Grandma Smith [Bob's mother] was a cold woman. . . . Once she came to the house, and we were all sick with the flu. Instead of pitching in, she went to bed, too![4]

Young Bob was sent to bed every evening at five o'clock. He went with a quietly obedient air that might have led some parents to suspect the worst. When he thought the coast was clear, Bob got up, dressed, and slipped stealthily downstairs and out the back door to join his friends. He was never caught.[5]

One could deduce from this information that young Bob Smith's sneaking out was an early sign of rebellion and leave it at that as the AA writer cited here apparently does.[6] However, it seems extremely strange that parents would send their child to bed at five in the afternoon. It also seems strange that they would *never* check on him and find him missing. It seems likely that "out of sight, out of mind" was the rule. Of course, a child treated like this thinks he deserves it, that his parental treatment is right. In spite of unloving, rejecting parents, Bob Smith describes himself, directly after his description of his parents as intelligent and church-going, like this:

Unfortunately for me, I was the only child, which perhaps engendered the selfishness which played such an important part in bringing on my alcoholism.[7]

AA's other co-founder, Bill Wilson, is reported to have had a close relationship with his father.[8] Bill's father, who had drinking problems, was himself a child of a heavy drinker.[9] His mother was in poor mental health and suffered a series of "nervous breakdowns" and went to a sanitarium at least once.[10] When Bill was six years old, he wrote a letter to his mother, who had already been away some months, probably "recuperating." In the letter, he indicated how he saw himself: "I want to see you ever so much. I try to be a good boy."[11] Evidently, as is typical of young children, he believed his mother's return, and his being able to re-experience her affection, to be contingent upon his being good enough. Bill remembered himself as being friendless at this time because "his shyness and awkwardness prevented him from developing close friendships . . ."[12]

Bill eventually got his wish and his mother returned home, at which time she announced that Bill's father had "gone for good." Bill didn't see his father again for nine years. The exact age this occurred is not given in Wilson's biography, but it was no later than age 10 or 11. Bill later told of hearing that he wouldn't see his father again: "It was an agonizing experience for one who apparently had the emotional sensitivity that I did."[13] He saw his sensitivity as being part of the problem. He could not, and apparently never did, see his sensitivity as being a perfectly natural and normal response to abandonment by the father he loved. He says, "I hid the wound, however, and never talked about it with anybody . . ."[14] Turning to his mentally disturbed mother was out of the question. She "lacked the warmth and understanding" Bill needed.[15] This may have been putting it mildly, because as Bill remembers her, "My mother was a disciplinarian, and I can remember the agony of hostility and fear that I went through when she administered her first good tanning with the back of a hairbrush. Somehow, I never could forget that beating."[16] His mother soon left after recuperating from some unspecified illness. Bill was now abandoned by both parents. He sank into a year-long depression.

Bill stayed with his maternal grandparents. He loved his grandfather, but also recognized that "they were not overpopular people."

At some point, Bill began to excel both scholastically and athletically. At 17, he fell in love with the local minister's daughter, Bertha. Unfortunately, she died "suddenly and unexpectedly." This great loss precipitated a "tremendous depression" which lasted for three years. His grades suffered and he no longer was an overachiever. As he later told it, "No athletics, no schoolwork done, no attention to anyone. I was utterly, deeply, and compulsively miserable, convinced that my whole life had utterly collapsed."[17]

As Wilson's biographer describes his sense of *helplessness* after Bertha's death:

> The evening after Bertha's funeral service, standing in the cemetery next to the crypt that held her body in screaming mockery of his inability ever to hold it again, the suddenly aged Wilson achieved a revelation of "failure": He knew now . . . His need, his loving, didn't matter a good goddamn. His wanting, his hunger and desire, meant nothing to the terrible ongoing forces of creation and he would never forget this truth which he saw and accepted that night.[18]

Bill was never again able to maintain success after this loss. He later told of his thoughts at this time, "I could not be *anybody* at all. I could not win, because the adversary was death."[19] While he certainly had been winning in scholastic and athletic terms, in the more important terms of parental love and romantic love, he had *always* lost.

One facet of the denial of prior abuse and the viewing of "the self as bad/parent as good" is that, quite often, the substance abuser is openly hostile toward one or both parents. While the very early childhood lessons are the ones most sacrosanct, other factors come into play. One is that maltreatment is more easily recognized in the teen years. Also, older children, having a more fully developed intellect, are not as locked into the position of seeing themselves as being wrong as are small children. It is the *emotionally unrecognized* abuse that teaches the child that he is bad or defective that does the most damage.

Another factor is that abused children often become most attached to, and identify with, the most abusive parent. An example of this is a man named Angelo who had begun irregularly attending AA meetings. Angelo, who was around 30 at the time, was extremely skilled at "proper" upper middle class social interaction. He dressed tastefully, was careful to use perfect grammar and pronunciation, and never used bad language. For several months he expressed great anger toward his stepmother, whom he characterized in negative terms, but his deportment and language was always "proper." He described his father and his relationship with him in glowing terms. For months, Angelo expressed great fondness for his father. I sat over coffee with him one night for three hours. During the entire time, he told me story after story about what a perfect father he had.

Not long afterward, I ran into him again at "after meeting coffee." His demeanor and behavior had changed radically. No longer was he worried about being "proper." He was boiling over with rage. Face red, eyes blazing with hatred, he spoke in an entirely uncharacteristic fashion, "That fucking bastard. He used to beat me every time he got drunk. I want to kill that fucking bastard." He went into detail about the sometimes bizarre, always cruel, punishment he had suffered at the hands of his father. After a long time of expressing his rage, as he began to calm down, he began reverting to the "old Angelo." He became concerned about his "unsightly display" and said he felt like some sort of horrible monster. Unfortunately, he was among a group of AA members who, although a little more liberal than most, shared the wisdom that he *was* "half-way" a horrible monster.[*]

For people with various learned attitudes of helplessness, distrust of intuition, contempt for their emotions, and a general basic distrust of *themselves*, drinking alcohol, as well as other addictive behaviors, can have much to offer . . .

---

[*] In AA theology, allowing oneself to experience anger is considered a sin and a leading cause of returning to drinking. Unfortunately, at the time, I was an AA member and had nothing to say. It might have been appropriate to ask who the horrible monster was, a parent who beat and tortured his child year in and year out, or the beaten and tortured child. As I'm writing, I wonder if Angelo ever "made amends" to his father for being angry with him as AA members are expected to do.

1. MacAndrew (1965)
2. AA (1980):171-172
3. AA (1980):12
4. Suzanne Windows, Bob Smith's daughter, in AA (1980):10
5. AA (1980):12
6. AA (1976):172
7. AA (1984):14
8. AA (1984):15
9. AA (1984):24
10. AA (1984):20
11. AA (1984):22
12. AA (1984):24
13. AA (1984):24
14. AA (1984):25
15. AA (1984):25
16. AA (1984):27
17. AA (1984):26
18. Thomsen 1975: 63 cited in Kurtz (1987):12-13
19. AA (1984):37

8: Drinking

In a purely physical sense, alcohol intoxication can be considered to be an across-the-board incapacitation of normal brain function. Depending on the degree of intoxication, people have difficulty speaking clearly, accomplishing tasks like driving and walking, thinking, remembering, and committing new experience to memory. The desire for this disruption of normal mental processes is at the heart of both social drinking and alcoholism.

While there are specific pharmacological effects of alcohol that contribute to social and alcoholic drinking, these are of little relative importance except as a general backdrop for *expectancy effects*. This is demonstrated in a rather humorous anthropological study done among the natives of the Truk Islands in Polynesia.[1]

Young males, not knowing one must *drink* alcohol to get drunk, became "intoxicated" by *sniffing an empty bottle*. They "lost control" of their behavior because they knew from seeing drunken outsiders what happened when people got drunk.

Because they were intoxicated, the village elders declined to punish them. Obviously the behavior was attributable to the alcohol, not the young men.

While this may seem farfetched, there is ample solid evidence that beliefs about the effects of alcohol, or other drugs, override to a very large extent the chemicals' actual physiological effects in terms of behavior and subjective experience.

In a study using hypnosis with heroin addicts, experimenters were able to produce, *by suggestion*, a drug "high" in their subjects complete with physiological changes such as altered pupil size and blood pressure.[2] They also produced the withdrawal state *by suggestion*. The subjects, when actually given drugs and drug-counteracting posthypnotic suggestion, behaved normally. In other words, people can become, for all practical purposes, high on drugs and go through withdrawal from those drugs *without ever taking them*. They can also *behave as though not high* when actually on drugs.

A special method called the *balanced placebo design* has been necessary to determine the effects of alcohol itself as opposed to the effects of believing that alcohol has certain effects. Subjects are divided into two groups. One group is led to *expect* that they are drinking alcohol. The other is led to *expect* that they aren't. Every effort is made to build expectancy, such as mixing the drinks in front of the subjects and demonstrating false "breathalyser" results. Both groups are divided in half again. Half of each group is actually given alcohol and half not. The four groups are:

1) believe alcohol, given alcohol
2) believe alcohol, given no alcohol
3) believe no alcohol, given alcohol
4) believe no alcohol, given no alcohol

Use of this experimental design has disproven many widely held beliefs thought proven in earlier experiments, one being that alcohol causes sexual arousal.

In a study with the balanced placebo design, male social drinkers were divided into the four groups listed above.[3] The subjects were wired to equipment which measured several factors in sexual arousal including penile tumescence, heart rate and skin temperature. After drinking, the subjects listened to tape recordings of heterosexual intercourse, forcible rape, and nonsexual sadistic aggression. The two groups who *believed* that they had drunk alcohol were more aroused by the rape and sadism tapes than the other two groups. Belief, not actual alcohol consumption, was the deciding factor.

Another experiment with the balanced placebo design used "dirty pictures" of varying types, some "deviant" and some "normal."[4] The subjects were timed on how long they spent looking at the individual pictures. Those who *believed* that they had been drinking alcohol, as a group, looked at the "deviant" pictures longer. In other data gathered from the subjects, it was found that only those who had a high level of sexual guilt were affected by the belief that they were drinking. This indicates that, rather than alcohol "unleashing perverted sexuality," *the belief that one has been drinking counteracts sexual guilt.*

The main effect of alcohol on human sexuality is to decrease physiological response. But *believing one has been drinking* more than counteracts decreased physiological sexual response by "giving permission" or "displacing responsibility" for one's behavior from oneself to the alcohol.

The belief that alcohol causes aggressive behavior is also common. In another experiment with a balanced placebo design, experimenters found that "the only significant determinant of aggression was the expectation factor. Subjects who believed they had consumed alcohol were more aggressive than subjects who believed they had consumed a nonalcoholic beverage, regardless of the actual alcohol content of the drinks administered."[5]

Another study found that those who *believed* that alcohol increased aggression were more aggressive when they thought they were drinking. This held true even after taking into consideration how hostile the subjects were to begin with. In other words, no matter how hostile a person may or may not be, if he *believes* that drinking will make him more aggressive, he will be more aggressive if he *thinks* that he is drinking.

The effect of expectancy on behavior when drinking is profoundly highlighted in different South American Indian tribes. Different tribes have different attitudes and beliefs which govern their drinking behavior. One tribe may use alcohol strictly on religious occasions. In a religious ceremony, the priest may get so drunk that he needs help standing up. However, nothing detracts from the completion of his priestly duties. There is neither aggressiveness nor licentiousness. No behavior is *expected* to detract from the spiritual nature of the occasion. None does.

A few miles away, another tribe, under more outside influence, may become rowdy when drinking at a nearby *cantina*. Another nearby tribe may behave piously when drunk at religious ceremonies and lose all restraint on social occasions.

The general attraction of alcohol in our culture is heavily based on its use as a "social lubricant." Alcohol, like Valium, the barbiturates and certain other drugs, is an anti-anxiety agent.[6] It decreases certain types of fear, such as fear of failure, punishment and frustration. A drink or two will lessen or remove the little fears which inhibit social interaction. For example, if someone is nervous about striking up a conversation with a stranger because they are worried about rejection or "saying something stupid," alcohol will weaken the fear and allow spontaneous interaction. Alcohol also narrows awareness in general and decreases awareness of the self.[7]

For instance, the attention of a partygoer is apt to be narrowly focused on the party. The frustrations of the workday, worries about tomorrow, and self-awareness fade away as attention is narrowed to the music, conversation, and food. This is the core of the expectations and goals of social drinkers.[*]

There is no one reason that some people see benefit to drinking excessively over other excessive behaviors. The following paragraphs present some of the more commonly perceived benefits of drinking. *The degree to which the benefits of alcohol are only perceived benefits and fail to fill real needs is the degree to which alcohol use is a problem.* For example, the light social drinker seeks only a moderate amount of disinhibition and "euphoria" from alcohol and only on certain occasions. He generally gets exactly what he expects. He is also likely to expect that alcohol will intensify all feelings, pleasant as well as unpleasant.

Heavy drinkers, on the other hand, perceive great benefit in drinking to excess. Unlike social drinkers who tend to expect alcohol to intensify whatever they feel, alcoholics commonly expect to feel better no matter how they feel.[8] Having such expectations, the worse one feels the more *reason* one has to drink. If a heavy drinker is fighting the emergence of unpleasant feelings of enough intensity and persistence, he may drink so much that his friends will have to tell him the next day how much fun he had.

Drinking to dull the awareness of undesired feelings does nothing to remove the cause of those feelings. A woman who drinks to suppress feelings of anger or jealousy over a suspicion her husband is having an affair will never, by drinking, find out if her suspicions are justified and will not deal with the situation appropriately. Instead, she may hold onto her suspicions, anger, and jealousy in perpetuity, thus "needing" to drink many times over one situation.

---

[*] This narrowing of awareness is not necessarily a pleasant experience. A social drinker usually drinks in a pleasantly stimulating environment. An alcoholic who is sitting alone in a bar, a situation a social drinker rarely finds himself in, may focus his attention on something sad and "cry in his beer."

Drinking alcohol can also be a way of temporarily evading *internal* restrictions. People "know" that alcohol causes aggressive, hostile behavior. Since "the alcohol causes it," a mild-mannered gentleman who never has an unkind word for anyone can, by getting drunk, give vent to his hostility. Everyone, including himself, "knows" that he would never act that way; it was the alcohol. He preserves his self-image. Alcohol serves a "useful" function.

Everyone "knows" that alcohol decreases inhibition and breaks down resistance to sexual advances in women: "Candy is dandy but liquor is quicker." With this knowledge, a prim and proper lady who would never be sexually seduced can be seduced into drinking and, the next morning when she wakes up in a strange bed, can tell herself, "I shouldn't have drunk so much. Look what happened to me." She knows she isn't a "loose woman." It wouldn't have happened if it wasn't for the alcohol.

It's true, though, that because of alcohol's scrambling of normal mental functions, a person might become extremely aggressive or promiscuous due in part to the effects of alcohol—one time. The issue here is not the spurious, one-time, freak incident, but the continual repetition of the same behavior.

The point is not that people consciously set out to use alcohol as an excuse, but that people who have been taught to deny vast areas of their own existence easily fall into a further trap. They come to attribute their own power and their own choices to *external forces*. For instance, the man who repeatedly gets drunk and beats his wife or the woman who gets drunk and "is taken advantage of" every Saturday night will tend to ruefully blame the alcohol and swear never to drink again.

However, no matter how sincere, neither is likely to keep their promise. They will try to be good in early childhood terms. They will work to keep their mental function disrupted. The angry and abusive man will try not to feel angry; the promiscuous woman will try not to feel lonely. Against the certainty that he or she will become angry or lonely, alcohol may seem a "good" solution. Alcohol may come to be "automatically" seen as the solution. The more incapacitated mental function is, the easier it is to be "good." Even if a failure occurs, such as becoming abusive or promiscuous, it can't be helped, "the alcohol was responsible." It is a better to risk becoming abusive or promiscuous than to face the certainty that anger or loneliness will reappear with no one but oneself responsible.

By considering emotions the problem and by believing that drowning them is the best possible choice, it is unlikely that proper associations will be made. The hostile man may never recognize the real causes of his anger or discover productive ways of expressing it. The promiscuous woman may never recognize her loneliness or find ways of relating to men that are more consistent with her values.

Repressed anger and intimacy problems often play a role in alcoholic drinking. However, the "misbehavior" is more often associated with temporary and increasingly futile attempts to escape from learned internal rules and regulations.

These internal restrictions—as opposed to "society's rules"—are ones that other people simply do not have. For example, if someone has been taught that he doesn't deserve to be happy, he can break the rule and be "happy" by becoming drunk. The anti-anxiety effects of alcohol decrease the fear of punishment and the alcohol can be *blamed*. If someone has learned to stifle spontaneity, by being drunk they have *internal* permission to be spontaneous. Again, the alcohol is responsible, not the person.

If someone is taught in childhood that he doesn't deserve to be happy, but to be punished, he can temporarily evade the injunction by getting uproariously drunk and having a good time, then spend the next day "making things right" by suffering a hangover.

Alcohol has many perceived benefits for heavy drinkers other than as permission, or as an excuse, for "misbehavior." People who have been led to believe that they are incompetent and thus fear the possibility of exposure, particularly to themselves, can use alcohol as protection from the feared "truth."[9] For example, someone who fears he is incompetent in the business world may prefer to risk causing failure by drinking too much rather than face the fear that he may indeed be incapable. It is a perverse kind of win-win situation. If he fails, he can blame the drinking. If he succeeds, he can give himself "extra credit" because it was so much more difficult with the handicap. For the serious self-handicapper, there is almost no limit to the variations of this method. It can be used at work, at play, and in relationships.

Perhaps the biggest motivation for excessive drinking is to cope with "negative" emotional states. Alcoholics and addicts of all types see the internal experience of emotion, as well as other integral parts of the self, as bad. The "solution" is to keep the offending emotions out of awareness.

At times when "bad" emotions are subject to being aroused, alcohol consumption increases. One interesting study investigated a group of 60 "heavy social drinkers"* who were provoked to anger with and without an opportunity to retaliate.[10] The drinkers were intentionally provoked to anger with insults about their intelligence, ways of dressing, and general appearance. The experiment, under the guise of a wine-tasting test, showed that those who had no chance to "retaliate" drank significantly more than those who had the chance. Imagine the situation of someone who learned in early childhood to *never* be angry. Without even the internal experience of anger, "retaliation," or even response, is impossible. Imagine the effect on drinking in daily life.

Another experiment with "heavy social drinkers" tested whether fear of being evaluated led to increased drinking.[11] Sixty-four male college students participated in this psychological experiment disguised as a wine-tasting experiment. Thirty-two were led to believe they would be in a second experiment where they would be *personally* evaluated by a group of women. Needless to say, this tended to be a rather intimidating prospect for young college men. Those who expected the evaluation drank considerably more than the other group.

In everyday life, people are constantly evaluated when meeting new acquaintances, applying for a job, or going on a first date. Imagine the intense fear generated and the corresponding increase in alcohol consumption of someone who has been taught, and who is keeping the secret, that he is basically "unfit for survival," "unlovable," and "inherently defective."

A review of the literature on expectancy and drinking behavior cites studies dating back to 1945 about alcohol use in relation to personal power issues.[12] These studies show that alcohol consumption increases in situations where a person feels powerless or incapable. In our culture, people often expect, and therefore often experience, a feeling of power or control when drinking. For someone whose life is pervaded with learned helplessness and who is constantly battling to keep feelings of powerlessness out of awareness, alcohol has great attraction.

Problem drinkers don't consider emotions a helpful source of information. It would be unusual for an alcoholic to appreciate his

---

* "Heavy social drinkers" was defined by dividing college students into five groups depending on the amount they drank. The heavy social drinkers were the top twenty percent in consumption.

feelings of sadness, loneliness, anger, or helplessness. Even if he'd get a glimpse of the meaning and purpose underlying them, having learned that he is helpless in important areas of his life, he would be unlikely to work to solve the problems behind those feelings. Instead, he would take direct action to make the feelings go away. Alcohol is a useful tool in such an endeavor.

For those who have problems with intimacy, alcohol has much to offer in terms of image if not substance. Alcohol sales campaigns often associate alcohol with "good times" and "warm intimacy." The alcoholic beverage industry sells its products in advertisements which usually feature either a couple in a romantic setting or a larger group of people enjoying good times and friendship. People who drink are never, of course, portrayed as lonely social misfits. Our cultural association of alcohol with both sexual and emotional intimacy and with enjoyable social interaction is not lost on the alcoholic.

Normally, someone who later becomes a "problem drinker" begins and maintains drinking on a predominately "social" drinking level for years. The problem develops gradually. For the person whose self-hatred allows only shallow interaction with other people, the image of alcohol becomes confused with the reality of intimacy. As frustration increases over the inability to fill the normal human need for emotionally fulfilling relationships, alcohol offers itself as a symbolic substitute. Significantly, people who give up excessive drinking or drug use often describe it in terms of giving up a lover or best friend.

Cultural beliefs about alcohol build the expectancy that alcohol has magical powers to cause behavior totally separate from a person's identity. This allows a person to engage in behaviors seen as contradictory to his self-image and that he would normally avoid. This function of heavy drinking can become an ever-more-attractive solution to life.

As use increases, real problems tend to get worse. As problems get worse, the subconscious struggles harder for attention, meaning it works to generate more intense emotion. If the "subconscious" learns that the solution to problems is to drink, what is perceived as an alien, uncontrollable force begins to impel a person to ever more self-destructive drinking.

There is nothing irreversible about the addiction process. Tens of millions have quit smoking, a large percentage of overweight people have managed to attain and maintain a desired weight, and at least two or three percent of alcoholics go into remission every year. The reason for these changes varies with the person. Younger substance abusers generally give up their habit as they grow older. They see it as inconsistent with an adult role as spouse and parent.

Often, altered circumstances lead to the change. Someone who drinks due to frustration over being unable to find suitable work may promptly moderate upon finding a new job. Someone who drinks due to the loss of a spouse through death or divorce may moderate or quit when he begins to date. Often alcoholics quit or moderate when they develop a physical intolerance to drinking. It is extremely difficult to maintain a pattern of heavy drinking if the first drink causes sharp stomach pains and the second one makes things worse.

A deep awareness that drinking is not the best choice is what precipitates change. It can take many forms, from one morning looking in the mirror and thinking, "Why am I doing this? This is not what I want to do," to waking up in a hospital after an accidental overdose and becoming aware that, "I will die if I continue this way."

The deep awareness that often precipitates a change in drinking patterns takes two general forms: a moment of clarity or a painful emotional ordeal. AA members aptly use the term "hitting bottom" to describe the tumultuous emotional ordeal precipitating a desire to change. The "moment of clarity" is often cast in "spiritual" terms and ascribed to an awareness of AA's Higher Power.

These deep awarenesses must be distinguished from "shallow" ones. A conscious, surface decision to change that doesn't reach to the depth of the subconscious decisions to drink will leave them unaffected and the drinking behavior "on automatic." A person who internally experiences an inability to stop drinking may be out of touch with the reasons he drinks. He may have learned that he is helpless, so his subconscious automatically fails to muster the resources necessary for the effort to quit or moderate. Or he may use "not being able to stop" as a way of protecting his self-image from the knowledge that he *wants* to drink.

However the decision to change develops and is experienced, it may be only the beginning of a protracted process. The addicted person has the job of finding new ways to fill, or of trying to fill, his needs. This often takes the form of substituting other addictions. With the blessings, assistance, and encouragement of their psychiatrists, drinkers often substitute Valium, Xanax, or other anti-anxiety drugs for alcohol.

Abstinent alcoholics often smoke a lot of cigarettes and drink a lot of coffee, and religious or sexual addictions often come to the fore.

Most people who have drinking problems want to moderate their drinking rather than quit altogether. Disease theorists and AA members consider this to be a symptom of the disease, "denial." While there may be a lot of denial on the subject of controlled drinking, the denial seems to be more a characteristic of the disease theorists and AA members than controlled drinking advocates. The truth of the matter is that, even after treatment that works to *sabotage* the ability to moderate, almost three times as many alcoholics *do* manage to moderate their drinking than manage to abstain.[13]

Treatment sabotages the ability to moderate by instilling AA's "One drink, one drunk" belief in those who already have drinking problems.[14] *This is teaching learned helplessness.* When people *learn* that they can't help but continue drinking, the subconscious automatically fails to marshal the resources to stop. Also, if someone *wants* to get drunk he can "accidentally" or "unwittingly" eat rum cake, use mouthwash, or take a sip out of the "wrong glass." By placing the blame on the alcohol and "innocent action," an "alcoholic" gets to drink *and* preserve his self-image. The alcohol is responsible, not the person.

Some excellent studies have compared the benefits of abstinence and controlled drinking as treatment goals.[15] One of these involved 70 alcoholics who, in order to qualify for the study, had to meet certain conditions: they must not have been AA members, must not have believed in the disease theory, and must not have been able to manage an extended period of abstinence. The 70 were randomly assigned to one of two groups, one with the goal of abstinence, the other with the goal of moderation. After treatment they were followed for two years. The findings strongly support moderation as a goal over abstinence.

Most of those assigned to the abstinence group objected to the goal. During treatment, *those assigned abstinence as a goal drank more* than those in the controlled drinking group. During the two-year follow-up, both groups drank the same in both quantity and frequency. An important point is that most of those assigned an abstinence goal moderated on their own. Perhaps most important is that while those who were classified as "lighter" drinkers did equally well in both groups, *those classified as "heavier" drinkers did better with controlled drinking treatment.*

Of course, abstinence is necessary for some people. People with health problems such as liver damage and diabetes must abstain. This is not because one drink inevitably leads to the next but because one drink is injurious to an already ailing body. Abstinence is also clearly necessary for those who believe "one drink, one drunk," because *for those who believe it*, one drink, or perhaps even using mouthwash, does lead to one drunk.

This discussion of the merits of abstinence is *not* intended to suggest that people who are successfully abstaining should drink. The point is that for *most* problem drinkers abstinence is an unrealistic goal. The "loss of control" hypothesis used to support a need for abstinence for "alcoholics" has been proven untrue. The person with drinking problems who wants to moderate his drinking, and who hasn't been convinced that he can't, in all likelihood will succeed. The situation is entirely different for people with heavy exposure to AA. They almost never moderate. As a matter of fact, *practicing AA's "spiritual principles" usually makes the underlying problems of alcoholics and addicts much worse . . .*

---

1. Marshall (1979)
2. Ludwig and Lyle (1964)
3. Briddell (1978)
4. Lang et al (1981)
5. Lang, Goeckner and Adesso (1975)
6. Gray (1978)
7. Steele and Josephs (1988)
8. Russell and Bond (1980)
9. Jones and Berglas (1978)
10. Marlatt et al (1975)
11. Higgins and Marlatt (1975)
12. Donovan and Marlatt (1980)
13. Polich (1980):102
14. Schaeffer (1971)
15. Sanchez-Craig (1980), Sanchez-Craig et al (1984), and Sanchez-Craig and Lei (1986)

9: Meetings

AA meetings are held in a wide variety of locations. Groups rent rooms from churches, schools, and community organizations, and treatment centers often give them free space. In most cities, AA members, separate from AA itself, band together to establish "club-houses"—storefronts or houses used exclusively for Twelve Step meetings and socialization by groupers.

The membership of groups varies widely. The most readily observable differences are in social and economic status and age. In wealthier neighborhoods, of course, the membership is wealthier, and in poor neighborhoods, poorer. There are also many exclusive meetings in private homes where an invitation is necessary and "undesirables," however they may be defined, are not invited.

The size of meetings also varies tremendously, from perhaps half a dozen groupers to hundreds. The larger, more prestigious meetings consistently have speakers with 20 or more years of Time. In Los Angeles, celebrities also lend prestige, and the amount of Time they have is of less importance than their celebrity status.

The larger, more prestigious meetings tend to take on the atmosphere of a great crusade and may have up to several hundred people in attendance. Members of the cheerful crowd greet each other with hugs and pleasantries, exchange bits of gossip about other members, discuss other meetings, and share anticipation of the speaker's message. In keeping with the traditions of the Oxford Group, everyone is on a first name basis. Large meetings normally have one or two speakers who give their "pitch." Sometimes, one-speaker meetings open the floor to questions on the Program for the speaker who, having Time, acts as an authority.

Most meetings are smaller, usually having substantially fewer than 100 people. They normally open up to "sharing" for witness and confession by individual groupers after the speaker finishes, exactly as was done at Oxford Group meetings. This "Gospel of Personal Experience," whether related by just one elder or by as many groupers as time allows, is the core of all meetings.

The reading of sacred text is also part of every meeting. The Oxford Group, being "more spiritual than religious," but still (in Christian countries) acknowledging its Christian roots, used the Bible for readings. Alcoholics Anonymous, being "spiritual, not religious," doesn't use the Bible at all; rather, it uses another sacred text, the inspired Word of God as expressed through Bill Wilson, the Big Book.[*] [**]

The Twelve Steps are read at almost every meeting. When taking collection, called "The Seventh Tradition," the Twelve Traditions are read, bringing a spiritual context to the collection of money.

Among the most popular readings is an abbreviated version of Chapter Five from the Big Book. In it, the recovery program of AA is laid out, beginning with "Rarely have we seen a person fail who has thoroughly followed our path . . .," through the Twelve Steps, and ending with AA's description of the predicament of the alcoholic and the solution to his problems:

a) That we were alcoholic and could not manage our own lives.
b) That probably no human power could have relieved our alcoholism.
c) That God could and would if He were sought.[1]

In continuing the traditions of the Oxford Group, AA uses elders as preachers. The quality of the speakers varies, but almost anyone with more than a few months of Time is a passable if not excellent speaker, able to "carry the message" skillfully, with sincerity, passion, and humor. The best speakers tend to have the worst "bottoms," both emotionally and behaviorally. Having the worst

---

[*] AA members never *say* "the inspired Word of God." The *do* however, *say and believe* that the AA Program and literature were "inspired by God." The present-day grouper may be disturbed at the suggestion that the Big Book is a sacred text, but he would likely be horrified if someone were to show irreverence for it.

[**] This is AA's present-day practice. The situation was somewhat different in AA's early years in Ohio. Dr. Bob kept a copy of the Bible on the podium at his meetings in Akron until well into the 1940s.

bottoms, they are living testimonials to the great recovery available to anyone through AA.

To hear the "best" speakers it is usually necessary to go to the more prestigious meetings. Since so few groupers manage to attain 10, 20, or 30 years of Sobriety, people with a great deal of Time are in great demand. In the competition for speakers, the larger, more prestigious meetings usually win out.

The speech itself is called "sharing," just as in the Oxford Group. It is the Oxford Group's "Gospel of Personal Experience," although it is now called "sharing personal experience," "Twelfth Step sharing," or "sharing experience, strength, and hope." This sharing, more aptly called a sermon, begins with a recitation of immorality, misery, and ruination at the hands of Devil Drink, now referred to as alcohol or alcoholism. It goes on to tell of "spiritual awakening" in AA. Unlike the Oxford Group, which claimed salvation and redemption by Jesus through the Oxford Group,* AA proclaims "recovery" by one's "Higher Power" through the Twelve Steps and Alcoholics Anonymous. The general format for the sermon is, "What it was like then, how I got here, and what it is like now." In order to "not preach," the speaker carefully restricts use of the word "you." The speaker couches almost all statements in terms of "I," "we," and "alcoholics."

The speaker opens the sermon by identifying himself by his first name and "disease" or "diseases." The diseases are usually identified as such through the existence of Twelve Step programs for those "suffering" from them. For instance, "My name is John and I'm an alcoholic and a junkie." Using only the first name is thought to protect anonymity and maintain humility. Labeling oneself as "alcoholic," with or without other diseases, is considered essential for beginners to help break through "denial" and establish humility. It is also considered essential in maintaining recovery because, unless humility is maintained, God will not protect the alcoholic from Devil Drink.

After identifying himself, the speaker may tell a joke on himself

---

* Evidently the Bible, and Jesus along with it, were discardable even before the rise of Alcoholics Anonymous. It was reported that in India in the 1920s and '30s, where local religious groups were offended by attempts at conversion to Christianity, groupers also dropped Jesus in order to more effectively win converts to their organization.

or alcoholics in general to warm up the audience before the real beginning of the sermon: "What it was like." He recites his past in terms of the "disease" of alcoholism. The word "sin" is never used, but the speaker's history is hardly a medical history as might seem appropriate to those who only know of alcoholism through *public* statements of people "in recovery" and treatment industry advertising; instead, the word "sin" is replaced with "defects of character." Unlike Oxford Group members, who confessed to having been "wretched" or "lost" sinners, today's AA groupers confess to having been "sick," "suffering," or "drinking" alcoholics.

The main theme of this part of the sermon is the confession (called "admitting" in AA) of "defectiveness" and "powerlessness" "from the beginning." Confession of the worst sins are usually made with little sadness, guilt, or penitence, and often in a joking, sensationalistic manner.* The recitation of sins may begin in childhood or with the first drink.

Sins of childhood generally cover three main areas: physical, emotional, and spiritual, since alcoholism is considered a physical, emotional, and spiritual disease. The physical aspect of the disease can include symptoms of "alcoholic thinking" and "reacting wrong" before ever having had a drink. For instance, I remember one speaker who told of being punished as an eleven-year-old for making a "B" on his report card instead of his customary straight "A"s. He was grounded and forced to stay in his bedroom for the next semester. He then told how he reacted wrong: he became rebellious.

Any childhood misbehavior is held up as a symptom of disease. Another speaker shared a rather popular theme. As a child, he thought he was adopted even though he wasn't. Among the emotional symptoms of the disease in childhood are having felt lonely, sad, angry, and different, as though one didn't belong. These "symptoms" are described in the context of "abnormal" or "alcoholic" sensitivity, as Bill Wilson said he displayed as a despairing child abandoned by his father to his mentally ill, abusive mother.

Often, the speaker will tell a story about himself to prove that he has always been defective. This story may be set at the time of the

---

* This refers only to the main speaker. Other groupers may later share for confession, called "Fifth Step sharing" which in stark contrast to "Twelfth Step sharing" is normally characterized by a penitent attitude and remorse.

first drink, but often predates it. One man shared that when he was 16 a girl he had been going with for a year broke up with him. "I felt abandoned," he said. "I've always been that way." Another speaker told how she had always had behavior problems. At two and a half, she would lie awake at night. "My father was a psychiatrist, so I know it wasn't anything my parents did." She knew she was defective from the start. Earlier, however, she had shared that her grandmother died when she was two and a half. Her wise parents told her that Grandma was asleep; they didn't want to upset her. When speaking of themselves in childhood, AA members *always* describe themselves, with all sincerity, as "bad."

The portion of the sermon which begins with the first drink ever taken and ends with finding AA is called the "drunk-a-log." Sermons often begin here, and the drunk-a-log often comprises almost the entire sermon. It is here, beginning with the first drink, that the speaker "qualifies." To "qualify" means to prove one's authority, wisdom, and right to preach to others by telling how incompetent one has been at using alcohol. Usually beginning with, "I drank alcoholically from the start," the speaker tells of loss of control over both drinking and behavior. Except for the seriousness with which the concept is held, the overall message is reminiscent of Flip Wilson's comic character Geraldine saying, "The Devil made me do it." The greater the "sins" committed while under the influence of Devil Drink, the more appreciation the congregation of groupers shows for the speaker. The speaker confirms for them the Powerlessness of an "alcoholic" in the face of the "cunning, baffling, and powerful" disease of alcoholism.

In speaking of the individual symptoms of the disease, the speaker outlines specific characteristics of alcoholics. These will vary somewhat from speaker to speaker. Among ones which may be heard are "I thought it was cool to drink," "I feel euphoric when I drink; alcoholics are different," and "I was angry at the world."

Whatever the particular symptoms given, the speaker paints everything in his past, prior to AA, in terms of "unmanageability," hopelessness, desperation, and "disease." All pre-AA hopes, dreams, emotions, and thoughts are now recognized to have resulted from "the disease."

To prove their powerlessness, speakers usually admit to futile attempts to stop drinking "alone," meaning without AA. Coming from "personal experience" they make jokes about the futility of trying various therapies. Speakers ridicule themselves for any attempts to stop drinking without AA, even if they succeeded for months or years longer than they have in AA. They also ridicule themselves for not admitting their disease and its "true nature," meaning their own Powerlessness.

This is often the point where impassioned pleas are addressed to the newcomer: "Alcoholics rarely recover on their own." The speaker may then point to the Twelve Steps posted on the wall. "Look, this is a 'we' program, not an 'I' program. You don't have to do it alone. Let us love you until you learn to love yourself."

The first-timer at a meeting may be awed by the sincerity, "honesty," and telling of intimate secrets. This is a direct result of the "humility" of the speaker as expressed through his admission of the "unmanageability" of his life before AA and his "powerlessness" in the face of alcoholism. The theme is expanded in clichés like "My best thinking got me here" and "I am my own worst enemy." The speaker will often admit his motivation for "working with others," including speaking, is to "stay sober myself." The speaker never suggests that there are good qualities within himself. All good flows from the Program.

The "how I got here" portion of the sermon maintains the humility of the speaker. First time attendees attribute their presence to a variety of reasons: court order, "intervention," or a friend's suggestion, among others. Even highly religious persons attribute their arrival to a variety of reasons. The person with Time, however, has always been guided by the direct intervention of God. God got them arrested, had their family intervene, or sent an "Eskimo" (an AA elder)[*] to "bring me in from the cold." Never, ever, have I heard an AA speaker say anything remotely resembling, "I thought I had a problem so I used the brains God gave me and sought help." The speaker is likely, with all due humility, to instead announce, "I thought. Ha! Ha!," to which the groupers respond with knowing laughter.

---

[*] The term "Eskimo" can also refer to any person involved in a "coincidence" arranged by God which leads a person to AA. AA members, like the Oxford Groupers before them, believe that "there are no coincidences" and they should constantly be on the lookout for what appear to be coincidences because they are clues to God's will.

The "what it is like now" portion of the sermon is an expression of gratitude toward AA and a demonstration of recovery in AA. This portion usually stresses the sincerely held belief that "AA saved my life." Examples are often given of people who, not having found the Program or not having stayed in the Program, eventually drank themselves to death. The speaker holds himself up as someone saved from inevitable "jails, institutions, and death" by Alcoholics Anonymous. Because AA rescued him, the drinking alcoholic, from the clutches of Devil Drink, the speaker attributes anything that he now perceives as good in his life directly to the Program, since without AA the speaker wouldn't even be alive. "I owe my life to Alcoholics Anonymous."

The speaker goes into detail about the benefits received by working the steps. Among the most important and frequently cited is the finding of Serenity. Serenity, usually portrayed by the speaker as a state of "evenness," is described as *not* suffering from the feelings presumably experienced only by drinking alcoholics. This "evenness" is due to no longer feeling resentments (anger) and self-pity (sadness, loneliness, or hopelessness). "Evenness" also means not feeling extremes of happiness, or feeling "too" good. The only human emotion that seems consistent with Serenity is Gratitude. This state is referred to as "utopia" in the Big Book.*

The speaker will tell how serenity is maintained "one day at a time" by working the Steps. He will perhaps give examples of how his serenity was temporarily lost or endangered by allowing an evil internal force (personalized as "My alcoholic told me . . .") to come between himself and his Higher Power.

If the speaker has told of "not being understood" in his "suffering alcoholic" days, he will now tell of the understanding found in AA. "I never felt I was understood. I didn't know I was an alcoholic. Normies can't understand an alcoholic. Only another alcoholic can understand."

"Being understood" is closely related to "belonging": "I never felt like I belonged. I belong here. I am an alcoholic." The speaker may tell of the love found in AA and describe AA as "my real family." Among the loving acts attributed to AA is that "they loved me

---

* "Utopia" originally was worded "heaven on earth." It was changed prior to publication in order to not overtly contradict Catholic beliefs. *(Pass It On*, p. 201)

enough to tell me the truth." This is another point where the speaker may implore the newcomer to "let us love you until you learn to love yourself." Evidence of how the speaker has learned to love himself is often expressed like this: "I get on my knees every morning and admit my powerlessness," "I work the steps," and "I force myself to go to meetings even when I don't want to."

There is a sharp dividing line between what is "good" and what is "bad" in AA. Everything good in life is attributed to "working a Spiritual Program." Everything "bad," such as troubling thoughts, emotions other than Gratitude, and wanting to drink are attributed, in part, to the "alcoholic self," to not following direction (Oxford Group's Guidance) from God, one's sponsor and other elders, to not attending enough meetings, to forgetting one's own Powerlessness, to not working the Steps, and to not "working with others."

The "what it is like now" portion of the sermon can be summarized as "no matter how 'bad' you are and have been, I was worse and AA keeps me 'good.' I don't feel pain. You can be good and not feel pain too."

The speaker models being good in many ways. He doesn't show "bad" feelings, and instead displays Gratitude, Serenity and good cheer. When speaking of past trauma, instead of expressing the feelings normally associated with tragedy, he laughs at himself and often, with a self-disparaging joke, invites the other groupers to join in. Laughing at his own pain and inviting others to join allows him to demonstrate how he has "recovered" in the Program.

The congregation assists the good speaker with unanimous responses to Program clichés and other ultimate truths. They don't often shout "Amen," but rather shout "right on" and "yeah," nod in agreement, and burst into applause or laughter at the appropriate moments. This is not to suggest that the groupers consciously work together to respond in a particular fashion, but that they all hold the same beliefs and view things from a similar perspective. If a speaker tells a joke about how he "thought," all the groupers, *knowing* how alcoholics suffer from "alcoholic thinking," are compelled to laugh along. A speaker may tell of a tragedy that befell him because he didn't take the first step seriously enough. Everyone *knows* what happens when powerlessness is not admitted, so they can nod in agreement. When a speaker says, "When I'm alone with myself I'm behind enemy lines," the groupers can all relate and laugh along because they know what it is like to be alone with themselves.

Speakers find it important to give certain warnings to the newcomer. These are consistent with the presumed three major components of alcoholism as a physical, emotional, and spiritual disease. The presumed uncontrollable craving that develops after the first drink or perhaps just a sip falls under the physical attributes. The warning clichés are "one drink, one drunk" and "don't drink or use no matter what."

Another area, which could be attributed to either the physical or emotional aspect of the disease, is "alcoholic thinking." Symptoms that the newcomer is cautioned to watch out for (dangerous thoughts) include thinking that you might not be an alcoholic, thinking that you don't need the Program, disagreement with someone with more Time, thinking that you don't need a sponsor, or thinking that you can stop at one drink. The speaker often uses himself as an example and may give the warning indirectly: "When I was new, they told me I needed to work the first step. I thought I didn't need to. Let me tell you, not everyone makes it back." The speaker may then go on to list AA members who drank themselves to death as a result of not following direction, of not "Surrendering to the Program."

Newcomers are warned against such emotional symptoms of the disease as feeling angry, sad, lonely, or afraid. These feelings are all ways that "cunning, baffling, and powerful" alcohol impels an alcoholic, against his will, to take the first drink. The speaker may say, "I can't afford to be angry anymore," or "Resentment is the number one reason for slipping." Sadness, loneliness and hopeless-ness, grouped together as self-pity or "being on the pity pot," are also symptoms of alcoholism and tricks used by "my alcoholic" (the Oxford Group's "Evil One") to "lead me to the first drink." According to the Big Book, "Sometimes we think fear ought to be classed with stealing. It seems to cause more trouble."[2] A speaker may caution the newcomer with "FEAR: False Evidence Appearing Real."

"Spirituality" is generally treated rather lightly at newcomer meetings because, as the Big Book cautions, "There is no use arousing any prejudice he [the pigeon] may have against certain theological terms and conceptions about which he may already be confused."[3]

One of the most popular cliches, which gives a warning of a spiritual nature, is "Don't leave five minutes before the miracle," meaning that Serenity is just around the corner. Warnings of what happens when one doesn't admit one's disease, doesn't work the Steps, or doesn't get a sponsor are also of a spiritual nature, although they may not be presented that way,

The warnings and aims of a newcomer's meeting are well summed up by one of the more popular clichés, "HALT: Don't get too Hungry, Angry, Lonely, or Tired." All four are considered to put an alcoholic at risk of taking the first drink. Hunger and tiredness can be attended to by the newcomer himself, but anger and loneliness are emotional symptoms of a spiritual disease that need spiritual attention. The newcomer is cautioned to either telephone an AA member or go to a meeting at the first sign of a bad emotion or wanting to drink. Going to meetings and getting direction from an Elder are both considered spiritual in AA, even if they are not presented to the newcomer as spiritual principles.

Normally, little direct advice is given at a newcomer meeting, but what is given is presented carefully. The most important step in rescuing the "still suffering alcoholic" is to get him to commit to attending more meetings. The only direct advice that may be given can be summed up by the cliché "90 meetings in 90 days." One popular way of expressing this and exhorting the newcomer to return is "Just stick around for 90 days and we will refund your misery." The suggestion may also be that "If you are new here, you are too new to know if you need AA, so just go to 90 meetings in 90 days and then you can decide."

Other common suggestions are to begin working the steps—"No one ever drank while working the steps"—and to get a sponsor. Those who doubt that they have the disease may be encouraged to "Just stop for a year. Only an alcoholic would have a problem with it or object to it."

Meetings often include the ritual of giving "chips" and observing "birthdays." Chips, tokens such as key rings or medallions, are given for varying lengths of "sobriety." The periods observed in this way are 30, 60, 90, and 180 days. Each honored member usually has a few moments to address the congregation. He expresses gratitude to the Program for making it all possible and exhorts those with less Time to "Keep coming back, it really works!"

Following the giving of chips, birthdays of one or more years of continuous abstinence are celebrated. They are a joyous occasions complete with cake, candles, and the singing of "Happy Birthday" by the entire congregation. For the AA member, birthdays are public acknowledgements of "working a good program" and a celebration of AA's most intensely held value, absolute abstinence. The AA birthday supersedes the importance of "natal" birthdays, which must be distinguished in conversation to avoid confusion.

While the AA birthday is a joyous occasion marking spiritual progress, "natal" birthdays are seen as days when the grouper is in special danger of drinking, as are all holidays celebrated by "normies." Real birthdays, Christmas, Thanksgiving, and New Year's Eve are all days on which one is particularly vulnerable to Devil Drink. One is warned that at these times it is wise to stay particularly close to the Program. To this end, marathon, 24-hour meetings are held on holidays.

Most meetings open the floor for witnessing and confession from the congregation. New groupers, with only days, weeks or months of Time, engage in the Oxford Group's "sharing for confession," now called "Fifth Step sharing." These confessions, known as "being honest" and "admitting defects of character" are, in contrast to the Twelfth Step sharing of the speaker, usually highly charged with anger, sadness, and remorse. Among the most emotional confessions are those of groupers who have had a drink of alcohol. The penitent will share his realization of Powerlessness and express great Humility. This is appreciated—humility and self-humiliation are always cheerfully applauded by AA members. These are qualities at the heart of AA spirituality and are held as essential to maintaining recovery.*

If the sharer deviates from AA doctrine, the audience may respond with derisive laughter, boos, stony silence, patronization, or expressions of fear for the sharer. Groupers with more Time will "help" the novice. For instance, if someone with three months Time should announce that he has stayed sober without working the steps, an Elder (someone with more than three months) may share how the

---

* To quote an "early and wonderful friend of AA," "Alcoholics Anonymous is natural; it is natural at the point where nature comes closest to the supernatural, namely in humiliations and in consequent humility." (Big Book p. 574)

Steps are but suggestions and no one has to work them if they don't want to. He will then go on to list all the pitiful examples of those who drank themselves to death because "their disease told them" that they didn't need to work the Steps.

Groupers with Time are interspersed with "beginners." Those with Time share in the same fashion as the speaker, often thanking the speaker for his wise words and, perhaps, testifying to the speaker's "having good sobriety." They will also give their own abbreviated version of "What it was like then and what it is like now," witnessing to their own miraculous recovery in AA.

There is no sharp dividing line between those who engage in sharing for witness and those who share for confession. A sharer may first make a tearful confession and then follow it with praise for the Program. Nor is a great deal of Time necessary to engage in Twelfth Step sharing. The difference is determined by a grouper's relative status in a meeting. In a treatment center, for example, perhaps no one has even 30 days of abstinence. Under these circumstances, those with the most Time, even if only two or three weeks, tend to take on the role of elder authority and witness to the success of AA-based treatment and the wisdom of AA. They also point out errors in thought and dispense advice to those with less Time.

One thing clear to the casual observer is the recovery evident in those with Time. They can laugh at things the newer grouper cries about. They have licked the alcohol problem and their good cheer and Serenity bear witness to the difference between themselves and those who have only begun in AA.

At the end of the meeting, someone is chosen to lead the closing prayer. This is usually the Lord's Prayer but may be the Serenity Prayer. At the close of the prayer, the members all chant with conviction, "Keep coming back, it really works!" This is the end of the meeting but may not be the end of the meeting experience. Groupers get together for coffee afterwards, and the newcomer is invited.

For the newcomer, much that the speaker says resonates at a very deep level. Whether he arrives under his own volition or court order, or even if he has already moderated or stopped drinking, he is in an extremely vulnerable position. His crutch, alcohol, which he has used for so long to reduce his awareness of emotions, to drown out his ability to think, or as a defense against attributing real or imagined misbehavior to himself, is not, at the moment, a viable option for him.

When the speaker and other sharers talk about "what it was like," the newcomer can relate to the feelings they suffered prior to AA. Without alcohol to dull mental function, he is likely to be fighting off overwhelming feelings of anger, sadness, loneliness, and "badness."

It is not surprising that someone who has learned to automatically suppress self-awareness would be at a loss to explain, even to himself, not only excessive drinking, but any aspect of his behavior. When he hears of the "Powerlessness" and "unmanageability" of alcoholics, that they are victims of a disease, it rings true. His subjective experience is that his drinking comes from somewhere outside himself, and lessons of learned helplessness carried forward from childhood leave him with a feeling of powerlessness.

Other characteristics of "drinking alcoholics" described at AA meetings are likely to hit home with the newcomer. Anyone whose self-hatred is so intense that he seeks to drown normal mental functioning and self-awareness feels unloved. By the same token, the newcomer to AA is likely to feel misunderstood. His self-awareness is extremely limited. The problem is not so much an inability of others to understand him, but an inability to understand and express himself. For instance, imagine a problem drinker who goes on a binge every time his feelings are hurt. The problem drinker may insist, especially to himself, that his feelings were not hurt. The drinking helps him be "not aware." If the drinker has achieved his aim of not being aware through drinking, he will not be conscious of his hurt feelings. Any suggestion by someone who actually does understand the situation that his feelings were indeed hurt would *prove* to him that he wasn't understood.

The newcomer is also likely to feel different from others. Having learned in early childhood that essential parts of his personality are bad and not to be acknowledged, he has never had the opportunity to learn that other people have similar feelings and thoughts, or at least might have if they had suffered similar upbringings. In AA, these feelings of being different are familiar to all. They are a symptom of "the disease."

The AA environment is a recreation of the addictive family system. The "bad" presented in an AA meeting is the same "bad" taught children in an addictive family system. One's awareness, emotions and thinking are presented as symptoms of a disease. The ideal modeled by the speaker and other elders is the ideal taught to children in addictive family systems. The AA value of Serenity, an emotional void fillable only with Gratitude, closely matches childhood's lessons of don't be angry, sad, afraid, lonely, or "too happy." Those "in recovery" present themselves to newcomers as having achieved this drug-like state of Serenity. ("Drug-like" is a fitting term, because drugs are the most efficient and popular way of suppressing normal human emotions.)

The speaker also models the ideals taught in the addictive family system by discounting his own thinking. The child wasn't ridiculed or punished for agreeing with his parents, but for having "bad thoughts" or, better stated, for questioning his parents' statements, actions, or attitudes. The speaker is a "good child." He discounts his own thoughts.

One very attractive concept for the newcomer is that, unlike in the past where he could blame alcohol for his behavior only when actually drinking, under AA's disease concept of alcoholism he can attribute *everything* troubling within himself to alcohol. Every feeling, thought, act, or shortcoming which he deems "bad" is merely a disease symptom. This even includes things that happened *before* he ever took a drink. For example, if he still feels guilty about poor grades in school, even if he didn't have his first drink until after graduation, he can now blame alcoholism. He is "good" and "innocent." He is a victim of a disease. He is also in a room full of people who are in unanimous agreement. They agree because they "understand."

A great deal is promised to the newcomer. The clearest and most overt promise is that "it really works." This means that the newcomer will be able to share the solution to the "alcohol problem" found by others who were, according to their pitches, usually far worse off than the newcomer.

Perhaps the most attractive promise is the Serenity claimed and modeled by AA elders. According to their statements and demeanor at meetings, they avoid or quickly dispose of "resentment" and "self-pity." They can, rather than *feel* pain, *laugh* at the most painful of experiences. Due to their Spiritual Program, they are above normal human emotion.

The newcomer is not necessarily overwhelmed by the meeting, nor is he necessarily eager to attend again. The only important point from the perspective of cult recruitment is that he does attend again, perhaps even making a commitment to attend 90 meetings in 90 days until he is "qualified" to decide whether he needs AA or not.

The first-time visitor is often overwhelmed. He may find it extremely difficult to remain unmoved by what he has seen and heard. In the space of an hour or two, stories of wrecked and healed lives are presented. Newer members pour out their anguished hearts and souls. The audience may move in quick succession from sadness, to anger, to joy, to gratitude. Wild applause and laughter echo from the walls. The newcomer may leave his first encounter with the impression that the groupers, in spite of holding some odd beliefs and using rather cryptic language, are extremely sincere, open, happy, and have found something that "really works." But this is only a small part of the dynamics of a meeting. The more important, *life-changing* effects of the meeting are much more subtle.

The most important part of recruitment in any mind-control cult is meeting attendance. One of the reasons for this was well demonstrated in a series of classic experiments done in the early 1950s by Solomon Asch.[4]

Various numbers of people in a room were given the job of determining which of two lines was longer, even though one was obviously longer than the other. Each participant gave his answer in turn. This was repeated several times. The catch was that all but the last to announce were confederates of the experimenter. They would all either give the right answer or all give the wrong answer. The purpose of the experiments was to determine the effect on the last person.

Only one in four of the subjects managed to remain independent and give the correct answer every time, even though the answer was obvious. Some of those who answered incorrectly were "just going along," but some actually believed the obviously incorrect answers they gave were correct. *Every one of them, even the ones who managed to stay independent, began to doubt their own perceptions.*

The effect of the majority's unanimity was to create distrust of one's own perception. In a large majority of cases it also changed the subjects' behavior. In the more extreme cases, it actually altered individuals' perceptions.

In everyday life, this phenomenon has little lasting effect. A Jewish person attending a Methodist church service will be confronted with many unanimous opinions directly contradicting his own. He may even wonder, for a moment, whether Jesus is the real Messiah, but he is extremely unlikely to change his beliefs. He ultimately trusts his own life, his own thought processes, and his own conclusions.

The situation is entirely different in a cult meeting. One of the major differences between legitimate organizations and mind-control cults is that, in cults, one of the unanimous opinions is that the potential new member is incapable of exercising good judgement. Any disagreement or disbelief of doctrine is treated as a sign of poor judgment. In AA, this is expressed in the term "alcoholic thinking" and the phrase, "hasn't been around long enough to know." It is also expressed in patronizing attitudes.

Patronizing attitudes are also reflected in the names that members use to describe targets of indoctrination. Scientologists refer to them as "raw meat," and Oxford Groupers referred to them as "lost sheep." Alcoholics Anonymous refers to them as "pigeons," "beginners," and "babies." Of course, all of these terms are used lovingly.

Being a minority of one is far from the only factor that influences the potential recruit. Further explanation of cult mind-control techniques calls for the use of a slightly expanded version of the model of the mind used in Chapter 5. As was discussed, the human mind is of two parts, the conscious and the subconscious. The conscious mind processes information and sends it to the subconscious for storage and later reference. One part of the conscious mind, which here will be called the "critical factor," is responsible for critically interpreting information before it is stored in the subconscious for later use.

Imagine again a Jewish man at a Christian church service. He is likely to hear statements and phrases in either the sermon or in the singing of hymns such as "Jesus is our Lord and Savior," and "Jesus lives." Statements about Jesus will be analyzed by the critical factor against ideas already held in the subconscious. They will be found not to be self-relevant, to be other people's beliefs, and will be stored as such. Just hearing the word Jesus would be a tip-off that the information being received referred to *someone else's* religion. Statements about Jesus would be stored for later recall as fact, not about his own reality, but about Christian belief. There is little or no chance that the man would convert to Christianity.

Of course, the response of a Christian in a Jewish service would be similar. The information received would be critically analyzed and stored in the subconscious, not as one's own reality, but as information about Jewish beliefs and practices.

Now imagine for a moment a person with no "critical factor." He would *unquestioningly* store every piece of information in his subconscious as a "bottom line" truth. After leaving a Christian service he'd be Christian. The next day, if he were to go to a Jewish service, he'd leave with the Jewish faith. Witnessing a political debate, he would switch sides as quickly and as often as the speakers changed. Every statement would be accepted uncritically. When he went to check his beliefs, he would find someone else's beliefs in place of his own. He wouldn't even recognize them as "not his." Thinking that they are his own, which carries the automatic implication that they are true, they are beyond questioning.

Of course, no one is so suggestible. Everyone has a "critical factor" which filters and processes information for storage. The important point for cult recruitment is to bypass the critical factor, the ability to analyze and alter information before storage in the subconscious. In Alcoholics Anonymous meetings this is done in various ways. Combined with the "minority of one" effect, these methods can have profound effects on the personality.

One of the ways the critical factor is bypassed is through the "humility" of the speaker. People are rightly a little suspicious of others who claim to be doing "good deeds" while expecting nothing in return. The AA speaker quickly lays this suspicion to rest: "I am doing this to stay sober myself." There is never any hint that this is not true. Body language proves the sincerity of the speaker. The simple statement of the speaker carries several implications which may bypass the critical faculty because of the acceptance that the speaker is indeed speaking to stay sober. These implications are: "Speaking at AA meetings keeps people from drinking"; "The speaker is abstinent"; and "There is no ulterior motivation (and therefore no danger) involved."

When the speaker discounts himself, it has the paradoxical effect of building credibility. It defies reason that someone would confess to terrible misbehavior and personal inadequacy and could then turn around and give, with absolute sincerity, inaccurate information about "alcoholics" or "recovery" to the unanimous approval and agreement of a room full of people, who obviously "understand" him.

One of the popular ways to establish humility is for a speaker to say he is a liar. How is one to analyze what he has to say? He is obviously very sincere. Starting with the statement that he is a liar, he either is a liar and is now telling the truth, or he normally is not a liar, but is lying now, so he normally tells the truth. There is obviously great truth and meaning in this statement, judging by the unanimous approval of the groupers. The problem is to find it. One's own credibility is reduced: "I don't understand." The speaker's credibility is increased: "What he is saying must have meaning."

With the speaker's sincerity established through "humility," he is virtually unchallengeable since *he says he is guilty*. Planting thoughts in the pigeon's subconscious becomes much easier.

Like a skilled hypnotherapist, a skilled AA speaker presents statements in a certain order. A statement which otherwise would be rejected has a much better chance of slipping into the subconscious if it is immediately preceded by two or three unchallengeable statements. For example, a hypnotherapist, while inducing trance, may say, "You can feel the weight of your body pressing down against the chair. Take notice of your hands, whether they feel warm or cold. Now notice how your breathing is becoming deeper and slower." The first two statements are unchallengeable and the mind is expecting another unchallengeable statement. In the third statement, the instruction to "notice how your breathing is becoming deeper and slower . . ." normally slips by the critical faculty and the subconscious will act on it. *The client will notice how his breathing is becoming deeper and slower.*

This same method is used by AA speakers. In keeping with proper humility, speakers make some statement about themselves, such as, "I thought I could stop alone." This statement is unchallengeable. Anyone listening would have *no basis* to make a judgement except on the already established sincerity of the speaker. The statement is likely to be followed by "Alcoholics usually won't admit they can't stop alone." This is also "unchallengeable." The newcomer has little frame of reference for the characteristics of alcoholics in general and must defer to the sincere "authority" and unanimous majority. "If you think you can stop on your own, let me advise you, you don't have to." Again nothing challengeable. The prospect is now ill prepared to challenge any statement. Should the next statement be, "Let us love you until you learn to love yourself," even if the newcomer thinks, "No thanks," several ideas may be planted in his subconscious. "Let us love you" implies that the speaker and other groupers are willing to love the newcomer. It also implies that they are capable of loving. Still another implication is that in AA one will learn to love oneself.

One of the more important suggestions implanted this way is done through the ever-popular clichés, "Alcoholics Anonymous requires no beliefs," and "The Steps are but suggestions only." The speaker, having made these unchallengeable assertions, now will likely tell how a dearly beloved friend died because he didn't work the Steps. The suggestion implanted in the subconscious is not that it is unnecessary to work the Steps, or to believe, but that one will die if one doesn't work the Steps.

Another method of bypassing the critical faculty is through use of double binds. One example is a statement such as, "If this is your first meeting, and you are wondering if you might be alcoholic, let me assure you that you are. You wouldn't be here if you weren't." Another example would be, "If you come into these rooms you belong here. Well, maybe one person in a million doesn't belong here but, if you think you're that person, then you really do belong here." The only way out is to discredit the speaker, but the speaker has already established his sincerity by discrediting himself. The only simple, "logical" conclusion is that one is an alcoholic and "belongs here."

At an AA meeting, the tendency is for the newcomer's critical faculty to be overwhelmed by hypnotic suggestion, double binds, being "a minority of one," and possibly also by being in an extremely emotional environment. He is also likely to be in an overwhelming, almost impossible, struggle to understand the language. Everyone speaks in clichés, and words seem to have unusual meanings.

The most complex and most trivial of life's problems are reduced to clichés in mind-control cults. One of the hallmarks of these groups is their cliché-ridden language. Clichés are thought by members to contain great wisdom and ultimate truths and are used to express enduring doctrinal values. However, in spite of the perceived value of the cliché, it short circuits critical judgement and thought. For this reason, the jargon has been called "the language of non-thought."[5]

In AA, a simple statement like "no one ever drank while working the steps" conveys the concept that working the steps prevents drinking and that the person who has been drinking was at fault. He wasn't working the steps. Of course this statement is about as true as any such simple statement can be. Its truth and wisdom stop further inquiry into the reason for someone's drinking, offer the doctrinal solution for drinking, and deflect consideration of any imperfection in AA. Of course, other unused but truer statements might be, "no one ever drank while scuba diving" and "no one ever drank on a space mission."

AA's most popular cliché is "One day at a time." While this is presented to the public as nothing more than a core belief about AA's method of maintaining abstinence "one day at a time," it also serves much wider purposes. Alcoholics are thought to concern themselves too much with the future and the past, which is a "disease" symptom. For instance, a relative newcomer may question being sick, having to attend meetings, and carrying out cult duties for the rest of his life. Of course, this is "alcoholic thinking." To help the newcomer, those with more Time gently remind him, "One day at a time."

The difficulty of early abstention is moderated by taking it "one day at a time," and the experience translates well to other difficulties. No matter how empty or painful life in the group may become, life's problems can be handled "one day at a time." Of course, following this cliché wholeheartedly excludes planning for the future or even having a vision of the future. It also makes leaving AA most unlikely.

Another popular AA cliché, "KISS: Keep It Simple Stupid," reminds the grouper that it is stupid to see the complexities of life and that he himself is stupid and powerless to competently run his own life—he needs a Higher Power to do that for him. This serves a vital purpose. As long as the grouper sees things in the simplest terms, "alcoholic thinking" can never fully take over. "Spiritual growth" is assured. Another way of phrasing this cliché, which would have the same meaning in practice, would be "You're stupid. Don't even try to think. You're only causing yourself problems."

Other clichés are used to obscure the obvious. The only thing more common among AA members than abstinence is binge drinking. An AA member is constantly confronted with other groupers "slipping," "relapsing," and being "out there." What is most disconcerting for many AA members is when those with more Time than they themselves have drink. Even those with many years of Time may find this disturbing. The real danger, however, is that someone new, either because of an "alcoholic fog" or "spiritual ignorance," might come to the conclusion that the program *really* doesn't work, or at least doesn't work *really* well. Many clichés are used to obscure this reality from newcomers and old-timers alike.

"Keep coming back, it really works," as mentioned earlier, takes a prominent position in many meetings as an after-prayer chant. In meetings where doubt as to the effectiveness of AA has been vocalized, elder groupers may ad lib at the end of the chant, "If you work it!" This affirms the perfection of the program and clears up matters for those who may be confused. People in the program, even if they have been working at it for years, don't drink because of a fault in the program; it is their own fault. They weren't *really* working it.

The cliche "I am a miracle" supports the deeply held belief that each day that an alcoholic doesn't drink is a miracle performed by God through AA. Drinking is to be expected among those who are "Powerless over alcohol." What one is supposed to consider remarkable is not how often AA members binge, but that sometimes some of them don't for many years. All members should be grateful for the time that AA gives them sobriety.

One particularly insidious cliché, which becomes more true with time, is "Only another alcoholic will understand." As the "loaded language" is adopted, communication with non-members becomes ever more difficult. For instance, if a new AA member manages to abstain for two weeks then drinks after being fired, he will be told, or perhaps has already learned, that, "I drank because I am an alcoholic." No other response is acceptable. While this phrase has great meaning to fellow groupers since it expresses the predicament of an alcoholic at the mercy of Devil Drink, it means virtually nothing to humanity at large. A family member or friend who inquires about the drinking episode, if told "because I am an alcoholic," will have extreme difficulty "understanding." He will perhaps think, "Of course you drank because you're an alcoholic. And an overeater would have overeaten." If he further inquires as to the cause of the drinking, he may be told, "I didn't admit my Powerlessness." Now the family member or friend is entirely lost. He really doesn't understand. The new grouper now understands the wisdom of this cliché. If he wants understanding, he must get it from other AA members.

This is entirely different from what the pre-cult conversation over a drinking binge would have been. The problem drinker would have likely answered, "I don't know" or "because I got fired." Of course, neither is a complete answer, but some degree of communication and understanding would have been possible. Adopting AA language makes being understood by a "normie" almost impossible.

Loaded language, the language of non-thought, entails more than clichés. Individual words are given meanings or shades of meaning entirely separate from their normal usage. For example:

Abstinence—Similar to standard English: refraining from drinking alcohol. This is stricter in AA because mouthwash, breath freshener, and freshly-baked bread all contain alcohol. The wise alcoholic in a spiritual program usually avoids all of them. Abstinence is Absolute.

Alcohol—A demonic creature from the "spiritual" world, a great dark force, the opposite of spirituality. Only some people are susceptible to its cunning, baffling, and powerful effects. Those who are susceptible need a spiritual program or they will either die or be institutionalized for life.

Alcoholism—A physical, emotional, and spiritual disease. Alcoholism kills. There is no cure. "Once an alcoholic, always an alcoholic." One must work a spiritual program one day at a time to avoid death.

Dry Drunk—A painful state characteristic of alcoholics who abstain without benefit of a spiritual program. Also characteristic of members of a spiritual program who don't take their program seriously enough. A state of insanity similar to that of the drinking alcoholic. One should be careful to note that no matter how happy, well-adjusted, and successful those without the program may seem, they are really just "whistling in the dark." They don't have a Program.

God—A supernatural being more powerful than Devil Drink. Giver of the Twelve Steps, a guide to living in accordance with His will. Unlikely to save alcoholics who are too willful to work a spiritual program. All available evidence indicates that God is unlikely to help those whose willfulness causes them to depend on a religious instead of a purely spiritual program.

Sobriety—A special state of grace gained by working the Steps and maintaining absolute abstinence. It is characterized by feelings of Serenity and Gratitude. It is a state of living according to God's will, not one's own. It is sanity.

Spiritual Program—A program of living in accordance with God's plan. Alcoholics must be careful to distinguish it from religious programs, which may be very nice but which are relatively useless for the alcoholic. Religious programs require beliefs. Spiritual programs are better because they are suggestive only. They only need to be suggested because alcoholics who don't follow them die. As far as can be determined, AA and other Twelve Step programs are the only *really* spiritual ones.

These meanings are not usually directly presented to the newcomer and may never be directly stated. For example, no grouper would ever refer to alcohol as a "demonic creature." It is just treated as such. *A grouper will tell of what alcohol did to him, not what his use of alcohol did to him.* Alcohol, a liquid that is no more capable of thought or independent action than a bottle of drain cleaner, is labeled "cunning, baffling, and powerful." It is given a life of its own. Alcohol is presented as having the power to seduce and overwhelm human beings: "John Barleycorn calling me from the mantelpiece." When a grouper drinks himself to death, groupers take it as a warning: "The alcohol got him."

The newcomer may give up trying to understand the loaded language. He may attribute his difficulty in understanding to the "alcoholic fog" the groupers imply he is in. Perhaps he will consider it wise to attend 90 meetings in 90 days. They say that is the smart thing to do. He can decide then.

This is the goal of the meeting with respect to the newcomer. He questions his own competence and wonders whether the AA members, apparently having recovered from their own incompetence, have something to offer.

---

1. AA (1938):58-60
2. AA (1938):67-68
3. AA (1938):93
4. Asch (1956)
5. Lifton (1961):429

10: On the Broad Highway

"If you wish, you can join us on the Broad Highway."
—The Big Book

It is indeed a Broad Highway upon which the AA beginner sets out. The way is as wide as the eye can see. No restriction of any sort in sight. AA requires no beliefs, not even in God. One can pick one's own Higher Power. It can be God, the group, anything. One man even stayed sober with a doorknob for a Higher Power.

Members don't have to do anything. No one has to get a sponsor. No one has to work the steps. They are only suggestions. Membership is so easy that it's only necessary to *want* to stop drinking. You can even drink and be a member. For the new or prospective member, there is only the *suggestion* to make a commitment to 90 meetings in 90 days.

But this soft sell has a purpose.

Information control is essential to cult indoctrination. The group must become the sole source of information about the self. Communal cults like the Moonies, Hare Krishnas, and The Children of God* manage this through physical separation from other sources of information. The Moonies do this initially at three-day workshops held ostensibly for "world peace" or some other good cause. During the "workshops," members use the influence of a unanimous majority and hypnotic techniques to create confusion and distrust of the self in order to get a commitment from the prospective member to stay for an even longer indoctrination period.

---

* The Children of God is a religious cult. It commonly has female members prostitute themselves in order to draw potential recruits into the organization.

In non-communal cults like AA and the Oxford Group, physical isolation may be used. The portion of the Oxford Group that became AA had its "hospital work," and AA has alcohol and drug abuse treatment centers where patients' contact with friends and family is extremely limited. This degree of isolation is, however, not entirely necessary. In AA, the commitment to 90 meetings in 90 days can greatly limit non-AA social contacts. During this 90-day period of restricted social contact with "normies," every effort is made to discredit non-AA sources of information. The groupers become the sole credible information source for the new member about himself.

Imagine, for example, a man who works a 40-hour week and whose daytime hours are spent on the job. After work he heads for a meeting. The meeting lasts for one or two hours. He is then invited to coffee. He has the option of turning down the offer of Fellowship, and may want to since he hasn't seen his family all day. But, in thinking of his family, he may remember a speaker telling of how he almost lost his family for not taking advantage of the Fellowship or how another speaker lost his family altogether because he didn't put the program first. In any case, the groupers are friendly and welcoming, and he may have questions. Rather than spending time at home, the newcomer may be off for another hour or two, perhaps longer, receiving what can be considered informal indoctrination.

The groupers do not see themselves as having an ulterior motive. They sincerely want to help and will do their best to do so in the same ways they were helped when they were new. They are fully prepared to "freely give that which was so freely given," partly because they know, at least in the back of their minds, that their lives depend on it.

AA newcomers are also encouraged to stay in phone contact with group members. To this end, the newcomer is encouraged to exchange phone numbers at meetings and to use them. With an obligation to call several groupers every day, calls to non-grouper friends and acquaintances decline.

The commitment to devote a great deal of time with groupers severely limits the time one spends with others and, more importantly, time alone with oneself to reflect on what is happening.

The newcomer who does manage to spend some time alone must deal with constant warnings about another symptom of alcoholism, the desire to "isolate." It is often considered one of the first symptoms of an incipient return to drinking. If someone misses a meeting he usually attends, he will be queried, out of genuine loving concern, about where he was. If he doesn't have an acceptable reason, he will be cautioned about the dangers of "isolation."

The newcomer adopts "the language of non-thought" little by little. Words gain new meanings and 12-step clichés begin to have more and more meaning. As the new language is adopted, a linguistic barrier goes up between the new grouper and "normies." Normies gradually understand less and less; the newcomer and the groupers understand each other more and more.

Another way the new grouper is separated from others is with the advice to "stay out of slippery places." This does not mean just bars, but also parties, barbecues, dinner parties, and any other kind of get-together where alcohol may be served. Since it is more the norm than the exception for alcohol to be served on social occasions, and this is especially true in the social circles of those who drink too much, the newcomer will probably feel it unwise to socialize with his old friends. He will depend on the other groupers to fill this gap.

The most sinister form of separation practiced in AA is purely psychological and can be summed up with the cliché, "Alcoholism is a family disease." The first and most important meaning of this cliché is that the alcoholic's spouse, children, and parents are sick too, perhaps as sick as the alcoholic. The alcoholic is, and knows he is, to blame.[1] He is warned that it is imperative, if he cares about his family, that he recover. To this end, he must put the Program first, even before his own family.* If he doesn't, he'll drink and lose them anyway. The family man who feels guilt over having put alcohol before his family is now encouraged to make up for it by putting AA before his family.

This, combined with adopting AA's loaded language, can drive a wedge between a man and his sick (insane, not under God-control) wife and children. But AA has a solution to this problem. The family should be encouraged to work a spiritual program so they too can recover. Of course, this means working the Twelve Steps in Al-Anon.

Through various methods, among them hypnotic suggestion,

* The roots of this are in one of the Big Book stories of "personal recovery" which is often paraphrased by groupers as, ". . . I decided I must place this program above everything else, even my family, because if I did not maintain my sobriety I would lose my family anyway." (p. 294)

sharing "personal experience" or "scientific fact," a new member may be led to believe that his family wants him to drink and hence, to die.* This belief is buttressed when family members refuse to be "in recovery," disagree with "spiritual principles," criticizing his AA involvement, or criticize the new "alcoholic self." This generates suspicion and distrust between the alcoholic and family members who refuse to become groupers. *Where AA can't control sources of information, it discredits them.*

With time, AA becomes the sole source of credible information about oneself. Information from the world of "normies" isn't credible because they "don't understand." One's family and friends, if they drink, are in need of "a program." Even if they don't drink, family members are sick (codependent) and in need. The only people who can give accurate information, the only sane, understanding people, are the alcoholic groupers because "they've lived it," "they have recovered," and "they have a spiritual program."

Information is also controlled in interactions between the elder groupers and the newcomer. During hours of informal indoctrination, such as at after-meeting coffees, the newcomer has the opportunity to ask questions of the elders.

If he asks the "right" questions, the newcomer gets direct, informative answers. Right questions are ones like, "How do I get a sponsor?" or "Where are there meetings on Wednesday nights?" The groupers will do their best to be as helpful and informative as possible in response to such questions.

Other questions call for the groupers to be helpful but not quite so informative. For instance, if a newcomer should ask about the religious tone of a meeting, he will be answered with the cliché, "AA

---

* Sometimes the family actually does want the new AA member to drink. Often the most serious problem the family has had with the excessive drinker is that he has been emotionally and physically unavailable a great deal, if not most, of the time. When he joins AA, he may be even more unavailable. Whereas before he might have binged and been away mostly on weekends, now he is gone *every night*. What may be even worse, he quickly reaches a point where he is practicing AA's "spiritual way of life," meaning, in part, that he responds to the needs of his family with clichés and a holier-than-thou attitude. The family may attribute all this to his not drinking rather than to AA. They may decide that they want the "old" person back and think that they'll get him if he returns to drinking. This rarely, if ever, works. Once the drinker has adopted AA attitudes, his drinking usually becomes much worse. This only serves to prove to the drinker, and perhaps to the family too, the wisdom of AA.

is spiritual, not religious," and that, unlike religious organizations, "AA requires no beliefs." The newcomer is not told that everyone in the group holds certain beliefs in common and that they hold the Big Book above both other religions and science, have special knowledge of God's Will, and believe that those who don't "come to believe" face inevitable "jails, institutions, and death." The newcomer is not told that the groupers consider his religious beliefs inferior to their "spiritual" ones and that, as he becomes more dependent on AA, great pressure will be brought to bear on him to change his belief system.[*]

Information control within the group is far from complete, though, and the newcomer will occasionally see and hear things that contradict the sacred doctrine being held up to him as *the* way to stop drinking and grow toward happiness, usefulness, and wellness. Perhaps someone with 20 years Time will tell of having just beaten his wife "for the last time." This, of course, will be told in the context of spiritual growth achieved through working the Program. If the newcomer questions the effectiveness of the Program or the speaker's "recovery," there are many ways that he may be helped to understand.

Such situations come up so frequently that there are many clichés to deal with them, among them: "He has Time. What can you say about yourself?"; "Alcoholics are too judgmental. You must consider where he started from"; and, perhaps most popular, "Point a finger at someone else, and you are pointing three at yourself." These clichés and others point out the deficiencies and low status of the newcomer. He must be helped to understand that he *can't* understand because he doesn't have enough Time yet. It is absolutely untrue that the Program has flaws—it is spiritually inspired. It is also unspiritual to be critical of others, especially of the Elders. He may be told, "You must never be critical of others, but always hard on yourself." The elder groupers may tell how they used to be judgmental and how it nearly caused them to drink and die.

If the newcomer doesn't accept the wise, helpful words offered, he may be told in a loving way that he is too new or not yet spiritual enough to understand. He may be told, "As the Big Book says, more will be revealed if you work the program." However, if the newcomer is persistent in seeking explanations of inconsistencies, the groupers

---

[*] The superimposition of AA beliefs over religious beliefs is covered in the chapter on the steps.

may point out the newcomer's obvious insanity with, "Well then, why don't you just go drink!" This is very strong language and is only used with the most obstinate cases. However, it does point out the truth of the Program: to think that one sees flaws in it is evidence of alcoholism's cunning, baffling, and powerful influence over the mind. Attempts at critical analysis of the Program, or criticism of the Elders, is merely alcohol's evil influence. The reason for it is obvious: the newcomer wants to drink.

One of the most potent forces of mind control is the subtle elicitation of public statements. The first statement elicited publicly from the newcomer is "I am an alcoholic." Depending on the structure of the meeting attended, the newcomer may say it at his very first meeting with little or no thought given to its implications. In some meetings, everyone in the room takes turns introducing themselves by their first name and "disease." Perhaps 25 or 50 people will identify themselves uniformly with their first name and "I am an alcoholic." Then it is up to the pigeon. If he doesn't want to stand out, there is only one choice: to say "I am an alcoholic." And, indeed, the pigeon may have his own idea of what an alcoholic is and may feel comfortable stating that he is "an alcoholic."

In well functioning mind-control cults, physical coercion is rarely used in the indoctrination process. Situations are staged so that people "choose" either the desired course or from among desired options. At AA meetings, the pigeon has the option of merely stating his first name. At this point in the indoctrination process, even this may be desirable. The pigeon may then wonder what he is doing at the meeting and whether he is suffering "denial." Often, out of deference to a room full of friendly faces gazing at him, he will splutter in embarrassment, "I guess I'm an alcoholic." All of the groupers smile knowingly and affectionately. They understand that this is a milestone in his "recovery." The pigeon doesn't have a clue.

This public admission of being an alcoholic, whether the newcomer knows it or not, is the beginning of the acceptance of the authority of AA. Since he is an alcoholic, and has publicly acknowledged himself as such, the pigeon must defer to the unanimous opinion of the alcoholism experts gathered around him for information on who and what he is. In AA, by definition, an alcoholic is someone who must work the Steps and follow other "suggestions" or die:

> Unless each A.A. member follows to the best of his ability our suggested Twelve Steps of recovery, he almost certainly signs his own death warrant. . . . We *must* obey certain principles, or we die.[2]

A newcomer would reject out of hand being told that if he didn't work the Steps he would probably die. To get by this, groupers continuously acknowledge the Steps as "suggestive only." They then proceed to tell how they nearly died or how others died because their diseased minds told them that they didn't need to work the Steps.

Another way the newcomer becomes afraid to not work the Steps is through sincere, genuine fear expressed by the elders through body language. For example, if a newcomer says in casual conversation that he doesn't need the Steps, that he's staying sober just fine without them, the groupers will fall silent. Bodies stiffen. All eyes, filled with fear, apprehension, or disapproval, will focus on the new-comer. Without verbally contradicting the newcomer, the message is given. Once the message has been nonverbally transmitted, the ice may be broken by an elder reminding everyone, "Like the Big Book says, the Steps are but suggestive only." This is a reminder to the groupers of the Big Book injunction against "preaching" and open coercion. It also ostensibly supports the newcomer's position. Everyone knows that the Steps are suggestive only. No one has to do anything they don't want to in AA. So, while the newcomer gets verbal "defense" for not working the Steps, he is also strongly reminded that working them is a suggestion. He knows that if he stubbornly continues to refuse to follow the "suggestion," he is "signing his own death warrant."

In adapting to his new social circle, the newcomer learns which comments bring approval and which bring disapproval. People are so kind, friendly, and understanding that it is, at the very least, impolite to upset them. The only way to avoid this is to agree with them. One quickly learns to express, if not quite believe, only acceptable ideas.

In the interest of "recovery," the newcomer is also encouraged to "share" at meetings.* First-time sharers usually have little to say, but others model sharing for them. The nervous newcomer can feel safe announcing how much Time he has. Announcing, "I have three days"

---

* I have heard (but not seen) that in some areas of the country, newcomers are not encouraged to share, but to "sit down, shut up, and learn something."

will be interrupted with a round of applause and perhaps shouts of approval. He is rewarded for telling how he has found the truth of a cliché or some other piece of doctrine. Sharing how the Program is working for him always brings warm applause and caring attention. The congregation will also approve any statement of confession or any statement derogatory towards himself: he is "getting honest" and showing "humility."

However, any statement contradictory to AA doctrine, even if it doesn't bring immediate boos or derisive laughter, will bring explanations, warnings, and "understanding" from the elder groupers who share later. The "understanding" usually takes the form of "He is still new and hasn't learned yet." The warnings are usually given indirectly, the elders all "coincidentally" focusing their sharing on other people they know who hold the same opinions. These "other people" have either died or are drinking and will die soon if they don't see the light.

Sooner or later, the newcomer comes to see the importance of working the Steps. To this end, he must find a sponsor because "This is a 'we' Program," and "It is dangerous to take the spiritual path alone."

The newcomer must ask an elder to be his sponsor. Among the suggestions on how to pick a good sponsor are to find someone who "has what you want," meaning someone you hold as an ideal. Also important is selecting someone who has a similar social status, drinking history, interests, and at least a year or two of Time. The newcomer is often cautioned against picking someone with too much Time because they are sure to be too spiritually advanced and recovered for the newcomer to relate to.

The newcomer, believing that doing so will keep him sober and will allow him to share in the recovery he sees in the meetings, is now ready to work The Twelve Steps of Alcoholics Anonymous.

---

1. AA (1938):123
2. AA (1957):119

11: The Road of Happy Destiny

"We shall be with you in the Fellowship of the Spirit as you trudge the Road of Happy Destiny."
—The Big Book

The Twelve Steps are the core of the Alcoholics Anonymous "spiritual program." They are held as "spiritually inspired," so they are beyond question. It is normal, however, for the newcomer to ask how or why they work. The answer is that, being "spiritually inspired," they are above human logic and understanding, but that it is logical to work them because they have been "proven" to really work. The newcomer is surrounded by the proof: the other cult members.

Sooner or later the newcomer feels a need to work the Steps. He comes to understand, since it is so often pointed out, how much benefit comes from working them. Whenever he approaches an elder with a problem, he is likely to be reminded that he hasn't worked the Steps, with the implication that this is the root of his problem.

The presumed benefits of working a spiritual program are formalized as "The Promises." Taken from the Big Book, they often take a central position in meetings either as a sacred reading or as a topic of discussion, "How have the Promises been fulfilled in your life?"

If we are painstaking about this phase of our development, we will be amazed before we are half way through. We are going to know a new freedom and a new happiness. We will not regret the past nor wish to shut the door on it. We will comprehend the word serenity and we will know peace. No matter how far down the scale we have gone, we will see how our experience can benefit others. That feeling of uselessness and self-pity will disappear. We will lose interest in selfish things and gain interest in our fellows. Self-seeking will slip away. Our whole attitude and outlook upon life will change. Fear of people and of economic insecurity will leave us. We will intuitively know how to handle situations which used to baffle us. We will suddenly realize that God is doing for us what we could not do for ourselves.

Are these extravagant promises? . . . They will always materialize if we work for them.[1]

The alternative to these Promises is "jails, institutions, and death." The newcomer wants to work the Steps.

AA co-founder Bill Wilson, author of the Big Book and the most celebrated case of recovery in AA, after more than 10 years of working them, wrote the definitive manual on how to work the Steps. In this manual, called *The Twelve Steps and Twelve Traditions*, Wilson describes the value of the Steps:

A.A.'s Twelve Steps are a group of principles, spiritual in their nature, which, if practiced as a way of life, can expel the obsession to drink and enable the sufferer to become happily and usefully whole.[2]

Eight years after he was "changed" by Ebby from the Oxford Group, and five years after he penned the Twelve Steps, Bill Wilson was somewhat less than "happily and usefully whole."

From AA's own literature:

He was plunged into an abyss of such bleakness and negativity as to make him suicidal.[3]

This depression lasted for 11 years, during which time he wrote the book designed to help others become "happily and usefully whole."

AA member Marty Mann, who was busy "educating America about alcoholism" with her National Council on Alcoholism, describes Wilson during this period:

It was awful. There were long periods of time when he couldn't get out of bed. He just stayed in bed, and Lois would see that he ate.[4]

From his personal secretary:

He would come down to the office many times and sit across from me and just put his head in his hands and really not be able to communicate . . .[5]

And from an AA (GSO) general manager:

There were some times when these horrible depressions would go on and on, for days and days.[6]

Apparently, no official account of Wilson's depression was given until the 1984 publication of *Pass It On*. No one seemed to have found it ironic that *a man suffering severe chronic depression was claiming to have the secret to becoming "usefully and happily whole."*

An indoctrinated cult member, Bill Wilson was incapable of questioning AA doctrine even though his personal experience was the opposite of that promised. An examination of the Twelve Steps shows why the thoroughly indoctrinated member is incapable of questioning the doctrine even when belief causes great harm.

There is much within the Twelve Steps that leads to severe emotional problems, including suicidal depression. Depression is characterized by feelings of powerlessness and helplessness. It is also based in the suppression of one's emotions, most particularly anger. Rather than being a prescription for becoming "happily and usefully whole," the Twelve Steps are a prescription for helplessness, self-alienation, and depression. *They result in the problem drinker becoming more addicted to furthering cult goals than he ever was to alcohol.*

Step One: *We admitted we were powerless over alcohol—that our lives had become unmanageable.*

This Step, for the AA sponsor or treatment center therapist, is what Bill Wilson referred to as "tilling the black soil of hopelessness."[7] It is made up of two distinct parts: an admission of "powerlessness" and an admission of "unmanageability." Unmanageability is admitted when the "baby," "pigeon," or "patient" lists, often in writing, how unmanageable his life is as evidence of his alcoholism. This admission of "unmanageability" includes anything that the pigeon has done contradictory to his own values or to society's rules. It usually covers nothing further back than the "first drink." The baby must figure out how *everything* that is not right with his life, its "unmanageability," is directly tied to alcohol and alcoholism.

The pigeon has the problem of resolving guilt over his past actions. He can either admit that alcohol is responsible for everything and gain status and warm regard, or insist that he is responsible and be "in denial" and lose status and regard.

Part of the admission of alcoholism may be preparing a list of one's history of alcohol and drug consumption including quantity and frequency. The goal of this exercise is to convince the newcomer to accept that his behavior was "not his," meaning that he was acting under the influence of an outside, controlling force ('the disease"). At the same time, he is pressured to give a public admission: "I am powerless." This admission can take various forms. In a treatment center it may be "getting honest" in a "group therapy" session. Outside of treatment centers, it may be as simple as getting down on one's knees and admitting one's powerlessness and unmanageability to God and the groupers present.

Exactly how this is done is unimportant. The important point is that confession is made. The core of this admission is that alcoholism is a disease with a life of its own. Devil Drink, "the rapacious creditor, bleeds us of all self-sufficiency and all will to resist." The "alcoholic" is totally at the mercy of Devil Drink. The admission of powerlessness is an admission that one is faced with death, and that nothing within oneself, nor any "human power," can help.

The Twelve Steps and Twelve Traditions ("12 & 12") suggests that those who doubt their powerlessness should be told to go ahead and drink. This is, of course, without encouraging them to get help for underlying problems or even acknowledging that such problems may exist. The intent is to "plant the seed" that the target for indoctrination will indeed be powerless (that is, he will learn helplessness), as happened with Bill Wilson after being "treated" by Dr. Silkworth. The 12 & 12 suggests that this is a highly effective method:

It was then discovered that when one alcoholic had planted in the mind of another the true nature of his malady, that person could never be the same again.

Following every spree, he would say to himself, "Maybe those A.A.'s were right . . ."[8]

In a treatment center, it is not possible to suggest that someone drink. However, there are other ways to convince the indoctrinees that they are incapable of moderating or quitting without AA. One of these is the "scientific" lecture. Medical "authorities" give lectures on "the disease." Using unnamed scientific studies, the lecturer presents, in the presumed context of a non-AA lecture, "the medical facts," just as was done by Dr. Silkworth. These lectures include the "scientific certainties" of genetic defects, brain differences, loss of control, denial and inevitable progression.

Those who come to believe AA's "one drink, one drunk" slogan can't moderate their drinking. Once a newcomer learns that he is "powerless over alcohol," he suffers from a form of learned helplessness. He "knows," just like the inner-city school children who "couldn't" learn to read, that any effort to moderate is wasted. He automatically, subconsciously, can't even try.

No one can reasonably argue that someone who drinks self-destructively shouldn't be helped to see the damage that he does to himself so that he'll stop. This is not what AA does. *AA convinces a newcomer that a force outside his control is killing him and that without AA he'll die:*

Under the lash of alcoholism, we are driven to A.A., and there we discover the fatal nature of our situation. Then and only then, do we become as open-minded to conviction and as willing to listen as the dying can be.[9]

At the end of working Step One, the new grouper has made a "public statement" of "powerlessness" and "unmanageability." He has confessed that he has no resources to stop the "inevitable progression" of alcoholism.

If the first Step has been worked properly, Devil Drink, alias alcoholism, begins taking its place as the primary driving force in the life of the new cult member. Before, the newcomer may have wondered why he drank the way he did. Now he "knows" that he has a disease. While fear of death from drinking is now the primary motivating factor in the newcomer's life, he may feel *relieved* at this point. He is no longer responsible, at least for the moment, for *anything* that he has done in his past. It is not his fault; he has a disease. Devil Drink made him do it.

If his sponsor and other groupers have properly "till[ed] the black soil of hopelessness," the new grouper is now "open minded" and ready for Step Two.

Step Two: *Came to believe that a Power greater than ourselves could restore us to sanity.*

Step Two, to the uninitiated, appears to be mostly about finding faith in God. While there may be some truth in this, working this Step is more a matter of defining God in AA's image. However, that is actually only half of the Step and, without first working the second half, one is not *ready* to "come to believe" the AA doctrine that will be presented.

"Restore us to sanity" implies that the newcomer is insane. While his insanity may be clear to the elder groupers who have worked the Steps, the "baby" must be helped to understand the full depths of his insanity. This takes help from his sponsor and the other groupers or a treatment center "therapist" because "Some will be willing to term themselves 'problem drinkers,' but cannot endure the suggestion that they are in fact mentally ill."[10] In other words, even if someone admits that he drinks too much, decides to stop, and goes for treatment, he still needs to understand that he is "mentally ill." By AA's definition, an alcoholic is insane. "No alcoholic . . . can claim 'soundness of mind' for himself."[11] From the Big Book: "The main problem of the alcoholic centers in his mind, rather than in his body."[12] Of course, it is reasonable to argue that drinking to self-destructive excess and the outrageous behavior that may accompany it is insane behavior. This Step, however, goes much further.

The "baby" or patient may be assigned to write out, in detail, all the evidence of his insanity. This generally begins with the obvious: prior drinking behavior. It also extends to "insane" emotions and "alcoholic thinking." The goal is to get the pigeon to accept that he is insane, must distrust himself entirely, and is doomed to death without "a spiritual program." He is to rely on the AA elders who, due to the Program, are "miracles of mental health."

Little did the pigeon imagine when he first acknowledged "I am an alcoholic" that he was acknowledging being insane. He may have had his own definition of an alcoholic, but he now learns that to be an alcoholic is to be insane. All of the other groupers admit to their insanity. Those with more Time, of course, are much less insane than the newcomer. Their acknowledgement of their own insanity when they were new makes it easier for the pigeon to see and to accept his insanity.

By accepting his insanity, the pigeon, already under the threat of death, becomes totally dependent on the elder groupers. Any difference in thought and opinion from the elders or the sacred text is now merely a sign of his insanity. The elders often, usually "lovingly," but sometimes not so lovingly, remind him that he is insane. *He can no longer trust his own thoughts and perceptions: he has the disease; he is sick; he is an alcoholic; he is insane.*

Believing that he is insane and will die without AA, the newcomer is confronted with the "fact" that he is "doomed to an alcoholic death or to live on a spiritual basis."[13] He is now ready to begin putting faith in a "Power greater than" himself. This Power is most often referred to in AA as "Higher Power" or "HP."

The job now for the AA sponsor or treatment center therapist is to have the "baby" accept AA either as God or as the only viable interpreter of God's Will.

AA literature and members frequently boast of the Program being "spiritual, not religious." This is partly because AA discarded the Bible. The core of their argument, however, is that no beliefs are required for membership. This is true, sort of. However, in order to bother with attending, one must believe that AA has something to offer. It is also necessary to confess to having the disease to attend many meetings or to fully participate in other than a newcomer's meeting. To fit in with AA's social system, to gain status and to avoid being patronized, shunned, ridiculed, or taking the "sicker than others seat," one must begin accepting AA doctrine; and the core of the doctrine is that one must work the Steps in order to survive the machinations of Devil Drink. And in order to work Step Two, one must choose a Higher Power.

For someone who believes in God, this would seem rather perfunctory: "God is my HP." For the atheist or agnostic, it appears to present a difficult problem, but AA has the simplest of solutions. You don't need to believe in God. You can make AA your "higher power":

> You can, if you wish, make A.A. itself your 'higher power.' Here's a very large group of people who have solved their alcohol problem. In this respect they are certainly a power greater than you, who have not even come close to a solution. Surely you can have faith in them.[14]

For the believer in God who has his own religion or denomination, things are a bit touchier. AA must elevate itself above the recruit's religion without leaving itself open to accusations of having done so. The 12 & 12 attacks the pigeon *himself*, not his religion, on the basis of "quality of faith." In typical AA "humble" fashion, the words "we," "us," and "alcoholics" are used in all accusations.

> [Our problem] has to do with the quality of faith rather than its quantity. This has been our blind spot. We supposed we had humility when really we hadn't. . . . The fact was we really hadn't cleaned house so that the grace of God could enter us and expel the obsession. In no deep or meaningful sense had we ever taken stock of ourselves, made amends to those we had harmed, or freely given to any other human being without any demand for reward. We had not even prayed rightly.[15]

These and other "discounts" (put-downs) of the newcomer's religious practice are immediately followed by attacks on his soundness of mind in the customary indirect "we," "us," and "alcoholics" fashion.

> Few indeed are the practicing alcoholics who have any idea how irrational they are, or seeing their irrationality can bear to face it . . . No alcoholic . . . can claim "soundness of mind' for himself."[16]

This is the way the pigeon will be dealt with from this point forward. Before he has a chance to think things through and present, even to himself, a reasonable argument against what he is told, he will be reminded that, as one of "us," an alcoholic, he is irrational, mentally ill, evilly motivated, suffering from "alcoholic thinking," and insane.

From the Second Step onward, he will be told how to relate to his "Higher Power." His religion may offer eternal reward, but if he doesn't follow "direction," AA's word for Oxford Group Guidance, Devil Drink will send him to that reward sooner than he cares to go.

In order to understand the Program and its relationship to religion, it is helpful to go back to AA's roots in the Oxford Group. The Oxford Group's goal was to convert the entire world to God-control, a goal easily accomplished through establishing the ideal govern-ment: "a theocracy . . . [or] a God-controlled Fascist dictatorship."[17] The Oxford Group's members were to attend churches, but not in order to worship God nor as a path toward closeness with Him. They didn't need it. They had Guidance, a direct line to God, and they had their own meetings. Their purpose was the "humble" goal of *reforming* the churches. They didn't attend various denominations out of a belief in their creeds. They were there to help the lost sheep, to guide them to the Oxford Group.

AA's relation to other religions is derived from this. Early AA recommended church attendance, and quite often, individual AA members and groups still do. Bill Wilson's views, published in *Pass It On*, were essentially that, in spite of all the terrible things religions have done, religions are good in that there is a great deal of spiri-tuality in religion. But, of course, AA is the only "purely spiritual" organization.

AA was very careful in its early literature to say nothing which would overtly contradict any Christian denomination. AA even made a point of defending organized religion (but only in the context of an attack on atheists and agnostics). AA never attacked religion itself, only its practitioners. In the lengthy quote above, the newcomer is attacked for his "quality of faith." When the pigeon accepts that he does indeed have shortcomings in this area, he isn't told to return to his church to "set himself right with God." He is told to continue with the Steps in order to "fit himself into God's plan."

The "observations" about alcoholics, better viewed as attacks on the pigeon, ostensibly deal with themes consistent with almost all religions. They are, however, actually peculiar in that they are charges, in AA's own language and terms, that the newcomer hasn't worked all of the Steps. For instance, "we supposed we had humility when we really hadn't," points out the need to work Step Seven, which specifically addresses "humility" in an AA context. The accusation of never having "really cleaned house" is a call to work Steps Four and Five, taking a "fearless moral inventory" and "admitting defects of character." "Never made amends" means that one needs to work Steps Eight and Nine. Regardless of how the pigeon takes it, the accusation of never having "freely given to another human being" has absolutely nothing to do with Christian, or any other kind, of charity. It has to do with working Step Twelve, which is "carrying the message." "The message," of course, has nothing to do with any religious or spiritual convictions the pigeon may have separate from AA. It is the Oxford Group's call to practice the Five Cs—to convert others to Oxford Group beliefs. This admonition to "freely give" is nothing more or less than a call to carry AA's message, to indoctrinate others into AA.

The accusation of not having prayed properly is perhaps the most insidious of all. By discounting and, most importantly, getting the pigeon to discount, his private communication with God, AA becomes the intermediary, interpreter, and authority of just what God has to say.

The nature and depth of this change to "God-control" becomes clearer with an understanding of the ensuing Steps.

Step Three: *Made a decision to turn our will and our lives over to the care of God as we understood God.*

Whatever "Higher Power" one has selected, in this Step the indoctrinee is to begin acting and thinking on the basis of the desire of this Higher Power and to begin depending on it for all things rather than upon his own *insane* thoughts and desires. Any objection to any part of this Step will bring a loving reminder of the Step Two admission of insanity and Step One admission of unmanageability.

According to the 12 & 12's discussion of this Step, resolute action is necessary to "cut away the self-will which has always blocked the entry of God . . . or Higher Power."[18] The reason one's "Higher Power" need not be "God" becomes clear:

Isn't it true that in all matters touching upon alcohol, each of them has decided to turn his or her life over to the care, protection, and guidance of Alcoholics Anonymous? . . . Now if this is not turning one's will and life over to a newfound Providence, then what is it?[19]

There is no distinction made between Alcoholics Anonymous and God in AA theology. Since AA's literature, particularly the Big Book and the Twelve Steps, is "spiritually inspired," and the existence of the organization itself is a direct act of God, *turning one's "will and life" over to Alcoholics Anonymous is the same as turning it over to God.*

After stating that turning one's will and life over to the care of AA is turning it over to Providence, the new grouper is customarily attacked: to argue against turning everything over to "Something or Somebody else" is the "process by which instinct and logic always seek to bolster egotism, and so frustrate spiritual development."[20]

The trouble with "this kind of thinking," thinking perhaps that God gave us our will and our lives as a precious gift, is, according to the "12 & 12," that it "takes no real account of the facts."[21] The Orwellian "facts" are that "the more we become willing to depend upon a Higher Power, the more independent we actually are. Therefore dependence, as A.A. practices it, is really a means of gaining true independence of the spirit."[22]

AA, like all mind-control cults, seeks to control the inner world of intellectual experience. This control isn't limited to loaded language. The new member is taught that he doesn't have a right to think his own thoughts. His thinking should be "on a higher plane": "How persistently we claim the right to decide all by ourselves just what we shall think. . . ."[23]

Not only does the AA member not have a right to his own thoughts, this restriction extends to emotional life, as will be detailed in Step Four. AA members are taught to disrupt their own thinking with thought-stopping techniques. The most popular way in AA is *ostensibly* through prayer, "Thy will, not mine, be done."* This phrase

* A member of Codependents Anonymous, an organization which, like AA, considers the Twelve Steps the inspired word of God, recommended to me another thought-stopping technique: to say to oneself, "Cancel, cancel, blue sky" and to then imagine the sky. It serves the same purpose, is considered spiritual, and has the same effect as the one-line "prayer": it interferes with thinking.

or an entire prayer is to be said "in all times of emotional disturbance ..."[24]

Among the times a newcomer is likely to suffer "emotional disturbance" is when a thought overtly contradictory to AA doctrine comes to mind. This is when the thought-stopping technique has its most powerful and negative effect. AA members sincerely believe that AA comes directly from God, and that critical thoughts about AA are evilly ("disease") motivated. The "disease" is to be suppressed in oneself, and this means suppressing "alcoholic thinking." The AA member quickly learns to "stop" all negative thoughts about AA. While there is some permission to think thoughts critical of certain members, particularly those with less Time, and even to think critically of some meetings, there is no capacity to think negative thoughts about AA doctrine or AA itself. AA comes to be seen as perfect. One doesn't see a flaw in the doctrine and alter the doctrine accordingly. One *thinks* (alcoholically, of course) that one sees a flaw in the doctrine and works to "understand" where the flaw is in oneself.

This is closely tied to "honesty" in AA. The doctrine, being "spiritually inspired," is perfect. If one's life experience doesn't fit the doctrine, it isn't the doctrine that is wrong; rather, the person whose experiences don't fit isn't *really* honest.

A great deal of "progress" in "getting honest" and "spiritual growth" has occurred in the first three Steps. In Step One, the pigeon has "gotten honest" in admitting the Power of alcohol and his own Powerlessness in the face of it. In Step Two, the pigeon has "gotten honest" in acknowledging that AA is a Power capable of defeating Devil Drink and acknowledging that he is insane and cannot trust his own thoughts. In Step Three, he must "get honest" about the need to turn his "will and life" over to AA/God. Out of "honesty," he begins to work for the "willingness" to discard the self which he learned in Step Two is insane. He is to work to make his own thoughts go away.

The consummation of this Step may be the recitation of the "Third Step Prayer." In this prayer, the grouper prays, "Relieve me of the bondage of self, that I may better do Thy will."[25]

The following two Steps, four and five, can be considered together.

Step Four: *Made a searching and fearless moral inventory of ourselves.*

Step Five: *Admitted to God, to ourselves, and to another human being the exact nature of our wrongs.*

Great expectations about working these Steps are built up in AA literature and in the meetings. Groupers bear witness to the life-changing effects of working them. They speak of new-found Serenity or a new awareness of their Higher Power. The Big Book promises that "we are delighted. . . . We can be alone at perfect ease and peace. Our fears fall from us."[26] The 12 & 12 promises "a healing tran-quility"[27] and holds out the promise of becoming "conscious of God as [we] never were before"[28] upon the completion of Step Five.

Step Four, the "moral inventory," is much more than a written confession of sins or "defects of character." In preparation for writing out the inventory, evil is redefined according to the AA world view. In the writing, one redefines oneself, and one's past, in the AA image. The stress is on evil or sin, usually referred to as "defects of character." This marks a complete switch from the "outsider doctrine"* of alcoholism being a medical disease; with this Step it becomes a "spiritual malady." In Step One, the alcoholic's problem is "external" in the sense of being "not attributable to self." The alcoholic has a "disease." His problems are due to the power of alcohol/Devil Drink. However, by the Fourth Step, the stress is on alcoholism as a "spiritual disease." Although rarely stated bluntly, this "disease" is believed to be caused by moral failings. Whereas in Step One the blame is on "the disease," by Step Four, the "baby" knows that "our troubles are basically of our own making."[29]

The Big Book discussion of the Fourth Step begins with "being convinced that self, manifested in various ways, was what had

---

*All cults have different levels of truth. "Outsider doctrine" refers to information and "truths" that are told to the general public. Complementary to this "outsider doctrine" is "insider doctrine" which is revealed to members alone, and then usually only gradually as they attain status. For example, the outsider doctrine of the Scientologists is that their organization works for mental health and human potential. The insider doctrine includes beliefs in past lives on other planets and in a super-powerful evil being known as Xenu. The reason for this separation of doctrine in cults is that it would be impossible to recruit if people knew what the organization really was about. The line is not always sharp and clear between the two "levels of truth." I have heard AA members on radio interviews speak in detail of alcoholism as a spiritual disease. Normally, all that "should" be said is that it is a fatal, progressive, and incurable disease. Saying "spiritual disease" is too much of a tip-off to the true nature of "the Program." It might turn away "those who could have been helped."

defeated us . . ."[30] Principle among the "manifestations of self" is
normal human emotion. Anger, usually referred to as "resentment,"
is considered the number one offender:

> But with the alcoholic, whose hope is the maintenance and growth of
> a spiritual experience, this business of resentment is infinitely grave.
> We found that it is fatal. For when harboring such feelings we shut
> ourselves off from the sunlight of the Spirit. The insanity of alcohol
> returns and we drink again. And with us, to drink is to die.
>   If we were to live, we had to be free of anger.[31]

One of the recommended ways to be "not angry" is to use thought-
stopping techniques. When one becomes aware of anger, one is to say
to oneself, "God save me from being angry. Thy will be done."[32]

AA members have two motivations for not allowing themselves to
experience anger. One is that it is "unspiritual"; it is a sin.[33] The
other, illustrated in the above quotation from the Big Book, is that the
grouper fears that he will die if he allows himself to experience his
anger. While fear is the primary motivation for the grouper to
suppress awareness of his anger, he is unlikely, with the accumulation
of Time, to *feel* afraid or even to be *aware* that fear is such a major
motivator of his behavior.

In Step Four, he also learns that he must suppress awareness of the
"evil and corroding thread" of fear. Although, beginning with Step
One, his primary motivation in life is fear, the grouper doesn't
maintain awareness of it. Being aware of what is going on within
himself would be "dangerous," "evil," "unspiritual," and "useless."
The areas of emotional life that are to be disowned, for one to become
unaware of, also include a broad range of emotions termed "self-
pity," including sadness, loneliness, and feelings of hopelessness or
helplessness.

Self-confidence is also considered a liability.

> Some of us once had great self-confidence, but it didn't fully solve
> the fear problem, or any other. When it made us cocky, it was
> worse.[34]

There are many direct correlations between AA's scorn for normal
human emotion and thought and the attitudes common to the
addictive family system. In the addictive family system, the child's

awareness and perceptions are discounted. In AA, the member's awareness is called "alcoholic thinking." The child is taught that experiencing various emotions is wrong. AA teaches the same. The child in the addictive family system is caught in the bind of figuring out how he is wrong. In AA, the grouper is in the same bind. The doctrine and the elders are never wrong—something is wrong with the grouper. AA emphasizes this "wrongness" and "badness" of the alcoholic. *Any time that the alcoholic is upset about anything, it is a sure sign that something is wrong with him.*[35] "Though a situation had not been entirely our fault, we tried to disregard the other person involved entirely. Where were we to blame?"[36]

With the various "manifestations of self" fully defined, the grouper is ready to write out a thorough confession of his sins from the perspective of the "alcoholic" or "bad child." Much more than a confession of sin, this confession is also a redefinition of the self and the adoption of a repentant sinner role. In writing one's "moral inventory," all important events in one's life are looked at and written about from the "I am a sinner" perspective.

Many versions of Step Four exist, from the original Big Book version, to its expansion in the 12 & 12, to various "recovery house" versions, to those unique to individual AA sponsors. They are all to be written and all are unanimous in that the "manifestations of self," whatever they are called, are to be identified. Each version opens doors to the possibility of guilt in various areas the author thinks likely to be overlooked by the indoctrinee.

This is an extremely emotional period for the new grouper. Not only is he bringing up painful incidents going all the way back to childhood that "proved" him "bad," but he must accept in his adult consciousness that he is, indeed, "bad." Every incident that provoked fear, anger, sadness, hurt, or loneliness is looked at from the perspective that, in some way or another, he alone was wrong. He is a sinner. He is guilty. It is easy, in terms of AA doctrine, for him to see how defective he is. Even if he displayed little or no "bad behavior," he certainly had emotional responses. If one of the major events in his life was the death of his parents, he certainly sinned and sinned greatly. Since the normal response of children who lose parents is to feel sad, lonely, guilty, hurt, helpless, angry, and afraid, it is obvious to the grouper that he was guilty of self-pity, resentment, fear, and "alcoholic sensitivity." The grouper now understands that allowing these emotions to exist is the "real" problem. This points to one of the main purposes of Step Four, the institution of emotional control. The indoctrinee is to work to understand that allowing the existence of "self" was the cause of all ill effects. For example, the member who lost his parents as a child *rationalizes*, from the AA perspective, and *comes to believe* that his childhood experience of "self-pity, resentment, fear and alcoholic sensitivity" was the *cause* of problems. In carefully defining prior emotional experience as bad, any current emotional awareness is also seen as bad. The grouper has new reasons to work to suppress it.

As the indoctrinee works on Step Four, he very likely can't help letting off a lot of steam from pent up emotions. As he writes of past traumatic experiences, he may share some of the pain with his sponsor, with fellow groupers, or at meetings. This is accepted, even encouraged, during the "honeymoon" period.* Later displays of nega-tive emotion will be seen as signs of not "working the Program," since the Program is supposed to make "bad" feelings go away.

As the time for the Step Five confession approaches, the grouper is likely to find that he has certain secrets that he would prefer to take to the grave. However, he knows that it is essential that he reveal these in order to avoid a return to the bottle and death. Fear of exposure adds to his emotional turmoil. He may consider only telling God. However, the 12 & 12 is very clear on the necessity of making confession to "another human being." One of the reasons is that "being alone with God doesn't seem as embarrassing as facing up to another person."[37] Another is that being honest with God alone is "largely theoretical."[38]

While the Big Book is very careful to suggest that "those of us belonging to a religious denomination which requires confession must, and of course, will want to go to the properly appointed authority. . .,"[39] the later 12 & 12 stresses the need for "someone who is experienced, who not only has stayed dry but has been able to surmount other serious difficulties. Difficulties, perhaps, like our own."[40]

Another difference between the discussion of Step Five in the older (1939) Big Book and the newer (1952) 12 & 12 is the

* Most cults have a "honeymoon period" for the new member, during which time he is tolerated and catered to. In many cults, as in AA, it lasts about six months.

reintroduction of the word "guidance" from the Oxford Group, but now without the capital "G." The word is missing altogether from the Big Book version of this Step, which was written at a time when AA was attempting to hide its association with the Oxford Group.

The resurrected word "guidance" explains the need to confess to another:

> People of very high spiritual development almost always insist on checking . . . the guidance they feel they have received from God. Surely, then, a novice ought not lay himself open to the chance of making foolish, perhaps tragic, blunders in this fashion.[41]

While admitting that checking guidance* may not be infallible, the literature makes it clear that it is better than one's own prayer and meditation:

> It is likely to be far more specific than any direct guidance we may receive while we are still so inexperienced in establishing contact with a Power greater than ourselves.[42]

Notice that those who "check guidance" are those who have more experience in "establishing contact with a Power greater than ourselves." It is another way of saying that those who check guidance are those with Time.

While working Step Four, there is usually a tremendous amount of emotional release, although the subjective experience may be that the more some feelings are expressed, the more other feelings mysteriously appear. "A conviction of the hideousness of his own personal guilt," combined with increasing fear as the time for confession approaches, creates an emotional peak of both guilt and fear. Coupled with this great guilt and fear is an expectancy of "Serenity" just around the corner.

If the confession has been thoroughly prepared and nothing is held back, the grouper may well have his expectations fulfilled. If so, AA has proved the Power of the Steps in bringing about Serenity. However, if he doesn't have some sort of peak experience, it is his

---

* An AA member would never say "check guidance," and would in all likelihood be only dimly, if at all, aware of the Oxford Group expression. He would say "get direction."

own fault. Perhaps he wasn't honest and thorough even if he thinks he was. Any time the grouper claims the Promises aren't being fulfilled in his life, he is opening himself up to group censure and is risking loss of status. If the Program isn't working, as the popular cliché "Some are sicker than others" suggests, the grouper is one of the sicker ones.

If he genuinely believes and insists that he was "honest and thorough," but isn't receiving the "payoff," his insistence suggests that he is one of the "unfortunates." As the opening of Chapter Five of the Big Book suggests, he may be "incapable of being honest" with himself. "Unfortunates" seem to "have been born that way." The wise grouper soon learns the wisdom of pretending. One of the more popular clichés is "Stick with the winners." If he doesn't "act as if" (that is, pretend) he is "happily and usefully whole" and the honeymoon period is over, the other groupers may decide he isn't a winner and, to protect their own precious Serenity, may decline to associate with him. At the very least, they will show scorn and contempt toward him or be extremely patronizing.

Even if the grouper has a peak experience, which most do, it is unlikely to last for more than a few hours or days. He has let off a great deal of emotional pressure, exorcised the fear of confession, and alleviated guilt. But he now has his *self* defined as "defective" or "sinful" to a degree that is rarely learned even in the addictive family system. Where in childhood the alcoholic learns that parts of himself are "bad" in a haphazard or random manner, in AA the definition of the self as bad and useless is extremely thorough.

A partial list of bad parts of the self, those which are "defects of character," includes anger, sadness, loneliness, fear, self-confidence, sensitivity, and being "too happy." Other manifestations of self include self-knowledge, having hopes and dreams (ambitions), one's own thoughts, and one's own will. Not only is most of the self defined as bad, but in a very bizarre, limited way, tiny parts of the self are defined as good or useful. Gratitude is good, as are humiliation and apparently, at least some-times, embarrassment.[43] The will, too, *can* be good. It is good when it provides impetus to work the Steps.

Working Steps Four and Five is not the end of guilt. With so much of the self defined as evil, the grouper will have much to feel guilty about without even counting overtly bad behavior. But he is still only beginning. Just recognizing all of his defects takes Time.

As the grouper becomes more skilled at identifying parts of himself as sinful or "defective," and learns to suppress awareness of the existence of these bad/alcoholic/sinful parts, the subjective experience of an awareness of God is likely to increase. When "sharing" at a meeting, he may be surprised to find himself saying "spiritual" things he doesn't recognize as coming from himself. It is "God" speaking through him. Of course, he is merely repeating AA beliefs he has heard from other groupers, read in AA literature, or knows "instinctively" because the dysfunctional beliefs responsible for his problem drinking are, to a large degree, held in common by other alcoholics. He has the *subjective* experience of God speaking through him because he is becoming less aware of his internal experience as he "turns over" his defects of character to God (that is, as he uses thought-stopping techniques).

As the grouper learns that certain thoughts are coming from his "Higher Power," he also learns that other thoughts and most emotions, those inconsistent with AA's definition of "good," are from the evil self which must be done away with. This "not AA" force, the self, is referred to as "my disease," "my alcoholic," or "John Barley-corn."

As the vital flow of information from the subconscious to the conscious becomes more restricted, Devil Drink assumes a mystical, magical, supernatural nature. Fear of the awesome power of Devil Drink, which is actually fear of oneself, intensifies dependence on Guidance from one's Higher Power. This Guidance is actually from AA doctrine and the AA elders, combined, perhaps, with the newly resurrected abusive-parent-defined God.

Step Six: *Were entirely ready to have God remove all these defects of character.*

The Big Book version of how to work Step Six is extremely simple. A person need only ask himself if he is willing to have his "defects" removed. For defects he would rather keep, he is to pray for the willingness to give them up.

Probably as a result of 13 years of practical AA experience, the 12 & 12's expanded discussion of this Step begins by cautioning the grouper not to expect much in the way of defect removal: "with most of them we shall have to be content with patient improvement."[44] Much of the discussion of this Step is about lesser sins, and about how everyone, if truly honest, can find many of them in themselves. After pointing out that most people don't steal, murder, rape, and aren't extremely lazy out of "self-interest, pure and simple,"[45] the 12 & 12 points out lesser degrees of these sins. For instance, a lesser degree of stealing is letting "greed masquerade as ambition." For murder, which is caused by anger, a lesser degree is "self-righteous anger." For rape, it's "imaginary sex excursions."A milder version of being lazy is to work hard in order to retire.[46] Evidently Sun City is Sin City. The intent of the comparison is to create guilt in the indoctrinee who has been working hard to retire or who has retired.

The goal of this Step is to further widen the definition of sin, to increase guilt, increase the need to purge that guilt, and increase the feeling of a need to change. Most important of all, however, is the direction of this change. The grouper is to "become entirely willing to aim towards perfection."[47]

A popular AA cliché, "progress, not perfection," and an acknowledgement in Chapter Five of the Big Book that "we are not saints. . . . We claim spiritual progress rather than spiritual perfection," seem contradictory to "aiming towards perfection." However, the statement in Chapter Five and the slogan merely acknowledge that the ideal of perfection can't be reached. In AA, as in all mind control cults, an inhuman model of perfection is held out which is impossible to reach. The member is to always work to "progress." He is *never* done with the battle of suppressing his self. To achieve this "progress," the grouper is to "abandon limited objectives," meaning his own, "and move towards God's will for us,"[48] meaning AA objectives. The grouper, as with most non-hypnotic AA "suggestions," is cautioned, "Delay is dangerous, and rebellion may be fatal."[49]

Step Seven: *Humbly asked Him to remove our shortcomings.*

The Big Book version of how to work Step Seven calls only for a simple prayer. The central theme of this prayer and this Step is "I pray that you now remove from me every single defect of character which stands in the way of my usefulness to you and my fellows"[50]

The 12 & 12's expanded discussion stresses "humility" as "a necessary aid to our survival."[51] Against the threat of death without it, the newcomer is promised that, with humility, he has a good chance of "becoming truly happy,"[52] *in the future.* *The major component of humility is "a desire to seek and to do God's will."[53] God's will, of course, is encompassed within the Steps, and the path to humility is modeled by the elders' own journeys. "But now the words, 'Of myself I am nothing, the Father doeth the works' began to carry bright promise and meaning."[54] This total discounting of each and every human being's innate value and God-given potential for growth and change is why AA members are so insistent that AA is responsible for not only everything good in their lives, but also for life itself.

The supposition in this Step is that, if one is humble enough, God will remove one's "manifestations of self." It never occurs to the grouper that perhaps God created us as feeling, thinking beings for a reason. It does not occur to him that perhaps the AA elders don't have a special consciousness of God's will. If such thoughts surface, they are quickly dispelled. They are the work of the "cunning, baffling, and powerful" one, the disease.

"Humility" is gradually achieved in AA. Each Step makes its own contribution. In Step One, the grouper admits that he is "powerless" and is incompetent to manage his own life. He then admits that he is insane, thoroughly discounts his own communication with God, comes to see himself as incompetent and evil, and accepts that he can't change himself. In Step Seven, "humility," the discounting, holding in contempt, and the disowning of the self, is held up as an essential end in and of itself.

Before AA, the grouper drowned out selected parts of his self—his thoughts, emotions, awareness, and potential—with alcohol. In AA, he intensifies his oppressive self-hatred with thought-stopping techniques, by adopting the "repentant sinner" role, and by telling others how sick he is. He ferrets out every aspect of self, redefining that which is "good" as coming from AA and that which is "bad" as being truly his.

Guilt arising from the existence of self leads the grouper into an

---

* All cults promise *future* rewards for compliance with doctrine.

orgy of "humble" confession. In this purging of guilt over being hopelessly defective, the grouper is no longer a lonely, wretched sinner. He is a wretched sinner with company. Everyone in a meeting suffers from pretty much identical defects even if some don't know it yet. By sharing his struggles, by confessing his "shortcomings," his "resentment," "self-pity," "willfulness," "alcoholic thinking," and "powerlessness," the grouper momentarily purges the guilt of existence and feels as one with the group, with the great moral crusade, with God.

Step Eight: *Made a list of all persons we had harmed, and became willing to make amends to them all.*

Step Nine: *Made direct amends to such people wherever possible, except when to do so would injure them or others.*

These Steps, like the others, mimic the spiritual principles of the world's great religions. However, in AA "making amends," elsewhere known as "atoning for one's sins," is perverted. The major motivation for making amends in AA is not regret, but fear of drinking and dying. Also important is the promise of being "catapulted into the fourth dimension of existence" through "painstakingly" working the Steps.

This distorts the purpose behind acts of atonement. When a grouper makes amends, he isn't necessarily sorry for anything he's done. Of course, any act he does regret will make his Step Eight list and he will make amends in Step Nine. However, a grouper is also likely to "make amends" that he wouldn't make if he valued his better judgment. In AA, if one's better judgment does not agree with that of the elders, it is merely "one's disease speaking." It is willfulness and self-centeredness.

This Step is often carried to ridiculous extremes. For example, one woman shared at a meeting that her sponsor had told her that she must make amends regarding a situation about which she had serious misgivings. While alone in a ladies room, she was confronted by a man standing in front of her masturbating. Shocked and frightened, she screamed at him to get out. He didn't blink. She screamed at him again. He still neither stopped nor left. Probably more out of panic than anything else, she hit him. Her sponsor told her that while what the man had done may have been wrong, it was her responsibility to "keep [her] own side of the street clean." She needed to make amends to him. Her "sobriety" was at stake.

While this example may seem extreme,* this woman's plight is not unusual in AA. It is entirely consistent with AA's view of the "alcoholic" as "bad child," sinner, or hopeless defective. Doubtless her sponsor saw, and she herself worried, that not wanting to make amends was a dangerous "manifestation of self." She was humiliated by the exhibitionist, and if she actually made "amends" to him she would have felt humiliated again. But in AA, "humiliation = humility." It is a good emotion.

The final three Steps, Ten, Eleven and Twelve, can be called the "maintenance" Steps. Their purpose is to maintain the cult hold upon the individual.

Step Ten: *Continued to take personal inventory and when we were wrong promptly admitted it.*

This Step is a call to continue the work of Steps Four through Nine in a regular, though perhaps less formal, manner. The inventory may or may not be written and may be done daily, weekly, or monthly. The important point in Step Ten is that the grouper continue to ferret out instances where the self rears its ugly head. Any such finding is to be immediately followed by confession.

Step Eleven: *Sought through prayer and meditation to improve our conscious contact with God as we understood Him, praying only for knowledge of His will for us and the power to carry that out.*

---

* The first AA member who criticized this as being an extreme example is a man who, as a child, was molested by a priest. In AA, he apologized to the priest for having been angry. I am also reminded of a woman who was gang raped. Her "spiritual advisors" tried to convince her it was her fault. Fortunately, she had sufficient sense of self to leave AA before being coerced into "making amends" to the rapists.

In Step Eleven, the grouper is to work for "conscious contact with God." Rather than being an entirely new concept, this is largely a continuation of Steps One, Two, and Three. The call to pray "only for knowledge of God's will for us" means that one is not to pray "selfish" prayers. It is essential to cult purposes that the answers that come from God or one's Higher Power are consistent with AA doctrine, or at least with one's immediate Elders.

When meditating,[*] one is to find a "good" thought to meditate upon. "We rest quietly with the thoughts of someone who knows, so that we may experience and learn."[55] This "good thought" may be given by one's sponsor. The general intent of this meditation is to "learn God's Will." However, whatever thoughts are used as a guide in meditation become firmly planted in the subconscious as unquestioned truth. Perhaps not by coincidence, this Step about searching for "conscious contact" and "praying for knowledge of God's Will" is immediately followed by a Step which answers those prayers. Step Twelve, from AA's point of view, is the ultimate expression of God's Will.

Step Twelve: *Having had a spiritual awakening as the result of these steps, we tried to carry this message to alcoholics, and to practice these principles in all our affairs.*

"Carrying the message" is the modern-day version of the Oxford Group's Fifth C, Continuance. It has a much broader meaning than directly practicing conversion. The particular tasks of "carrying the message are divided, although not by a sharp line, between new-comers and elders.

The newcomer is encouraged to "make a commitment" to help with the meetings by making coffee, setting up, or cleaning up afterwards. For the newcomer, this is helping to "carry the message" since "rescuing the alcoholic who still suffers" is every group's

---

[*] In my studies of hypnosis, I have found the only essential difference between a hypnotic trance and the meditative state is the source of the suggestions. In both, the critical faculty is diminished. Those accustomed to frequent meditation only need to be asked to meditate in order for them to quickly enter a hypnotic state even if they have never been hypnotized before.

"primary purpose." Having newcomers do the menial chores frees the elders to make their own efforts to carry the message. For an elder to get a newcomer to make such a commitment is also "carrying the message." This is usually done by telling him that it will help keep him from drinking. The newcomer, although perhaps just emptying ashtrays, feels part of the great crusade to rescue the alcoholic who still suffers.

Newcomers are also expected to "take chips" and say a few words about how it wouldn't have been possible to achieve 30, 60, or 90 days of abstinence without AA. They are encouraged to share their trials and tribulations as a result of their disease. Confessions of shortcomings or difficulties are sympathetically heard and any credit given to AA is warmly applauded.

The reticent newcomer will be told how essential sharing is to "recovery." If the newcomer still won't budge, he may be given the suggestion that he could be dooming someone newer than himself by being so selfish. Rare is the individual who spends more than a few weeks going to meetings who doesn't get caught up in the orgy of confession and praise, pouring out his heart and soul to the congregation in sincere penance for his shortcomings and expressing deep gratitude to AA for salvation.

In the eyes of those who are brand new, the Fifth Step sharing of the newer groupers is in stark contrast to the Twelfth Step sharing of the elders. The newcomer really is helping to carry the message. He is telling and showing how sick he is. People with Time, on the other hand, have already overcome the worst imaginable problems and no longer suffer from unpleasant emotions. The message is clear. Time in AA makes one well.

The accumulation of Time changes the presentation given at the podium. As the honeymoon period wears off, the grouper finds that sharing anything other than how AA has made him "happy, joyous and free," or at the very least how AA is helping him progress, is received very coolly by the elder groupers.

As a person accumulates Time and works the Steps, he learns that it is *selfish* to share about his problems. There are newcomers to be saved from jails, institutions, and death. If his life isn't all that he wants it to be, it's his fault. He obviously isn't working his Program well enough. Any bad feelings or thoughts are the work of Devil Drink. "My mind is telling me things are bad. Better to let God speak through me." It is wise and spiritual to "act as if." There's no point in dooming others who have come for help.

There are many rewards for "carrying the message." Telling about how much the Program has helped is indirectly and "humbly" pointing out one's progress toward sanity and spiritual growth. There is also status in being a sponsor. But other reasons for "carrying the message" have more to do with avoiding punishment.

The most important driving force in AA is the fear of Devil Drink. AA attributes its very existence and the survival of all AA members to Bill Wilson's revelation that an alcoholic needs another alcoholic (to save) in order to stay sober (saved). However, "giving that which was so freely given" is often used as a method of ignoring problems. For example, the Big Book advises that "if sex is a problem, throw yourself all the more into helping others." Sponsors often advise their "babies," when they are having problems of any sort, to "help those less fortunate." In other words, the problems which were ignored by drinking are now ignored by working to convince others that AA is the solution to their problems.

Another driving force behind the obsession to convert others was expressed by the Oxford Group as "keep[ing] the conversion experience real." This is typical of all totalitarian groups. The cult member is in a bind. No matter how well he was indoctrinated, he is always "in danger" of becoming aware of inconsistencies and having his whole world, a world based on the perfection of the sacred doctrine, fall apart. He is reassured of the validity of the doctrine by convincing others. This is aptly called "the psychology of the pawn."

It is difficult to categorize people who have been indoctrinated into AA. One thing that *can* be said about them, and that they will agree with, is that they do not drink moderately. While members are very vocal about having found "a solution to the alcohol problem," only a very small percentage of "true" alcoholics in AA—probably less than 5 percent (the number most frequently cited at meetings)—manage to *not* die from "their disease." Most members go through seemingly random-length periods of abstinence and then, *without having any real clue as to why,* set off on a suicidal drinking binge, or even attempt suicide.* Many members "go in and out" for years

---

* I have kept some degree of contact with six of about twelve people in my "therapy" group four years ago. Three have attempted suicide. Two succeeded.

and eventually give up on quitting drinking because they know that "AA is the last house on the block," meaning that if AA doesn't work there is nothing left to try.

Drinking by members is used to point out the dangers of "halfway measures" and as proof of how well the program works. The frequent suicides are passed off with "the alcohol got 'em," and serve as warnings to members to be humble, obedient, selfless, and to take direction from the elders who are further along the Spiritual Path.

In spite of the differences among those who have worked the Steps, there are many common characteristics. . . .

1. AA (1938):83-84
2. AA (1952):15
3. AA (1984):293
4. AA (1984):293
5. AA (1984):293
6. AA (1984):293-294
7. AA (1957):13
8. AA (1952):23
9. AA (1952):24
10. AA (1952):33
11. AA (1952):33
12. AA (1938):23
13. AA (1938):44
14. AA (1952):27
15. AA (1952):32
16. AA (1952):33
17. Birnie (1936)
18. AA (1952):34
19. AA (1952):35
20. AA (1952):36
21. AA (1952):36
22. AA (1952):36
23. AA (1952):37
24. AA (1952):41
25. AA (1938):63
26. AA (1938):75
27. AA (1952):62
28. AA (1952):62
29. AA (1938):62
30. AA (1938):64

31. AA (1938):66
32. AA (1938):67
33. AA (1952):48
34. AA (1938):68
35. See "Acceptance" in the Big Book, p. 449, and in the 12 & 12, p. 90
36. AA (1938):67
37. AA (1952):60
38. AA (1952):60
39. AA (1938):74
40. AA (1952):61
41. AA (1952):60
42. AA (1952):60
43. AA (1952):60
44. AA (1952):65
45. AA (1952):66
46. AA (1952):67
47. AA (1952):69
48. AA (1952):69
49. AA (1952):69
50. AA (1952):76
51. AA (1952):74
52. AA (1952):70
52. AA (1952):72
53. AA (1952):75
54. AA (1952):100

12: Miracles of Recovery

Of the small percentage of those with significant exposure to AA who manage to remain abstinent, the vast majority continue to participate fully in cult activities, particularly "carrying the message" as speakers and sponsors.

A typical AA speaker is very adept at using confession to convince others of their powerlessness, insanity, defectiveness, and need for AA. The speaker often has motivations other than a sincere desire to help, but it is doubtful that the speaker is aware of them, since such awareness is inconsistent with being "spiritually awake" and would incite use of thought-stopping techniques. I have never seen an AA member so transparent in this regard as a woman I'll call Debbie.

Debbie has almost 15 years of "sobricty." She was a prostitute in her younger days and uses this to great advantage when speaking. "Do you know what I used to do? I used to sell my ass. Yes, that's what I used to do." Her "humble confession," which is typical of elders in all mind-control cults, is anything but truly humble. To quote Camus, "[I] . . . practice the role of penitent to be able to end up as a judge . . . the more I accuse myself, the more I have a right to judge you."

Debbie is different from the ordinary elder only in occasionally saying "you" to the congregation instead of always using "we" or "alcoholics." She tells them, "You may think you're the cream of the crop, but I'll tell you what you really are, you're the cream of the crap. You're sick. You're alcoholics." She continues at great length, always ending her tirades against "alcoholics," meaning all present, with a warm smile and "I love you all. Keep coming back." The congregation always responds with warm applause. She obviously does love them very much. She "loves them enough to tell them the truth."

Another, more or less typical example of an AA alcoholic or "judge-penitent" is Georgia, a very popular speaker, not only because she has 35 years of Time, but because of the earthy "honesty" she has acquired during those years. The congregation is always awed by her "recovery." She has no reservations in labeling herself a sinner. She isn't at all guilty of "rationalizing" or "justifying" her behavior, which would be symptomatic of "the disease." Her great recovery is clearly evident in her free confession of sin and defectiveness. Her story of alcoholic ruin and salvation by AA is frequently interspersed with, "I was (or am) nothing but a whore." Although she never was a prostitute, nor even particularly promiscuous, she did marry more than once. In AA, one can't be more "humble" or "honest" than by putting one's past actions in the worst possible light. Georgia' great humility and 35 years of Time testify to the Power of the Program. With her credentials established, she bears witness to the defects of all alcoholics. She is unrelenting in her indirect "we" and "alcoholics" judgments of the entire congregation.

These women benefit, as do all elders, from playing judge-penitent. To quote Robert J. Lifton, the world's foremost authority on the "psychology of totalism"*:

[Assuming this role] becomes a vehicle for taking on some of the environment's arrogance and sense of omnipotence. Yet even this shared omnipotence cannot protect him from the opposite (but not unrelated) feelings of humiliation and weakness, feelings especially prevalent among those who remain more the enforced penitent than the all-powerful judge.[1]

In other words, in the AA environment, where the member is forced to acknowledge his "powerlessness," "insanity," and defectiveness, and to humiliate himself in other ways, he can feel less insane, defective, powerless, and humiliated (feel his "higher power") by merging himself with the all-powerful, sane, perfect Program and *becoming the humiliator.*

---

* The psychology of totalism refers to the methods and psychology of "totalitarian groups." Among groups which can be considered totalitarian are the Red Chinese Communists, the Nazis, the parts of the Catholic Church involved in the Inquisition, the Moonies and Hare Krishnas, and, of course, Alcoholics Anonymous.

While AA speakers boast of how the Promises have been fulfilled, their boasts have little relevance to their personal lives other than that they *probably* are not drinking or drugging.

Paul, for example, has been "sober" for over ten years. When speaking at meetings, he presents himself as entirely "together." "The Promises" have been fulfilled in his life. He not only has more than ten years of "sobriety," he has Serenity. When a friend of mine heard him speak, he was so impressed with Paul's "recovery" that he asked him to be his sponsor. As it turned out, this paragon of AA virtue, absolutely abstinent and on a "spiritual path" for more than ten years, was hardly a person who should be "giving direction" of any kind to anybody.

Paul still has serious problems and during his period of "sobriety" has developed some new ones that he chooses to avoid "confusing the newcomers" with. He has no friends. He rarely leaves his apartment except for AA meetings, and he spends most of his free time alone with his television. He beat up his former male lover so badly that the man needed hospitalization. He was also arrested for procurement in a public park and has become grossly overweight. While these particulars may seem extreme, the dynamics of Paul's case are not out of the ordinary.

It is not unusual for people who quit an addiction without dealing with the underlying problems to substitute another. It seems apparent that this man is now, in Twelve Step jargon, "using" sex, food, and perhaps television. He also serves as an example of the dangers of "turning over" anger to one's "higher power." In plain English, "turning it over" means repressing it.

It may be difficult to imagine how he can justify the difference between his actual personal life and the one he presents from the podium, but, having adopted the "spiritual principle" of "Powerlessness," the quality of his life has little to do with him. He's powerless. The bumper sticker on his car is apt. It bears the AA slogan, "SHIT HAPPENS."

Scores of examples can be cited of people with Time beginning, or continuing, to do things destructive to themselves or others, but such characterizations don't prove anything except that such people exist. An AA member would respond that they had problems before they came to AA, which is undoubtedly true. The important point is the credibility of the "AA successes." Are those who have worked the

Twelve Steps "miracles of mental health" as they claim? Do they have a special knowledge or wisdom about alcoholism?

One interesting and celebrated example of what "recovery" is all about is Kitty Dukakis. Dukakis is a self-described alcoholic, addict, and manic-depressive. She has been hospitalized several times over eight years and has lectured on addiction and alcoholism with the intention of helping others. She has written an autobiography, *Now You Know*. Her story, other than the portion involving her husband's race for the presidency, is far from unique in AA.

She was raised by a mother who had serious problems. By Kitty Dukakis's own account, her mother taught her some very destructive lessons, which she learned well: you have no personality; you're worth less than the "red weasel" (the nickname given her sister because she was thought to be ugly); you are the cause of my rage; you are to be perfect; you are not worthy of praise; if others should compliment you it is meaningless; you can never win an argument; and, by example, it is bad to have fun.

Her father appears to have been more indirect. He is described as "plagued by self-doubt,"[2] and is cryptically referred to as "[someone who] naturally makes everyone around him feel good, even when he's punishing them."[3] He also had a strange sense of humor. He liked to introduce his two young daughters saying "one is much better than the other" and let the two little children figure out who.[4] Her father was also a practical joker.[5] When she got her first job in a record store, on her first day at work, he called and asked her for Beethoven's Tenth. She spent hours looking for it. As Kitty told it, "'You dimwit,' laughed my dad, 'Beethoven only wrote nine symphonies.' Dad pulled stunts like that on me the whole time I worked there. He always liked to make people laugh."[6]

It seems strange that a father would play that kind of prank on his insecure daughter's first day at work. Was he giving the message that she was stupid or incompetent? Was he, like when he was overtly punishing her, making her enjoy it? Was he merely amusing himself and his friends at his daughter's expense? Or was it, as humor often is, a veiled way of expressing hostility?

Her father's humor and punishment could well have been "crazy making." A father who works to make a child "feel good" when being punished is putting the child in a terrible bind. A small child feels bad when he has displeased a parent. A parent who builds the expectation in the child that not "feeling good" while being punished will further disappoint the parent teaches the child an extremely destructive lesson. The child's only available conclusion, since the parent must be right, is "my feelings are bad." The same goes for when a child is the butt of a parent's jokes if the parent expects the child to enjoy it. To be angry at being ridiculed is "bad." The small child again concludes, "my feelings are bad." The child learns to suppress the feelings in an attempt to be "good." The child may even learn to "feel good" when being punished, or to "enjoy" being ridiculed. But, out of sight, and out of the conscious mind of the obedient child, the anger and rage boil away.

While there is no way to be certain of the exact nature of the destructive lessons she learned as a child, Kitty Dukakis makes it very clear how she felt:

> My childhood was stacked with remorse; most of the time I walked around feeling I'd done something wrong. I lived under a Damoclean sword of accusation, and at any given moment it could drop and cut off, if not my head, my confidence.[7]

Her mother told Kitty that she had one thing going for her, though it wasn't something that she should feel good about. Unlike the "red weasel," she was attractive. In her teen years, she began gaining weight and thereby lost the only thing that she was allowed to value in herself. Following her mother's example, she began taking diet pills. Her mother disapproved of her "boundless energy" and "talking too much" and warned her to stop, but she didn't quit. She took one diet pill a day for the next 26 years.

After only a few weeks the body develops tolerance and, for all practical purposes, the pills would no longer have had an appreciable physical effect on her.* However, there may have been important psychological reasons for taking them.

Kitty Dukakis was living "under a Damoclean sword of accusation." She constantly felt guilty over what she might have done

---

* This is not to say that discontinuance would not have caused transitory discomfort but that due to the body's adjustment, one wouldn't be, after continued use of a small amount of a drug, appreciably more energetic or talkative or anything else due to *pharmacological* effects. After taking her daily pill, she would only feel as she would have if she had never taken them.

or would do. As long as she took diet pills, the pills were responsible, at least in her own mind, for her behavior. She was free to be talkative, active, and "silly." As long as she took the pills she had permission. One of her coping methods was to stay busy: "I could run away from my thoughts, from my feelings, and from my fears."[8] Believing that the daily pill would keep her active, and being able to attribute any "silliness" or imperfection resulting from her activity to "the drug," it is easy to imagine that her one-a-day pill habit was an effective, though far from productive, way of coping with life.

In discussing her 26 years of "drug addiction," Kitty D. outlines the history of an "addict" from the Twelve Step point of view. She has no real horror story of what "the drugs made me do." She tells of the events in her life—unhappy first marriage, pregnancy, divorce, and later remarriage—from the perspective that the daily diet pill was somehow extremely relevant. "In December of 1956, I started using."[9] "I was still taking my morning pill."[10] "Only one thing had remained constant throughout those four years, my addiction."[11]

As a Twelve Stepper, Kitty D. looks at her past in terms of what the drug did: "We had some tough moments, times when I would fly off the handle to such an extent that Michael would wind up not speaking to me. Of course he didn't know it was the pills talking."[12]

Perhaps we are to believe that, just like the little girl in *The Exorcist*, Kitty Dukakis was seized by a demon and forced, against her will, to say rageful things to her husband, that it wasn't her talking. Perhaps she wasn't ever, in those 26 years, angry at anyone.

But maybe anger was one of the feelings she ran from. Maybe she felt guilt over her natural, normal human response. Maybe, during the years she spent running to keep it out of her awareness, her anger grew into an ever more frightening rage. Maybe it sometimes caught up with her, but she had worked so successfully at ignoring it that she couldn't recognize it as her own. Or maybe it was just easier to pretend that it wasn't hers.

Whatever the case, while "using" she attributed all good she did to the pills: "Everything I accomplished during that quarter of a century plus I attributed to the chemicals ruling my body. I actually felt that without them, none of these achievements would have been possible."[13] It seems but a small step to attribute all that she disapproved of in herself to the same cause.

Her "bottom" as an "addict" came at her daughter's eighth grade graduation. As Kitty D. confesses, "I was talking loudly and snapping," "I squirmed in my seat." Knowing that her behavior was "indefensible," and attributing it all to the diet pill, she took action.

After 26 years of suffering an "addiction" which made her basically no different from anyone else, Kitty Dukakis got "help." She spoke to her brother-in-law, who had "always been open about his own alcoholism and subsequent recovery."* Kitty Dukakis, in July of 1982, began treatment for drug addiction.

Kitty D. claims that during her 28-day, AA-based treatment she was helped. "I accepted the fact that I was addicted to pills." The "acceptance of her addiction" actually means that she took the First Step and accepted 12-step/treatment center doctrine on the nature of addiction: that she was "powerless" and her life was "unmanageable."

She was advised that she was also an alcoholic in spite of the fact that she didn't have a drinking problem. While in treatment, Kitty D. was expected to identify herself as an addict and alcoholic. In spite of being warned that she was also an alcoholic, it seems that Kitty's "disease told her" that she was only an addict. After treatment, she refused to identify herself at meetings as an alcoholic. She would only say, "My name is Kitty and I am an addict."

Her problem with identifying herself as an alcoholic was based in the fact that she didn't have a drinking problem. Her "chronology of alcoholism," up to this point, was getting sick once from two glasses of spiked punch in high school, getting sick once from "a few too many" in college, and getting sick from drinking one Zombie in Mexico during her first marriage. These three instances were in her distant past.

After leaving treatment, she remained abstinent from both pills and alcohol and attended "support group meetings." She also began eight years of depression which she attributes, of course, to the pills. Believing that the pills enabled her to be active and to run at a safe distance from her feelings, she may well have felt "helpless" without them. AA taught her that she was powerless, insane, had "bad"

---

* While nothing is said in her autobiography about the brother-in-law convincing her that her less-than-perfect behavior was due to the daily diet pill or that he had been working on her to convince her of the need for help, the statement "had always been open about his own alcoholism" does imply that he was "fishing" for a convert. As a grouper he would have felt a moral obligation to "help": "Through confession we may win his soul."

feelings, and that being angry could kill her. If having her crutch taken away wasn't enough to bring on depression, it is easy to imagine that AA indoctrination was.

Kitty D. was soon on drugs again, but this time, the kind psychiatrists prescribe.* After a few months she quit going to meetings and began drinking moderately. However, she continued to lecture as an authority, "as one who knows," on drugs and addiction.

She managed fairly well over the next few years. She didn't have a drinking problem. She involved herself in numerous activities. Everything seemed to be going fine until April 1987, when Michael Dukakis formally announced his run for the presidency.

The campaign trail is extremely stressful. As the wife of a presidential contender, she had to give up her own work and interests. She had to hand over the management of her life to staff assistants who told her when to get up, when and where to eat, where to go, who to talk to, what to say, what not to say, and when and where to sleep. Her day began at 5:30 am and ended around 2:00 am. Duties included speaking to groups, answering questions and, perhaps most importantly, always being "up" for the ever-present cameras. There was never a moment's privacy. She took great care in everything she said and did. A mere slip of the tongue on her part could have cost her husband the presidency.

Such a schedule would quickly take a toll on anyone, but Kitty Dukakis had two additional strikes against her. First, she didn't like herself; she felt like a fake. Being constantly under the watchful eye of the cameras must have been terrifying. Someone might see who she thought she really was. The other was that, in the treatment center, "the seed had been planted." As Kitty tells it, "Buried way back in my brain was a warning I had received at the Hazelden Clinic back in 1982." The warning, perhaps better termed "AA suggestion," was that she was an alcoholic and would *eventually* "lose control."

At the end of each day, the campaign team got together to relax over drinks. Kitty joined in. During the campaign, she had one drink a day. The entire staff looked forward to the end of the work day, to

---

* She was seeing a psychiatrist who was "in recovery" himself. To quote an early psychiatric "friend" of AA, Dr. Harry M. Tiebout, the therapist's job is "breaking down the patient's inner resistance [to AA] so that which is inside him will flower . . . under the activity of the A.A. program."

being able to kick back and finally relax out of the glare of the TV cameras and have a drink. Kitty, however, with the seed firmly planted, felt as though something was wrong with her if she looked forward to that drink. She knew alcohol's power. It was Devil Drink that was good about the end of the day. Being out of the spotlight, having the pressure off, being able to relax and socialize, and being able to be herself without ruining anyone's career were irrelevant. It was Devil Drink that made her feel better.

The two-year campaign ended with Michael Dukakis's defeat. Kitty, having given up much of what was important to her, had nothing to fall back on. She had even quit taking her antidepressants. Even worse, during the entire campaign, she had dealt with the stress by working even harder than usual. She ran from her feelings and, as they threatened to overwhelm her and disrupt the all-important presidential race, she ran even faster. Now, with the campaign over, with nowhere to run, Kitty soon caught up with Kitty.

The dynamics of Kitty D.'s two-month drinking career may be evident to the reader of her book, although perhaps not to her. Kitty D. virtually dropped all outside activity. In her inner world, she battled with great success against "negative" thoughts and feelings. Loss of the election and whatever else was or wasn't going on in her life *called for* such thoughts and feelings. Since she had given up much of what was important to her, what made her feel good, she was left with *nothing* on the inside: "I was faced with a gaping emptiness I could not endure."[14]

Normally a person recovers from such a situation over time since sooner or later their feelings catch up with them. But Kitty D. knew from "treatment" that she was suffering symptoms peculiar to the disease of alcoholism. From her campaign experience, she knew alcohol had a special power to make her feel good. In treatment, she must have heard countless stories of the great painful emptiness peculiar to the alcoholic. She also knew, since the seed had been so firmly planted, what she could do to fix it—and what was expected of her. She could drink. She must also have known, at least in the back of her mind, that she would end up in treatment again. Perhaps being in a hospital is what she wanted more than alcohol, because it didn't take her long to get there.

While it is difficult to follow the number and dates of all her treatments, she seems to have gone through shorter and shorter periods of relative stability. The last self-destructive incident she reported was drinking hair spray, again resulting in treatment.

Her last AA-based treatment, like the previous ones, had its effect on Kitty D. In her 1982 treatment, she "accepted" that she was an addict, the seed was planted that she was an alcoholic, and she began suffering depression. In early 1989, she "accepted" her alcoholism and began a series of extremely self-destructive acts. In late 1989, she got further "help." Now the outside observer might conclude that the "help" she had been getting seriously aggravated her problems. But this is "unspiritual thinking." The Program is perfect. There was simply one more thing wrong with Kitty D., something which she "accepted" in her most recent treatment.

Kitty D. Accepted that she is manic-depressive. That means that she *must* be on drugs, not merely one diet pill a day, but lithium. So now, Kitty D., recovering alcoholic, addict, and manic depressive, has finally acquired the promised Serenity. She has been given "The Keys to the Kingdom": the Twelve Steps of Alcoholics Anonymous *and a bottle of highly potent pills.*

Between hospitalizations, Kitty D. kept busy educating others about addiction and alcoholism. She still wants to carry the message. At last report she had visited the former Soviet Union to give that which she was so freely given.

---

1. Lifton (1961):427
2. Dukakis (1990):41
3. Dukakis (1990):23
4. Dukakis (1990):42
5. Dukakis (1990):78
6. Dukakis (1990):78
7. Dukakis (1990):107
8. Dukakis (1990):243
9. Dukakis (1990):86
10. Dukakis (1990):97
11. Dukakis (1990):101
11. Dukakis (1990):140
12. Dukakis (1990):13
13. Dukakis (1990):249

Chapter 13: How Far Carried?

AA has been much more successful than the Oxford Group. In its heyday, the Oxford Group reached more than 60 countries. AA is active in more than 120. To understand this phenomenal growth one must understand the nature and purpose of "not AA" organizations.

To keep AA purely spiritual, what appear to be severe restrictions are placed on members' efforts to "carry the message." They can't solicit or accept money from outside sources. They can't ally themselves, as a group, with other organizations. They must, as AA members, remain anonymous in the media. And they can't, as AA members, take a public stand on any political or social issue.

However, there are no restrictions on AA members acting alone or in concert *outside* of AA to promote AA and its ideology. There are no restrictions placed on their *founding* outside organizations allied with AA or *moving* existing organizations into alliance with AA. As members of outside organizations, AA members can solicit funds and take stands on social and political issues. They can also "educate the public." In fact, a "not AA" corporation can do whatever it sees fit to "carry the message" except use the AA name and/or identify itself in public with AA. In a legal, corporate sense, AA doctrine has been spread more by "not AA" organizations and "not AA" people than by AA.

The most innocuous of these "not AA" organizations are the corporations operating AA clubhouses. Major cities have many locations operated, staffed, and used exclusively by AA members (and sometimes members of other 12-step groups) for meetings and socializing. These clubhouses are "not AA." In keeping with The Traditions, mixing "property and prestige" with the "spiritual" is not allowed. AA would never ask for or accept money from outside sources, but AA members can band together to establish "not AA" clubhouses. These "not AA" clubhouse corporations solicit public money for "people in recovery from alcoholism and drug addiction," not for AA.

Another "not AA" organization is the publicly funded treatment center. These centers are very often managed and staffed by AA members, and the "treatment" offered is AA indoctrination, but they are "not AA." Being "not AA," they are free to solicit public funds.

This represents only a small part of AA's influence. It begins with AA's approach to medicine and religion. (The individual AA member, even though he humbly knew he was more capable of helping alcoholics than either doctors or ministers, was advised in the 1939 Big Book to "cooperate; never criticize.")[1]

At the time of AA's founding, religious and medical organizations were failing in their attempts to get excessive drinkers to moderate or quit. AA members, boasting of a personal "cure" for the "disease," found fertile ground. Indoctrinated members, whether they drank or not, agreed on the nature of the disease. Those who were abstinent at the moment pointed to "a simple program" as the cause of their success. Those who continued to drink or whose drinking became worse could point to their own willfulness, stubbornness, self-centeredness, or lack of honesty for their failure, and still praise AA for its sincere desire to help. Those only partially indoctrinated, who didn't want to continue going to AA, were explained by co-founder Wilson: "Initial rejection of A.A. is part of the denial mechanism."[2] Against this background, it was difficult to be critical of AA. Those associated with AA were full of praise for it, and those who didn't like it were suffering a disease symptom. Casual observation showed sincere, successful people trying to help others and themselves.

AA has neutralized almost all criticism from organized religion. Because of AA's stress on a "higher power," the early suggestion that members affiliate with a church, and the insistence that it is a "spiritual, not religious" program, most religious organizations were swayed in AA's favor in the 1930s and 1940s, and remain so today. It would have been extremely difficult for a religious leader to criticize AA in the early days. His awareness of AA was mainly through new members attributing church attendance, and the solution of serious problems, to a new-found awareness of God brought about by AA. It would also have been difficult for a religious organization to criticize AA when AA was apparently so full of praise for religious organizations. As with so many things in AA, its criticism of organized religion was and is indirect.

It is difficult for a non-member to catch the hidden criticisms of other religions in AA literature. But they are there. For example, in the AA book, *Pass It On*, Bill Wilson expresses his thoughts on religion:

> The ungodly might not be expected to know any better. But men of religion should. Yet history shows that they just don't. It seems to me that the great religions survive because each has a sound core of spirituality. They survive because of their spirituality . . .[3]

The casual reader would see this as a lukewarm defense of religion; the "great religions" have "a sound core of spirituality" which outweighs their "history." However, the indoctrinated cult member is aware that organized religion is good to the degree that it incorporates the pure substance of AA, because AA is purely spiritual and not at all religious. AA requires no beliefs. Beliefs are essential to religion. AA doesn't need to require beliefs because those who don't "come to believe" AA's beliefs will die. This means that AA is the pure embodiment of all that allows organized religion to be *somewhat* good, and that AA is more powerful and has a more direct line to God than any religion. AA also has no "history" other than that "[AA's] world arteries . . . carry the life-giving grace of God."[4] Ironically, only a few fringe religious groups, with techniques similar to those of AA, have recognized AA's true stance toward religion and have warned their members against AA. As far as I know, the only religious groups which have been vocal in their criticism of AA are some of the more extreme fundamentalist Christian groups.

AA's modern relationship with other religions can be summed up by a conversation that I overheard at an AA meeting among a half-dozen or so groupers:

> "Did you read the article that said AA was taking the place of religion?" Some groupers indicated they had. "She shouldn't have said it," he continued. "But it is true," one grouper protested. "Yeah, but she still shouldn't have said it." All heads nodded in agreement.

While AA has been extremely successful in its relationship with most religions, its influence on medicine has been much greater.

Some members of the medical establishment are among its greatest boosters. A doctor who has been indoctrinated into AA or Al-Anon cannot speak "at the media level" about alcoholism *as a member of AA*. That would be "breaking anonymity." He can, however, "carry the message" *as a medical authority*.

In the medical school text, *The Treatment of Alcoholism*, the student is taught:

> Every effort should be made to introduce the patient to AA. Schedules of local AA meetings should be kept in the office and given to each patient. The physician should know several recovered men and women active in local AA who are willing to meet with a new patient, share their experiences, and take the patient to an AA meeting.[5]

If the excessive drinker would rather quit on his own, the doctor is to suggest that the person who tries to quit "by himself . . . usually fails"[6]—*as if people who go to AA have a lower failure rate than those who quit on their own*. The psychiatrist is advised that his "primary goal" is to establish a "therapeutic relationship" with the patient in order to use it as "leverage" to get him into AA.[7]

None of this is surprising, because the book was written with the admitted goal of getting people into AA[8] by a man who got his information from the "insights" of "recovered" alcoholics, going to AA meetings, and friendships with AA groupers.[9] The author claims "a deeper understanding of alcoholism, an understanding that is not approached by the usual process of medical education."[10]

This medical textbook and its acceptance would not have been possible if the AMA had not declared alcoholism a disease in 1956. Based upon the amazingly faulty work of E.M. Jellinek,[*] the medical establishment has given medical legitimacy to the disease concept, a concept which defines the "disease" as incurable, progressive, characterized by "denial," and fatal without "help."

This declaration was made with the best of intentions. Undoubtedly, some imagined the results would be that alcoholics would get effective treatment, and that the declaration would have a major impact on the nation's alcohol problems. The results, however, have

---

[*] See Chapter 3, "Disease Theory."

been at odds with these desires While there has been no decrease in alcoholism attributable to its being classified (and "treated") as a disease, there has been a dramatic increase in the growth of AA.

With alcoholism now an officially sanctioned disease, states began forcing insurers to pay for treatment, thus creating the multi-billion-dollar treatment industry. The treatment offered was, and still is, unproven, ineffective, AA indoctrination.

The ramifications go much further: *AA has become America's quasi-official religion*. In the midst of great public discussion over many church-state issues, an increasing portion of the federal government's budget has gone to pay for Twelve Step indoctrination under the guise of treatment. The 1991 federal budget alone calls for almost *four billion dollars* for "treatment." State, county and city governments, at the urging of "those who know," each contribute their own share.

Although almost one-and-a-half million people go through treatment every year, there has been no decrease in alcoholism or drug addiction rates. There has, however, been a great increase in the power and influence of Twelve Step groups.

Governmental agencies, particularly the courts, routinely coerce people into AA indoctrination. The choice is frequently AA or jail, in spite of research that shows that coercion into AA/treatment increases problem drinking.[11]

Members in good standing of the Moonies, as with almost any other cult, don't have alcohol or drug problems, regardless of their status before indoctrination. What would be the public's response if this year's budget called for four billion dollars for indoctrination centers for the Moonies or Hare Krishnas? The only real differences between these groups and AA is that they are honest about being religious groups and, at least with the Moonies, members moderate rather than abstain.

AA has also been extremely successful with the mass media. Rarely if ever is a story even slightly critical of AA published or shown on television. The media instead report successful "recovery."

Typical of television news was Los Angeles station KCAL's special report on alcoholism in the early 1990s. The report claimed that there are an estimated 22 million alcoholics in the United States with another 82 million persons affected by the alcoholics. "If left untreated alcoholism, like other addictions, gets progressively worse," the report warned. A Twelve Step cult member then testified that alcohol nearly destroyed her and that treatment saved her.

An alcoholism treatment expert from a local hospital-based treatment center explained, in "outsider doctrine," what AA is:

> It's a real simple program of fellowship. The Twelve Steps involve working with other people, being honest with other people and learning to accept help from outside of themselves.

Listeners were then given the phone number of Alcoholics Anonymous for more information. The newscaster thanked the researchers who "only wanted to help" for the report.

Television and movies invariably show alcoholic characters in the AA disease-theory mold. They suffer the consequences of, and all of their bad behavior is attributable to, their "disease," until they're saved by AA. In a recent episode of "Beverly Hills 90210," one of the main characters, a teenage boy, threw a party while his parents were out of town, got drunk, and wrecked the family car. The situation was resolved when a warm, understanding, wiser teenager, who had "lived it," brought him to an AA meeting. He went home with acceptance of his alcoholism and, presumably, lived responsibly ever after. No mention was made of a lifetime commitment to attend meetings, an obsession to get others to join, the rest of the family being sick and needing "help," or any other aspect of AA "spirituality."

Television dramas and sitcoms give the impression that once a person has joined AA, drinking problems, presented as the source of all problems, are solved almost as simply as just remembering "One Day at a Time." Never do the rigors of indoctrination result in a return to drinking. The pressures people are put under to change their concepts of God and to accept the Big Book as divinely inspired are not shown. The mass media never presents characters, real or fictional, who drink more, or commit suicide, following AA involvement. In a word, TV character portrayals are often quite unrealistic.

According to the Big Book, Bill Wilson was planning to save the entire world as early as 1938. One early AA member said Bill Wilson and another early member "were not only going to save all the drunks in the world but also the so-called normal people!"[12]

Their humble plans are being fulfilled.

The major difference between the Oxford Group and AA is that

AA concentrates its indoctrination efforts on only those with one "spiritual disease." Oxford Group members knew that they needed to save others, any others, in order to stay saved. AA members know that only saving other alcoholics will keep them saved.

Decades ago, many AA members found that, even if they managed to not drink, other addictive behaviors became problems. Since they attributed their not drinking to the Twelve Steps, forming Twelve Step groups for these other addictions seemed logical. This was first done for other chemical addictions with the founding of Pills Anonymous, Narcotics Anonymous, Cocaine Anonymous, and Marijuana Anonymous among others. As well, the Twelve Step movement has spread to cover non-chemical addictions with groups like Gamblers Anonymous. These groups all center around the "proven" Twelve Steps. In Step One, the word "alcohol" is replaced with the appropriate object of addiction. In Step Twelve, "alcoholics" is replaced with "addicts" or "compulsive gamblers," etc.

Members of Gamblers Anonymous follow the same pattern as do AA members in their efforts to "carry the message." A recent PBS program, "Lucky Number," used "recovering" gamblers and treatment industry personnel as experts on compulsive gambling. The first part of the program featured a "recovering" gambler who explained his compulsive gambling: "I needed to gamble just like the drug addict needed to put a needle in their arm." Statistics were presented to show the seriousness of the problem.[*]

The program lamented the fact that there are only 26 treatment centers for compulsive gamblers. A treatment center employee claimed a success rate of 85 percent for Gamblers Anonymous.[**] The only question deemed worthy of discussion was who should pay for more "treatment," the gaming industry or the government.

The Twelve Step religion has spread to almost every group of

[*] Compulsive gambling is a serious problem and growing worse with more states legalizing various forms of gambling and even running promotional campaigns showing the state lotteries as a *solution to problems and a source of wealth and joy.*

[**] The success rate was "for those who follow aftercare." There was no definition of success and no evidence was given for the seriousness of the individual cases. No figures were given for those who didn't follow aftercare and nothing was said about the nature of aftercare. In a 1988 study of Gamblers Anonymous only 7 percent remained abstinent from gambling for two years. See Stewart and Brown (1988).

people who suffer from any disease, illness, or problem which has a high rate of natural remission. It has even spread to people who have no particular problem except that they are normal human beings. Twelve Step groups have been formed for schizophrenia, depression, and mental illness in general. Other groups have been formed for people who eat too much, cheat on their spouses, have too much sex, are "addicted" to love, mismanage their money, have cancer, or are homosexuals. Many programs have parallel programs for family and friends who are, of course, sick too. There are now more than 200 different Twelve Step programs, each with its own particular "disease" used as leverage for conversion.

These are casually referred to as "support" groups. Even though most of them deal with temporary "diseases," or with only the spouses or friends of those with the "diseases," none accepts that people can ever get well and leave. They all call for lifetime dedication to the Steps, meetings, and converting others.

For instance, a depressed person may be told that he needs a support group. If he goes to what one generally imagines is a support group, he will receive help and understanding from others who are learning to deal with their depression. Members will leave when they no longer feel the need for special support. The Twelve Step "support" group, however, will make every effort to convince the person that he is powerless, insane, and incompetent, that the group is God (or His interpreter), and that he must "work the program one day at a time." If he asks how long before he is well and can leave, he may be told that worrying about such things is a disease symptom and must be repressed. If the depressed person doesn't "get well," he may be told that it is because he isn't "working with others"; he'll be happy only if he convinces others that they'll become happy by joining the group.

One of the newer Twelve Step programs is the most inclusive. It is for a newly recognized "disease" suffered by, according to one authority, 96 percent of the population because of the way they (we) were raised. According to another authority, the 4 percent who weren't raised under those conditions are sick from having to live with the rest of us. This new "disease," from which *everyone* suffers, is codependency. The spiritual program where one must go to recover from this "sometimes fatal malady" is Codependents Anonymous, familiarly know as Coda.

The authorities on codependency do not quite agree on a definition of it, although they do agree that most everyone has it and would benefit from joining Coda. (A non-member, Alan Marlatt of the Addictive Behaviors Research Center at the University of Washington, defines codependency quite accurately as "what used to be called caring for others."[13]) The "Codependency Movement" holds that codependents, in not understanding their powerlessness, make their lives unmanageable by always trying to please and help others. This is the root of the most widely accepted definition—relationship addiction. The symptoms include, but are not limited to, feeling sad, angry, disappointed, rejected, lonely, or abandoned at the end of a relationship, or not wanting a relationship to end.

There are many symptoms directly related to romantic involvement, but "the disease" takes other forms, the most cunning and baffling perhaps being *not* being involved romantically. Other symptoms of the disease are working as a nurse, doctor, therapist, or in any of the helping professions. People pick these professions because of their disease. While perhaps not everyone in these professions is sick, most show obvious symptoms. They become upset when a patient dies, commits suicide, or does poorly in any other way. Codependents get upset when they can't "control" other people by helping them.

The solution to codependency, of course, is the Twelve Steps. In Step One, "so-called normal people" are to admit that they are "powerless over others," that they can't really help anyone, and that they must give up their "rescuer" role. However, in Step Twelve, they are to go out and dedicate themselves to rescuing everyone they can by getting them to join Coda.

Codependents Anonymous is split between two seemingly opposing membership factions. One is "traditional AA." The other, which may be termed "psychological AA," is made up of people who have many of the characteristics of "traditional AA," but includes therapists in its members. The second faction blends modern psychology with the "old time religion" of AA. Which faction predominates is quickly obvious at any meeting. At "traditional" meetings, the sharing is characterized by "I'm so sick that . . ." In the generally upper-middle-class, "psychological" meetings, the sharing is characterized by pop psychology terms like "my inner child" and "dysfunctional family."

The suggested reading lists highlight the split. *Twelve Steps and Twelve Traditions* appears on the same list as pop psychology bestsellers on codependency. As yet, Coda has no Big Book.

Coda's indoctrination techniques are more varied and, in many ways, more clever than AA's. The "traditional" faction is more likely to use fear: "The disease kills." The "psychology" faction adds newer, more sophisticated methods. Many of Coda's founders are trained psychologists who, having "recovered" in AA, thought that there must be another disease because they had gained no Serenity. Once they found codependency, they set to work with skills adopted from modern psychology to carry the message.

The most potent techniques fall under the blanket phrase, "work with the inner child." Some of these techniques were used on the television talk show, *Sally Jessy Raphael*. Guest John Bradshaw, 25 years "in recovery" from alcoholism and codependency, and a guru of the codependency movement, did some "demonstrations" for the television audience. The most powerful was a hypnosis session in which the home audience was invited to participate.

Bradshaw instructed the audience members to close their eyes and go back to the earliest house they had lived in as children. "Notice the detail of it . . ." He suggested that they see their mothers and fathers and then "find the little child you once were." The suggestions were designed to bring into focus any childhood conflicts the audience members may have had with their parents:

> Tell him [the child you once were] "I know what you've been through." Look at your Mom and Dad and tell them you have to leave now because you have to have a life of your own. I am no longer going to carry your pain for you. I am no longer going to be an extension of your ambition. I have a right to my own life.

The messages given here are obvious: you (as a child) had unpleasant experiences, and it was Mom and Dad's fault. They wouldn't let you have a life of your own, they expected you to carry their pain, and they made you an extension of their ambition. Under hypnosis, a person will do his best to make the suggestions real. Appropriate unpleasant childhood memories are tied to the suggestions.

The next step in Bradshaw's hypnotic session was the separation of a person from "Mom and Dad." The audience was given the suggestion to "start walking away, you and that child." As the audience "leaves Mom and Dad," their replacement becomes apparent. "You and this child can . . . have your own life. If you don't have a support group in your life, tell your child, "I'll get you one, a new family of affiliation." Needless to say, it would be difficult for someone to find a support group or "new family of affiliation" for their "inner child" that wasn't Codependents Anonymous.

The session ended with a typical hypnotic suggestion to "go to the most special place you know," in order to leave the hypnotic subjects, no matter what emotional turmoil they may have been through, "feeling good" and wanting to repeat the experience.

With the birth of codependency, everyone is sick, insane, and in need of "a spiritual program." It is the disease of "so-called normal people." *Everyone needs to be saved.*

After 60 years, the "recovery" movement has come full circle. When AA separated from the Oxford Group, one of the defining differences between them was AA's belief that alcoholics should rescue only those committing the same sin, that is, other alcoholics. Everyone else was more or less irrelevant to AA. Today's "recovery" movement, however, has returned to the Oxford Group belief that *everyone* not belonging to a 12-step group is a sick, wretched sinner and in need of "a spiritual program."

With the combined membership of all Twelve Step groups, there are now perhaps up to 15 million believers dedicated to "carrying the message" in America. (Membership estimates vary radically.) While the social phenomenon of the Twelve Step cults might seem unique, not too long ago a similar group with nearly identical techniques shocked the Western world.

Upon the release of Western civilians held in Red Chinese prisons in the mid-1950s, it was found that some of them kept "repeating their false confessions, insisting upon their guilt, praising the 'justice' and 'leniency' which they have received, and expounding the 'truth' and 'righteousness' of all Communist doctrine."[14]

Most shocking to the American public was that many of these had been Christian missionaries. The press made much of "brainwashing" and torture, but careful investigation found that those who were tortured, or even saw others severely mistreated at the hands of the Communists, didn't convert. The common thread among those who did convert was that they all believed in the sincerity of the

Communist authorities and their cellmates. They believed that these individuals were sincerely trying to *help*.

The Chinese Communists, unlike their Russian mentors, had a program of "re-education" for "reactionaries." Most of this re-education was voluntary, but the more severe reactionaries needed "intervention." Among these were Westerners, mostly missionaries, who had stayed in China after the revolution.

The re-education of these "reactionaries" parallels that of the American alcoholic coerced into "treatment."* The experience of "thought reform" in the Chinese population directly parallels that of the American alcoholic who voluntarily enters treatment. The "treatment modality" is the same. In both situations, people are removed from any positive support for their identity and are "educated" by a unanimous majority about the nature of their "disease." The new prisoner or patient is to confess and accept his identity as a diseased person in need of a "cure."

He is no longer a doctor, businessman, or priest. He is a "reactionary" or "alcoholic." A prisoner's or patient's peers, having admitted their own disease, are absolutely sincere and know the importance of helping. Having been helped themselves, they know how to proceed. "Errors in thinking and judgement" and "alcoholic thinking" are pointed out. As the indoctrinee begins to see the world and himself from the viewpoint of his peers, he begins to see his own guilt and identifies himself as a guilty person.

The guilt one comes to feel is not so much over being a "reactionary" or "alcoholic" in the usual senses of the words; it is, rather, over one's previous existence as a nonbeliever as defined by the doctrine. For instance, the "reactionary" or "alcoholic" who had worked hard in order to retire sees himself as *guilty of selfishness and self-centeredness*. He hadn't worked for the cause. He had only been concerned with himself. The "spy" or "alcoholic" who had done what he once considered unselfish things, learns that he was in the service of evil. The missionary who had helped to feed and clothe the poor is now guilty of "deceiving the people" by making "reactionary

---

* It isn't much different from proto-AA (while still part of the Oxford Group) and its "hospital work" either. One poor soul, a prisoner who was a Protestant minister and had been a grouper, was reindoctrinated by the Communists. He reports that he "was struck by its similarity with the Moral Rearmament [Oxford Group] movement."

forces" look good. In the same way, the grouper who bought a hungry man lunch is guilty of "enabling."

Perhaps the most motivating form of guilt in terms of identity change is guilt arising from disappointing "those who are only trying to help." Emotional attachments can be quite intense in both thought reform and alcohol treatment center environments. Special meetings foster these attachments. In China, they are called "struggle meetings." In the U.S., they are called the "hot seat." In this "therapeutic technique," a recalcitrant "sick" person is chosen for special attention. His peers, in order to help him, tell him, in the strongest terms, how unlikable, sinful, and useless he is. While this "therapy" sometimes results in psychotic reactions, the intent is to cure, not destroy. The effect is to shake a person's sense of identity enough to create a desperate need for positive confirmation. To get this from his peers, he must adopt the "repentant sinner" role. He will also develop closer emotional ties with those who were harshly critical but are now willing to help by being understanding. At the very least, he will be more willing to accept help from those "more advanced" in order to avoid another struggle session.

"Re-education" also includes a written confession identical to AA's Step Four. In writing his confession, the "reactionary"" redefines his past and himself in terms of the infallible doctrine. Both "treatments" have meetings in which sacred literature is studied. For the Chinese, it might be readings from "the Little Red Book." For the AA indoctrinee, it is readings from either the Big (blue) Book or the 12 & 12. In these study meetings, participants tell how elements of the doctrine are true and how they apply to themselves. If a participant doesn't think that a point applies to himself, or perhaps isn't true at all, the unanimous majority helps by pointing out his "reactionary" or "alcoholic" thinking. Other Chinese Communist meetings are for self-criticism and for expounding on the Communists' devils, capitalism, and reactionary forces, as the sources of all evil. AA meetings combine the two approaches. One may hear someone confess to a character defect and, in the same sentence, attribute the shortcoming to alcoholism.

In both Chinese re-education and the Twelve Step treatment center, the world is painted as a battleground between two forces, one pure good and one pure evil. The ultimate good for the Chinese Communists is the Party, the doctrine as interpreted by the Party, and everything else associated with the Party. In AA, the ultimate good is AA, the doctrine as interpreted by AA's elders, and everything else associated with AA. Where one's experiences, thoughts, desires, or behavior are not aligned with the "ultimate good," they are in the service of evil.

After both re-education and treatment, the prisoner and patient are thankful for the intervention of "history" or a "higher power" (that is, AA/God). They feel gratitude toward the bearers of the great wisdom which transcends ordinary human concerns. For the "new man" and the "recovering alcoholic" the goal is the same: to spread the sacred doctrine. The Red Chinese had the benefit of political power to "help" hundreds of millions of Chinese to "understand history" in a very short time. The work of "helping" sick Americans is going much more slowly, but there are ominous signs on the horizon. In the chilling words of an interview in *Sober Times*, a newspaper for people "in recovery":

> People who are chemically dependent and codependent have a huge obligation to society to band together [politically], because we've been there and we know what the needs are in the community . . . Recovering people must flex their united muscle . . . We have to teach kids . . . intervene.[15]

---

1. AA (1938):89
2. AA (1982)
3. AA (1984):283-285
4. AA (1952):129
5. Nace (1987):148
6. Nace (1987):60
7. Nace (1987):124
8. Nace (1987):xix
9. Nace (1987):xiv
10. Nace (1987):xiv
11. Ditman et al (1967) and Brandsma et al (1980)
12. AA (1976):245
13. Cited in "Are we a nation of 'addicts'?" *Long Beach Press- Telegram*, Nov. 18, 1990
14. Lifton (1956)
15. *Sober Times*, September 1990, p. 29

14: The Plight of the Grouper

When AA members return to drinking, as they frequently do, it is usually to much worse drinking than before their initial AA contact. Since the program is held as perfect, the drinker and other groupers attribute this to the nature of "the disease."

Often a person quits attending meetings because he is angry over being pressured to accept a particular point, or presumed point, of doctrine. For instance, a Jewish person may be told that his prayers are no good because he doesn't pray on his knees. "God won't listen unless you show humility."*

While the admonition in and of itself may have little effect, if a member's "willfulness" becomes an object of group "help," great pressure will be brought to bear. Speakers and sharers may tell how their own refusal to pray on their knees caused them great harm. Or a speaker may tell how his "terminal uniqueness," thinking that he was different from other alcoholics, caused him to think that he didn't need to pray on his knees. Proper praying position may become a frequent topic of "casual" conversation at after-meeting coffees.

Pressure also takes other forms. For example, if a Jewish man should seek direction on a particular problem, he may be asked if he has prayed about it and then be asked if he prayed on his knees. If the answer is "no," he may be met with silence and body language that suggest, "Well, that explains it."

The subject may be kept at the forefront of discussion for days or weeks until someone else's crisis becomes the focus of "help," the errant grouper sees the error of his ways, or he becomes angry and

---

* Kitty Dukakis, who is Jewish, discussed this issue in her book. In her last treatment center she learned that *as an alcoholic* she must pray on her knees. This is an excellent example of the AA-alcoholic identity superseding the religious one.

decides that he doesn't need AA.

If he should angrily decide that he doesn't need the program, it may be only the beginning of a process in which the errant grouper learns the depth of the wisdom of AA. The grouper has already adopted large chunks of AA doctrine, and rejecting just one small part leaves him extremely vulnerable.

In AA, one learns that anger, sadness, loneliness, and other emotions are the work of Devil Drink and must be repressed. Most of the methods of repression an AA member has learned can't be used outside of AA. For instance, if one is "in danger" of becoming angry, the "resolution" may include going to meetings, public confession, working the steps, reading the Big Book, getting counsel from one's sponsor, or convincing others of the miracle of recovery in AA. The person who leaves AA can't continue to repress emotion in the same ways. He also fears he will, and is unanimously expected to, return to drinking. Upon leaving, the errant grouper is likely to notice the "symptoms" of his "disease" get worse—he experiences strong feelings of "self-pity," "resentment," and fear. There are many reasons for this, but none have anything to do with any disease.

During the indoctrination process, barriers went up between the new grouper and his pre-AA friends. His social group now includes predominantly or only AA members. Upon leaving AA he is *at best* left friendless and "suffering self-pity" (that is, being extremely lonely).

In all likelihood, however, his grouper friends will, out of genuine concern and fear for him, respond to his plight in a way that sabotages his ability to remain abstinent.

The most dangerous way this is done is with sincere body language which transmits the expectation of failure combined with verbal expressions of cautious optimism. For instance, if the errant member should state that he can remain "sober" without meetings, bodies will stiffen and apprehensive eyes will express genuine fear and the expectation of failure. The accompanying verbal response may be, "As long as you have a spiritual program." Of course the errant grouper knows that AA is the only spiritual program for alcoholics. His self-doubt and fear increase.

Grouper friends may also confess to how they had left the program and had had the same thoughts as the errant grouper. They will tell of the grief and danger it caused until they returned to the program. If a grouper has no such personal experience to confess, he may, out of loving kindness, tell how someone else, preferably someone who died, did exactly what the errant grouper is now doing.

The errant grouper's "disease symptoms" grow worse.

He is locked into an identity as an alcoholic. His "disease" has long since been proven to him, and he will find it extremely difficult to imagine that he could be anything but a "drinking alcoholic" or "in recovery." Unable to even imagine that there are other possibilities, or even that he may not be an alcoholic, he is trapped.

AA worked to shatter his ego, allowing ego support only through belief in AA doctrine. When he leaves AA, he can no longer speak as someone who has special knowledge of God's will. He is no longer part of the great moral crusade. He no longer has special wisdom to share. He is unable to tell others how he has found a solution to their problems.

When he leaves AA, the ex-grouper is left with his frightened, disoriented, discounted, sad, betrayed, disease-defined self and an extremely shaky ego at war with his "disease." His only remaining ego support is his abstinence.

The presence of strong emotion and the unanimous responses of his grouper friends are not the only evidence to the errant AA member that he will return to self-destructive drinking. Other evidence comes from society at large, where people, influenced by 60 years of propaganda, encourage him to return to AA, thinking that his distress (and, in a sense, accurately so) is because he stopped attending meetings. He shouldn't be angry with AA; his fellow groupers are only trying to help.

With even non-grouper friends, acquaintances, and authorities suggesting, "You should go back to the meetings," the errant grouper is caught in a bind. He can either return to meetings and humbly acknowledge his "willfulness," or he can decide that "the whole world is wrong and I am right." But he will probably recognize this thought as a disease symptom.

At this point of extreme pressure, the errant grouper often begins drinking or commits suicide. Knowing that he is "powerless over alcohol," he may decide to delay his "inevitable" return to AA in the only way he knows of: drinking will remove the intolerable "symptoms," at least for a while.

Once he takes the first sip, all his Time, his sole remaining ego support, is gone. He can no longer say, "Well, at least I'm sober." He is now living proof of AA doctrine.

At this point, the errant grouper may have so little sense of self left that he returns in terror to AA with proper penitence, or proceeds to turn his anger inward by drinking himself to death. If his efforts to maintain "spiritual principles" and stay "sane," as defined by AA, are particularly successful, he may manage to be "not angry." This often ends in schizoid breaks and suicide. Whatever the outcome, his reactions prove to his grouper acquaintances the power of the cunning, baffling, and powerful "disease" and the wisdom of AA.

However, the errant AA member may find that he doesn't want to, or even like to, drink. This is not surprising since most people first go to AA because they don't want to drink anymore and only attended AA because they believed that they needed to in order to stop. The former member may decide, "I am not an alcoholic."

Under such circumstances, though, his AA belief system remains intact except for the one point of doctrine which he is angry about. With a basic belief that he is helpless, inadequate, and in danger of being overwhelmed by evil forces, he is extremely vulnerable to, and may even seek, another cult or cult-like group. Any similar group which understands his basic "badness" or "sickness" may be acceptable. The easiest and most frequent transition is to other Twelve Step groups. Codependents Anonymous is perhaps the most often chosen.

An AA member may question and become angry at some of his peers or elders over the interpretation of a particular point of doctrine. It would be extremely unusual for him, however, to question the "spiritual principles" themselves. By joining a similar group, he is merely exchanging social groups. He is choosing one which won't pressure him, at least for the moment, on the particular point on which he takes a stand.

The grouper most often returns to excessive drinking without being overtly angry with AA. His most outstanding characteristic is the intensely held belief in the goodness of AA and the badness of himself. Having unquestioned belief in the doctrine, and knowing that he is "powerless," he can't conceive of, and doesn't even attempt to, moderate or stop until he is ready to return to meetings.

While perhaps paying lip service to some external event, the grouper centers on his evil self as responsible for his drinking. The errant grouper need only pick and choose which "manifestations of self" are most responsible.

Many such people are actually extremely angry at AA elders, peers, or doctrine. However, they "know" that their anger is wrong. The Big Book stresses that "resentment is the number one offender," the number one symptom. Perhaps most convincing is the obvious sincerity and unanimity of the other groupers. A grouper has difficulty grasping the possibility that people who act out of sincere loving concern can be wrong. The fault must be within himself. And he represses his feelings of anger.

Verbal assault on the doctrine is met with extreme anger, and the errant grouper will be verbally assaulted. The errant grouper may ultimately accept the doctrine as true, and may even end up being grateful to those who verbally assaulted him. Telling someone "the truth" is a sign of the great love in AA. Telling someone "maybe you have good reason to be angry" is an obvious sign of spiritual ignorance. It is dismissed out of hand.

The errant grouper may drink himself to death, but since excessive drinking is its own punishment, he will probably reach a point where he wants to stop. Being thoroughly indoctrinated, he "knows" that he must return to AA.

Upon his return, if the other groupers know he has been drinking, he must show proper humility and penitence. He may, however, if no one knows that he has been drinking, decline to confess until he has reacquired 30 days of Time with which, in most meetings, he can confess and, at least with the newest of the newcomers, resume his status as an elder authority.

Many people go back and forth between abstinent meeting attendance and being "out there." When a grouper is not attending meetings, he is drinking. When a grouper is attending meetings, he is not drinking. This is proof to all concerned that the program "really works." The more often a grouper relapses, the more skillfully he adopts the repentant sinner role and the more "personal experience" he has to share about his own "sickness," the wiles of "the disease," and the wisdom of AA.

During indoctrination, words and slogans acquire highly charged emotional associations. This is partly due to the unanimous emotional responses and body language of the other groupers to the loaded language. Another, more important way that strong emotional associations with words and slogans are instilled occurs during the Fourth and Fifth Step redefinition of the self. Everything which has meaning—all experience, thought and emotion—is redefined in terms of the loaded AA language. AA language elicits emotion; emotion elicits AA language.

Information contradictory to the doctrine no longer registers properly. For example, if a family member points out to a grouper, *who never had a real drinking problem*, that he never was really an alcoholic, the grouper cannot seriously consider the possibility. The family member is a "normie" and "doesn't understand," or, if he is a drinker or an alcoholic, abstinent or not, it is his "disease speaking."

If the grouper should think that he may not be an alcoholic his thought is, *by definition*, a disease symptom. His thought is a dangerous one that evokes fear. Feeling fear, another trick of Devil Drink, means that he is veering too far from the "spiritual." To be safe he must not think the thought. It can only lead back to the bottle.

AA's loaded language includes many words with twisted and blurred meanings—entirely different from normal usage—that carry strong emotional associations. The word "sober," for example, is commonly associated with moderation, and when used in reference to alcohol can also mean "not drunk." To the grouper, however, "sober" means absolutely abstinent and in AA, because AAs believe that those who "don't have a spiritual program" are on a "dry drunk" and do not have "emotional sobriety."

When an AA member asks another person if he is "sober," he is not asking if he is feeling the effects of intoxication. He is asking if he is maintaining absolute abstinence and, perhaps, if he is free of strong emotion as well.

A person who leaves AA, even if he remains abstinent, cannot claim "true sobriety." In time, he may recover from the crisis of leaving and be happier, calmer, better adjusted, and abstinent, but he cannot measure up to the doctrinal standards of "sobriety."

Just hearing the loaded language can cause an errant grouper to either drink to excess or return to AA. What sometimes happens can perhaps best be described as "switching" or "flipping over" into the cult personality.* It is like becoming trapped in a maze. In this maze, there are many ways in (words, thoughts, and feelings) but few ways out. Once within this "other personality," thought- and emotion-stopping techniques "automatically" kick in.

But the situation is far from hopeless.

There are many things that one can do to ensure success in leaving AA. Perhaps the easiest and most immediately important is to break the closed loops making up the language by practicing new associations. In other words, rather than allowing a word or slogan to continue evoking AA associations, one can evoke other, more customary associations until they become automatic and the language loses its power.

For example, the phrase "in recovery," in common usage, implies "getting well." However, AA usage implies a lifetime commitment to AA. *"In recovery," as AA uses it, means staying sick forever.* "In recovery" means "in a cult." The word "program" refers to something suitable for a machine, perhaps a computer or a robot, not a human being. One can allow other loaded words to evoke new responses. When a grouper asks, "Are you sober?," one can respond, "Are you speaking English and asking me if I'm not intoxicated or are you speaking Programese and asking me if I'm practicing abstinence?" If you hear a reference to "emotional sobriety," you can think of the more unbalanced members of AA, particularly ones with a great deal of Time, including Bill Wilson, with his 11 years of severe depression while in AA. You can then note that AA uses "sobriety" in a sense peculiar to itself as a cult term. You can replace the term "resentment," which in common usage is not a fatal feeling, with more common and appropriate words like irritation, anger, and rage.

The word "love" carries strong emotional associations. The word is extremely difficult for ex-groupers to redefine, since there is no clear English definition which covers the feelings of warmth, affection, and desire, acts done out of love, and the results of those acts. In AA, "love" is often the motivation for acts destructive to oneself and others. "I love myself enough to force myself to go to meetings." "We love you enough to tell you the truth. You're the cream of the crap, that's what you are." A direct parallel comes to

---

* Steve Hassan discusses this in detail in relation to the Moonies and their language in his book, *Combatting Cult Mind Control.*

mind—the Medieval man who took his sick wife to a physician to be bled. Did he love his wife? Of course, but that doesn't mean he wasn't killing her. The uses and meanings of the word "love" can become more sharply focused and removed from the cult context by substituting the less ambitious word "respect." Am I *respecting* myself? Are they *respecting* me? Am I *respecting* them?

Perhaps the word which is most difficult to redefine, and which has the widest range of definitions and associations, is "spiritual." One definition which most helped me was "that which gives feelings of worth, belonging, and connectedness." While I have found no organization which is perfect on all three counts, by this definition, AA is grossly unspiritual on all counts. AA teaches that the self is worthless, and AA confers "belonging" (as a "diseased" person) only at the cost of connectedness with most of the human race (we "alcoholics" and you "normies"). Even though they tout their own humility, isn't it *arrogant* for Twelve-Step members to assume that they and they alone are sane and purely spiritual and that everyone else is insane and needs their "spiritual" help?

The clichés also need new associations. Since most are exclusive to AA and would never be used in ordinary conversation, all that is necessary to deal with most of them is to come up with a few associations that show their logical flaws. Making fun of them is particularly appropriate because ridicule is the opposite of the reverence in which they are held, and it saps their power. For example, to combat the cliche "Alcoholics rarely recover on their own," one might try thinking, "Alcoholics rarely recover on their own, unless, of course, they are shipwrecked alone on a desert island." Or, "Alcoholics rarely recover on their own; alcoholics *never* recover in AA." (According to AA doctrine one is always "re-covering," never recovered.) And to deflate "No one ever drank while working the steps," try "No one ever drank while working the steps, but they usually drink a lot more afterwards."

This is not to suggest that one should ridicule the groupers. The point is, *especially* in one's own mind, *to neutralize the power of AA's language.* It is also important to protect oneself from interacting with groupers in a way that creates confusion and leaves one open to suggestion.

Language and identity mix in the words "I am an alcoholic." In all Twelve-Step groups, members adopt a "disease" as the core of their identity. This identity can be exchanged for broader, more accurate, self-definitions. First and foremost, most general and inarguable, one can say, "I am a human being." While this may seem obvious, for the grouper it is a radical concept. Beyond that, one may *partially* identify oneself in an almost infinite number of ways, including profession, relationships with other people, political, social, religious affiliations, and by interests and hobbies. People are not their "diseases."

15: Moderation and Abstention

There is some evidence that abstinence is an easier goal for most older, married persons, and that moderation is easier for most younger, single people. But, what *may* be easier is just one factor, and not in itself grounds for a decision. There is no authority, other than a physician pointing to specific disease conditions such as diabetes and liver problems, who can tell someone whether they must abstain rather than moderate. Someone who belongs to a church that uses wine in communion services won't want to be, and doesn't need to be, *absolutely* abstinent. Other than the exigencies of health and religion, the most critical factors in choosing a goal are what a person *believes* that he can do and what he *wants* to do.*

The only serious problem with abstinence as a goal is its difficulty for most people. An advantage of the goal of moderation is that the option is always open to abstain if one later decides that that would be *easier*, which for some people it is.

Perhaps the best way to begin moderation is by abstaining for two weeks or so.** The benefits of a short-term period of abstinence are twofold. First, tolerance decreases and a relatively small amount of alcohol will give an appreciably greater effect. Second, by paying careful attention to oneself, to the feelings and thoughts that arise while abstaining, the role of the excessive drinking comes more clearly into focus.

For example, a person who feels extremely lonely when he abstains will be able to focus his attention on finding better ways of

---

* Beginning moderate drinking after long-term abstinence has many pitfalls and is not recommended. Why tamper with success?

** Moderation Management, a support group for those who wish to moderate rather than abstain recommends 30 days.

interacting with others. If he feels helpless or powerless, he can look for ways to regain the perception of control in his life.

It is important that a person who has been drinking to great excess see a physician. Medical advice can be helpful and perhaps even life saving, but any suggestion by one's doctor that "people rarely recover on their own," that one should go to AA, or than one should meet someone "in recovery" should be ignored. It is also important to take note of the doctor's body language and, if it seems to discourage one's decision to quit or moderate without "help," to consciously discount the source.[*]

Although one may experiencestrong emotion, abstaining or moderating is not necessarily difficult. While it may seem over-whelming to decide to "never drink again," it is relatively easy to ignore "never" and merely postpone or delay a decision to drink—to just do something else. For example, someone in the habit of drinking after work, instead of worrying about the difficulty of abstaining forever, will find it far easier to just go to a movie, watch TV, meet friends for dinner, go on a date, or read a book.

Central to maintaining moderation or abstinence is having or developing motivation and a "can do" belief system. Motivation can perhaps be best thought of in terms of what you would *rather* do. Humans rarely have clear-cut motivations and goals. For example, someone who is planning a vacation may want to go to two mutually exclusive places. Perhaps he wants to go to Europe and to South America, but only has two weeks off work and a limited budget. He *wants* to go to both, but what he actually does is based on "what he would rather do."

The same is true when choosing whether or how much to drink on any given occasion. Mixed emotions often play a part. *Wanting a drink is not a sign of looming failure.* Comfortable success in abstention or moderation doesn't necessarily depend on feeling horror or revulsion at the thought of drinking, but on the development of

---

[*] Many physicians just don't know. Traditionally, they have had little education about problem drinking since it wasn't considered a disease until fairly recently. Now that it has been voted a disease, their "education" about drinking problems originates with members of the medical profession who are also AA members. If you have, or wish to have, a long-standing relationship with your doctor, you may want to loan him this book. It is helpful to have a supportive physician rather than one who is trying to be supportive by suggesting what can only lead to failure.

"would rathers." For example, someone who has decided to abstain may have an urge to go out on Saturday night for a few drinks at his old hangout. This is no big deal and need not lead to "relapse" or failure. All he needs to do is to find one thing that he would *rather* do. Then he not only doesn't drink, he doesn't feel cheated.

It is important for the abstainer, when "craving" (wanting) a drink, to have alternative ways to *better* meet the needs behind the "craving." Someone who has been abstinent for several months may find himself looking forward to the day he can "control" his drinking. Of course, people can and do control their drinking when they want to, but they are less likely to want to as long as they remain blind to the reasons why they drink. The most important point is to not waste time pining for what is not available, but to recognize and take full advantage of present opportunities. By finding better ways to accomplish what one did in the past through drinking, the desire to drink progressively diminishes.

Taking accurate notice of the costs and benefits of excessive drinking also helps develop motivation. For example, a man who is angry with his wife may gain a sense of control by storming out and getting drunk. He feels "in control." She isn't. But while a sense of control of one's life is essential to well-being, by recognizing and carefully weighing all alternatives, better choices can be found which give the perception of control without doing harm, and perhaps are even constructive. He may decide that he would rather honestly discuss the underlying problem with his wife, work out a compromise, go for relationship counseling, or get a divorce. By being aware of, and carefully considering, all possible alternatives, one can find something one would *rather* do than drink.

The person who drinks as a substitute for real intimacy can work on intimacy problems and, though he may *want* to drink, he may find that he'd not only *rather* share real intimacy, but that he is more than capable of doing so.

Developing motivation and a sense of competence and capability are mutually supportive. The more one wants to quit or moderate, the easier it is to do. Realizing that one would rather not drink powerfully counteracts lessons of learned helplessness concerning drinking. The more obtainable the goal of stopping or moderating seems, and the less grief expected in reaching the goal, the more desirable a course of action it becomes.

Thinking in terms of how one will *succeed* instead of how one will *fail* is essential to developing a sense of competency. "Slips" or "relapses," should they occur, can be thought of as failures, *but they can't occur without success*. They can also be great learning opportunities. One can ask oneself, "Why did I?," "What did I expect to be the advantage?," "Was there a 'pay-off'?," "What are the disadvantages?," and, most importantly, "What better choices are there and how will I make them the next time?"

Drinking more or behaving worse when drinking upon deciding to quit or moderate can be good signs. *The higher the price paid for drinking to excess, the more difficult it is to continue.*

It might seem odd to suggest that someone with a drinking problem should work to enhance the drinking experience. However, excessive drinking is heavily based on false expectations. The more clearly a problem drinker discriminates between those occasions when drinking is pleasurable and productive and when it is unpleasant and destructive, the more difficult it is to continue excessive drinking.

Two entirely different drinking styles point out the benefits of drinking for maximum pleasurable effect. Imagine a man in a bar who, on an empty stomach, slowly sips two drinks and feels pleasantly "high" for a couple of hours. During that time, he may enjoy conversation and music. If he is having a good time, he may stay a little longer. If he is not enjoying himself, he'll leave. After drinking, he eats and quickly becomes unintoxicated. The next morning he wakes up sharp and alert, ready to take advantage of the day.

In contrast with this social drinker, imagine a man who customarily drinks large quantities of alcohol. Due to his steady high consumption, he needs to drink a lot to feel a little effect. When he drinks on a full stomach, he needs to drink even more. In the morning he is groggy and hung-over, so he guzzles huge amounts of coffee. This creates a need to drink even more when he does drink to feel an effect. While he may have some pleasant experiences while drinking, he stays "high" long after the pleasure is gone and will continue drinking whether or not he is enjoying the experience. This also disrupts his ability to sleep well. He suffers hangovers and the long-term health consequences of excessive drinking.

It is important for the moderater to carefully discriminate between a desire to drink for a pleasant experience and drinking to avoid undesired feelings and to ignore problems. Before drinking, one can ask, "Do I feel good?" and "Do I have unpleasant feelings I want to drown out?" If the answer to the latter is "yes," drinking is never in one's best interest. And if the goal is abstention, the question to ask when feeling good is "Do I want to risk changing it?"

While drinking, it is important for the moderater to notice whether he is enjoying himself and whether the environment is pleasantly stimulating. When it is not, it helps to develop the habit of stopping drinking and doing something else. For some people, since so much of drinking behavior is merely the habit of sipping or gulping, it is helpful to have a glass of water or soft drink to sip on. It also helps to do "intoxication checks," to frequently take careful notice of the physical and mental effects of drinking. It is rather pointless to drink for the "high" and to not pay attention to one's body. The more attuned one is to the effects, the less one needs to drink to feel them.

Paying close attention to emotional states and their effect on drinking helps. If an angry or sad thought comes to mind, what is its effect on your drinking behavior? Do you reach for the glass? Do you take bigger gulps? Just noticing the behavior and the futility of it can help maintain moderation.

Taking notice of the environment is closely related. Drinking in an unpleasant environment is likely to be an unpleasant experience, while drinking in a pleasant environment is likely to be pleasurable. Much of the enjoyment in drinking comes not from the alcohol itself, but from the environment and one's own mood and expectations.

Of course, if someone clearly would rather get very drunk or clearly would rather drink moderately, not much will make a difference.* However, people are usually somewhere between the two extremes and any little substitute habit, awareness, or effort can have dramatic effects.

When drinking more and enjoying it less, it is important to ask oneself what one would *really* rather do, what would be more fulfilling? There is no real benefit to alcohol except as a mild social lubricant. It fills no real needs.

In studying drinkers whose goal was abstention, researchers found that those who succeeded felt confident and capable and had

---

* For someone to recognize that he would rather drink excessively, even if he then does so, can be a good start in getting a handle on the problem.

"multiple ways of dealing with stress." Those who "relapsed" drank over frustration, anger, social pressure, and interpersonal conflict.[1] In other words, those who returned to self-destructive drinking did so in response to more or less everyday stress. Those who succeeded had multiple ways of responding in stressful situations.

The stresses leading to excessive drinking are chronic, although perhaps intermittent. To a large degree, the responses to those stresses are subconscious and automatic. The dynamics of a particular situation may be entirely out of the conscious awareness of the problem drinker. He may be mystified by his own drinking.

There is no single way to deal with stress, nor is stress itself the problem. For example, imagine a man in a forest being chased by a pack of wolves. That certainly is a stressful situation. What does he do to deal with the stress? Does he meditate, exercise, or practice relaxation techniques? Or does he deal with the *problem* at hand and climb a tree?

Parallel situations exist in everyday life. A man who has an unsuitable job becomes "stressed out." There are many things he can do to deal with the stress, to make the undesired feelings go away, including drinking or meditating. That takes care of the stress. It doesn't, however, solve the problem. He still has unsuitable work. Or he may feel "stressed out" over an intolerable relationship. The stress can be "dealt with"; it can be made to go away. He still, however, has a bad relationship.

The problem drinker who is having continued trouble moderating or abstaining needs a greater awareness of his underlying problems, of his choices for solving them, and of his power to make those choices. The tools for this greater awareness lie within the problem drinker's much-scorned and disparaged self.

---

1. Marlatt and Gordon (1980)

A: Notes on Finding Assistance

For someone who wants outside help, a great deal is available. There are many forms, but since psychologists are the most popular, this appendix centers on suggestions and cautions in finding a psychologist to work with.

If friends or family can't recommend someone, most counties have psychological associations which can refer you to a therapist.

Shopping for a therapist is like shopping for a used car. You might get lucky and like the first car you see, but often you need to look at more than one.

Therapy has limitations, and knowing those limitations can help avoid disappointment. Going to a therapist with the attitude, "I drink too much. It is your job to stop me," is a waste of time and money. A therapist can't do it for you.

Psychiatrists have entirely different training than psychologists. While there are competent and capable psychiatrists, they tend to look at problems in living as the result of "brain disease." It is much safer to go to a trusted psychologist and, if he recommends drug treatment, continue psychological treatment while seeing the psychiatrist for medication.

Asking for treatment for "alcoholism," a drinking problem, or drug use is asking for a twelve-step "therapist." Going to an alcoholism or addiction "expert" is tantamount to going to a grouper. Even if not a grouper, the experts in the field tend to be very strongly influenced by grouper ideology and to be ignorant of recent advances in related fields. For example, one of the leading and most respected authorities in the field is totally ignorant of developmental psychology:

And, of course, there is the old standard Shedler & Block, who were able to identify kids who would have problems with AOD when they were about 7 years old—hard[ly] much development to have been arrested by that point!

Needless to say, he, and others like him, would be useless to those with deep-rooted problems based in early-childhood learning.

A therapist who believes in the twelve steps finds nothing un-ethical in spending months establishing trust in order to convince a client of his powerlessness and his need for "a support group." He is following a higher authority and a higher code of ethics than his profession and its code of ethics. He is following "God," as revealed through twelve-step scripture.

One of the most popular tricks used unwittingly by groupers is giving a test to determine if you are an alcoholic. AA literature suggests telling someone, "Why don't you just try to drink moderately for three months and then you'll know." The key word is "try." A hypnotherapist uses the word "try," as in "the more you try to open your eyes the tighter they will lock shut." The word "try" implies failure. The hypnotherapist uses the word in this context to *suggest failure*. Moreover, the test proves that either on has "the disease" or doesn't. There are no suggestions to deal with underlying problems or even acknowledgement that they exist at all.

There are also written tests that pick up on bad reasons for drinking, frequency of over-consumption, and severity of over-consumption. The purpose of these tests is to identify someone with a "progressive, incurable disease" characterized by "denial."

Any effort on the part of a therapist to prove "alcoholism" is a clear signal to immediately terminate the relationship and find a new therapist.

Words used by the therapist can be keys to his or her twelve step status. Among these are "codependency," "inner child," "sobriety," and "recovery."

A suggestion to attend just one meeting to see if you like it or to see what AA is really like is grounds for immediately terminating the relationship. The most powerful influence in cult indoctrination is making someone a "minority of one." Among those most easily influenced in this situation are those who believe that they won't be influenced.

Use of the words "spiritual" or "spirituality" is also a danger sig-nal. While not all who use the words are groupers, many religious groups, particularly some New Age groups, do not consider themselves religious and hold their religious (spiritual) views as "universal truths" above and beyond religion. If someone is advertising "spiritual" therapy or bringing up "spiritual issues," make sure that their religion is compatible with yours.

Once you find a suitable therapist, one you have confidence in, are able to establish a rapport with, *and who has confidence in your ability to moderate or abstain,* it is time to take gambles with openness. While there are many types of therapy, the key to success is the same as if you're not in therapy. This is *learning to be more honest and open and developing the courage to look within oneself deeply enough to like what you see.*

Appendix B: Sources of Help
(Non-cult Organizations)

Abstinence oriented

Rational Recovery
P.O. Box 800
Lotus, CA 95651
Phone: 916-621-4374 or 916-621-2667.
http://www.rational.org/recovery/

SMART Recovery
24000 Mercantile Road, Suite 11
Beachwood, OH 44122
Phone: 216-292-0220
http://home.sprynet.com/sprynet/mike888/

Secular Organizations for Sobriety
6632 Grosvenor Blvd.
Marina del Rey, CA 90066
Phone: (310) 821-8430

Women for Sobriety
P.O. Box 618
Quakertown, PA 18951
Phone: (215) 535-8026

Moderation oriented

Moderation Management Network, Inc.
P.O. Box 27558
Golden Valley, Minnesota 55427
http://comnet.org/mm/

C: The Substance Abuse Proclivity Profile (SAP)

The SAP is an excellent example of the use of an extremely useful tool, the MMPI, to "prove" AA doctrine and to gain acceptability for AA language. The SAP successfully discriminates between young male substance abusers, putative normals, and non-substance-abusing psychiatric outpatients. It is useful for those between the ages of 13 and 26. Validity falls off rapidly afterward.

The scale is divided into three "factors": "Extroversion," "Rebelliousness" and "Self-Pity." While there is room for criticism of designer MacAndrew's analysis of the first two factors, the third is most interesting.

AA doctrine asserts that the alcoholic is guilty of self-pity. The SAP scale proves it. Substance abusers score high on "Self-Pity." A look at the 10 questions which make up the self-pity factor, however, shows more ideology (or perhaps theology) than "Self-Pity."

My Webster's Dictionary defines self-pity as "pity for oneself." It defines pity as "sympathy with the grief or misery of another." The dictionary definition does not discriminate between what we may find distasteful or pathological from what is expected and considered normal and natural.

What MacAndrew refers to is related to a distasteful or pathological "pity for oneself." This is made clear in his statement, "Since it is Self-Pity that unifies this 'litany of lamentations,' that is how I have labeled this factor."

Three of the self-pity factor questions deal with vague fears.

#543: Several times a week I feel as if something dreadful is about to happen.
#494: I am afraid of finding myself in a closet or small closed place.

#365: I feel uneasy indoors.

Substance abusers are more likely to answer "True" to the three questions. MacAndrew holds this as substance abusers' inclination to "portray themselves as victims."

If young substance abusers have these vague fears in disproportion to other groups, which apparently they do, they have two choices when *asked* if they do. They can either tell the truth and prove "self-pity" by marking these questions "True" or they can prove another doctrinal point about alcoholics. They can lie.

#202: I believe I am a condemned person.
#484: I have one or more faults which are so big that it seems better to accept them and try to control them rather than to try to get rid of them.

MacAndrew holds the tendency to respond "True" to these as again "portray[ing] themselves as victims." It seems much more accurate, given the situation of taking the MMPI, that respondents are merely expressing honest beliefs about themselves based in learned helplessness. There are also other possibilities. The respondents are *in treatment* where they are being pressured to admit that they are "powerless over alcohol." They are constantly being pressured to admit the flaws which prove their disease. They are also learning that they can't change their faults and must wait until Step Seven, "Humbly asked God to remove our shortcomings," for the program to change them. Rather than "self-pity," perhaps the answers to these questions reveal treatment "success."

Since those who abuse alcohol and drugs often come from disordered homes and have a high frequency of one or both parents being alcohol or drug abusers, "accurate estimation of circumstances" may well be a better interpretation of the "True" response given by young substance abusers to the following questions.

#157: I feel that I have often been punished without cause.
#338: I have certainly had more than my share of things to worry about.

It would seem that just *being in treatment for substance abuse* is more than most people have to worry about. To state such *when asked* is hardly part of a "litany of lamentations."

Answering "True" to the remaining three questions can also be viewed as evidence of "self-pity." "True" answers to these questions can also, however, be seen as the result of growing up (or partially growing up) in a family in which there was intense competition between siblings for limited parental attention, approval and affection.

#469: I have often found people jealous of my good ideas, just because they had not thought of them first.

#331: If people had not had it in for me I would have been much more successful.

#507: I have frequently worked under people who seem to have things arranged so that they get credit for good work but are able to pass of mistakes onto those under them.

MacAndrew sums up the information provided by the SAP scale:

From a remedial perspective it would seem, . . . that when this sort of mordant self-absorption is detected, 'treatment' might profitably focus upon its radical transformation.

No doubt many young substance abusers would benefit from therapy in which they learned to clearly recognize their fears and put them in a proper perspective. Anything which counteracted their pervasive sense of helplessness, their lack of self-efficacy, would be helpful. They would benefit from support for their *rightness* in a *wrong* environment. They could learn that the jealousy and competition that exist in their home environments are far from universal, and that as they grow up they have increasing power to choose their associates.

MacAndrew's analysis leads to a diagnosis of substance abuse with a definition of the substance abuser as more or less a self-pitying wretch. This logically leads to "treatment" for learned helplessness which begins with confessing "I am powerless" and to "treatment" for vague fears which consists of learning that fear is "an evil and corroding thread." Success at suppressing fear would make the young substance abuser more like his adult addict and alcoholic counterparts. After "treatment," he would be more likely to respond "True" to the MMPI's "Evil spirits possess me at times" than prior to "treatment."

Young male substance abusers do differ from "putative normal" college students. But it is questionable how much they differ from the average young person. The "Self-Pity Factor" shows that they are having difficulties growing up, but longitudinal studies show that they do grow up. That is, of course, unless they get what MacAndrew himself needs to put in quotes, "treatment."

Regardless of how high young substance abusers score on the Self-Pity Factor, "self-pity" is a gross misnomer and is of scant diagnostic value in treatment. The grouping of the above questions under the title "Self-Pity Factor" only serves to lend an air of respectability to AA doctrine and to give respectability to AA's loaded language.

D: Further Reading

Alcoholism and Addiction

Stanton Peele
The Meaning of Addiction: Compulsive Experience and Its Interpretation is the most comprehensive work on addiction available. Social psychologist Peele gives a detailed and thoroughly documented account of the broadest range of addictions.
Lexington, Massachusetts: Lexington Books, 1985.

Herbert Fingarette
In *Heavy Drinking: The Myth of Alcoholism as a Disease,* philosopher and former consultant to the World Health Organization on alcoholism Fingarette is simple, direct, and to the point.
Berkeley: University of California Press, 1988.

Self-"Recovery"

Audrey Kishline
Her book, *Moderate Drinking,* is the handbook for Moderation Management, a group whose goal is moderate drinking rather than abstinence.
New York: Crown Books, 1995.

Stanton Peele and Archie Brodsky
The Truth About Addiction and Recovery is a scientifically grounded do-it-yourself book on how people can overcome a wide range of addictions.
New York: Simon & Schuster, 1991.

Jack Trimpey
Rational Recovery: The New Cure for Substance Addiction explains Rational Recovery's Addictive Voice Recognition Technique for controlling addictive behavior.
New York: Simon & Schuster, 1996.

Cults/Totalitarian Groups/Indoctrination

Charles Bufe
Whereas *The Real AA* approaches its topic largely from a psychological perspective, the very well-researched and complementary *Alcoholics Anonymous: Cult or Cure?* approaches the same topic from a sociological and historical perspective. An enlarged second edition with a great deal of new information is being published simultaneously with this book in January 1998 by See Sharp Press.

Peter T. Furst
Hallucinogens and Culture. Although the discussion centers around the use of hallucinogens in primitive religion, it lends a context for understanding the Oxford Group conversion techniques and the 1950s use of LSD by Bill Wilson and others for "spiritual experiences" for both himself and hospitalized patients.
Novato, California: Chandler & Sharp, 1976.

Steven Hassan
Combatting Cult Mind Control. In writing of groups he describes as "destructive cults," Steve Hassan builds on his experience as a Moonie. The groups he writes about are predominately communal cults. The methods used by these groups are more sophisticated than those of the Chinese Communists and more directly parallel twelve-step "treatment." Also covered in detail is how to assist someone involved in a cult.
Rochester, VT: Park Street Press, 1988.

Robert J Lifton
Thought Reform and the Psychology of Totalism: A Study of "Brainwashing" in China is the classic work on thought reform and totalitarianism. First published in 1961, this book has become more

relevant with time. It has been used by both those founding totalitarian groups and those working to understand them. The techniques used and the environment and internal experiences of those who escaped the Chinese Communists are familiar to all who have a brush with modern American cults.
Chapel Hill: University of North Carolina Press, 1989.

Stanley Milgram
Obedience to Authority: An Experimental View. A classic study of the extent to which most individuals will go in violating their own consciences while obeying authority figures.
New York: Harper & Row, 1969.

Edgar Schein (with Inge Schneier and Curtis H. Barker)
Coercive Persuasion: A Socio-psychological Analysis of the "Brainwashing" of American Civilian Prisoners by the Chinese Communists.
New York: W.W. Norton & Company, 1961.

Margaret Singer
Cults in Our Midst takes up where Robert Jay Lifton leaves off. Written by a psychologist who has made study of cults her life's work, this book provides probably the best definition of cult characteristics available. The similarities between acknowledged cults and the 12-step "treatment" industry are striking.
San Francisco: Jossey-Bass, 1995.

Journals and Journal Articles

Solomon E. Ashe
"Studies of Independence and Conformity: I. A Minority of One Against a Unanimous Majority," *Psychological Monographs: General and Applied*, 70(1956):1-70

The Journal of Rational Recovery
The *JRR*, Rational Recovery's bi-monthly journal covers not only material of interest to those who practice *AVRT*, but also has lengthy articles on the treatment industry, historical perspectives of AA and

Oxford Group, news on current legal battles, and a very interesting letters section.

The Oxford Group

Tom Driberg
In The Mystery of Moral Re-Armament: A Study of Frank Buchman and His Movement, Tom Driberg traces Frank Buchman and his movement from the earliest days to the 1960s. The pro-Nazi sympathies of the movement and its political association with some of this centuries worst despots is discussed.
London: Secker & Warburg, 1964.

Marjorie Harrison
Saints Run Mad is an analysis of the Oxford Group from a Christian perspective. Harrison's observations about the group and the doctrine still read amazingly well more than 60 years later as a criticism of present-day groupers.
London: John Lane the Bodley Head Ltd., 1934.

A. J. Russell
For Sinners Only was the Oxford Group's "Big Book." Extremely tame in comparison to much of its other literature, this book's primary purpose was to attract new members.
London: Hodder and Stoughton, 1937.

H. A. Walter
Soul-Surgery is the instruction manual for practicing the Oxford Group's 5 Cs.
Oxford: The Oxford Group, 1932.

Psychiatry

While the bulk of the books in this section were written by psychiatrists, all of them are particularly outstanding people in the field. The works by Thomas Szasz and *Thou Shalt Not Be Aware* by Alice Miller in "The Self" category offer blistering criticism of vast

segments of the profession. With all due respect to the many remarkable people in the field, I must state that I do not hold a member
of a profession with one of the highest suicide rates as particularly
competent to help others with emotional issues by virtue of that
membership. Traditional psychoanalysis has lost its credibility but,
unfortunately, the ideas that have supplanted it are no better.

Patient to psychiatrist: "I have been really sad this week."
Psychiatrist: "Let's try a change in your medication and see if that
helps."

Thomas S. Szasz
*The Manufacture of Madness: A Comparative Study of the Inquisition
and the Mental Health Movement.* The comparison is chillingly
detailed and documented.
New York: Harper & Row, 1977.

In *The Myth of Mental Illness: Foundations of a Theory of Personal
Conduct,* noted psychiatrist Szasz debunks the dogma of "brain
disease" as an explanation for socially unacceptable behavior.
New York: Harper & Row, 1974.

The Self

The following authors present different perspectives on "the self."
While there is great divergence in their views and the models used,
all are removed from the "because I (you) are bad/sinful/sick" as an
in-depth explanation of personality and behavior. Rather than being
a list of books to help someone find out what is wrong with them,
either directly or indirectly, they can be used to find one's inner
strength and wisdom.

Edgar A. Barnett
*Unlock Your Mind and be Free: A Practical Approach to Hypno-
therapy* presents a positive approach to recognizing and resolving
internal conflicts.
Glendale, California: Westwood Publishing, 1979.

Eric Berne

Games People Play: The Psychology of Human Relationships. Eric Berne is the founder of Transactional Analysis, the most popular school of pop psychology of the 1970s. Berne intended to break down barriers between therapist and client by developing a language of therapy that facilitated communication and replaced the language therapists used to talk about clients among themselves. Many forms of therapy in use today are based upon the TA concept of parent, child, and adult ego states . Codependents Anonymous, blending the language of psychology with twelve step doctrine, acknowledges two of them, parent and child. The "adult" ego state is not acknowledged; the individual must look to the group and elder authority.
New York: Ballantine Books, 1973.

Nathaniel Branden

How to Raise Your Self-Esteem is a "do it yourself" book. Mr. Branden's concept of self-esteem is far removed from today's "self-esteem movement." He does not suggest standing in front of a mirror trying to convince oneself, "I am handsome," "I have a relationship" or "I am tall." His concept of self-esteem has to do with learning the value of what is real within oneself.
New York: Bantam, 1987 .

The Disowned Self is a must.
New York: Bantam, 1973.

Alexander Lowen

The title, *Narcissism: Denial of the True Self,* is misleading. When we think of narcissism, we think of someone who is obsessed with his good looks. Remember, Narcissus was so taken by his *image* in a pool of water that he starved to death looking at it. He obviously wasn't a pretty sight as he approached starvation. The reflected image, not his own substance, was what was important. In Lowen's model of narcissism, "good" images share the stage with "bad" images. Excellent in delineating what is image and what is substance. The development and price paid for the valuation of image over substance is detailed.
New York: MacMillan, 1985.

Also by Alexander Lowen is *The Betrayal of the Body*.
New York: MacMillan, 1967.

Alice Miller
For Your Own Good: Hidden Cruelty in Child-Rearing and the Roots of Violence clearly documents the damage done, not only to individuals, but to society at large by commonly accepted methods of child rearing. Using the three main examples of Adolf Hitler, a child-murderer, and a drug addict, Alice Miller makes the origins of their behavior and what *we* must do to stop making destructive and self-destructive people abundantly clear.
New York: The Noonday Press, 1990.

Alice Miller's *Thou Shalt not be Aware: Society's Betrayal of the Child*, notes many of her discoveries in her years as a psychoanalyst. One of the most important points is that when people come to terms with childhood trauma they get well remarkably fast and don't need decades on the couch. Especially recommended for those who have had limited or no success with therapy. This book is difficult to categorize because not only is it a classic criticism of psychoanalysis but serves equally as well as providing the necessary information and intellectual framework to be able to recognize, and overcome, one's own internal barriers to awareness, independence and competence.
New York: Penguin, 1986

The Untouched Key documents the effects of childhood experience on later life for a number of well-know people including Kafka, Nietzsche, and Buster Keaton.

Ashley Montagu
Touching: The Human Significance of the Skin is a detailed account of human development from the perspective of the importance of the skin and touch. A revolutionary account of what it is to be human.
New York: Harper & Row, 1986

Frederick Perls (Ralph F. Hefferline and Paul Goodman)
Gestalt Therapy: Excitement and Growth in the Human Personality
is in at least its 25th printing. The exercises presented, particularly the
first few, are excellent for increasing one's awareness of emotions and
feelings. This not only directly counteracts cult indoctrination but
also opens the door to understanding many of the earlier influences
which left one vulnerable to addiction and mind-control techniques
in the first place. Highly recommended.
New York: Dell, 1951

Martin E. P. Seligman
Helplessness: On Depression, Development, and Death is a detailed
account of research on learned helplessness.
New York: W. H. Freeman and Company, 1975.

Claude Steiner
Games Alcoholics Play looks at alcoholism from the TA perspective.
New York: Ballantine Books, 1974.

Frank Sulloway
In *Born to Rebel: Birth Order, Family Dynamics and Creative Lives,*
Sulloway describes his findings from 26 years of research on how
childhood environment influences who we grow up to be.
New York: Pantheon, 1996.

Bibliography

AA 1952, *Twelve Steps and Twelve Traditions*.New York Alcoholics Anonymous World Services

AA 1938, *Alcoholics Anonymous*. New York: Works Publishing

AA 1957, *Alcoholics Anonymous Comes of Age*. New York: Alcoholics Anonymous World Services

AA 1976, *Alcoholics Anonymous*. New York: Alcoholics Anonymous World Services

AA 1980, *Dr. Bob and the Good Oldtimers*. New York: Alcoholics Anonymous World Services

AA 1982, *AA as a Resource for the Medical Professional*. New York: Alcoholics Anonymous World Services

AA 1984, *Pass It On*. New York: Alcoholics Anonymous World Services

AA 1987, *AA Membership Survey*. Alcoholics Anonymous World Services

Armor DJ, Polich JM, and Stambul HB, *Alcoholism and Treatment* (The Rand Reports two-year follow-up). New York: Wiley, 1978

Aronson H, and Gilbert A, "Preadolescent Sons of Male Alcoholics." *Archives of General Psychiatry* 8(1963):235-241. Cited from Tartar (1988)

Asch SE, "Studies of Independence and Conformity: I. A Minority of One Against a Unanimous Majority." *Psychological Monographs: General and Applied* 70(1956):1-70

Bennett R, Batenhorst R, Graves D, Foster TS, Baumann T, Griffen WO, and Wright BD, "Morphine Titration in Postoperative Laparotomy Patient Using Patient-Controlled Analgesia." *Current Therapeutic Research* 32(1982):45-52

Bigelow G, Liebson I, "Cost Factors Controlling Alcoholic Drinking," *The Psychological Record*, 22(1972):305-314

Birnie WAH, "Hitler or Any Fascist Leader Controlled by God Could Cure All Ills of World," Buchman Believes. *New York World-Telegram*, Aug26(1936). cited from Thornton-Duesbury(1964):130-133

Brandesma JM, Maultsby MC, and Welsh RJ, *The Outpatient Treatment of Alcoholism: A Review and Comparative Study.* Baltimore: University Park Press, 1980

Briddell DW, Rimm DC, Caddy GR, Krawitz G, Sholis D, and Wunderlin RJ, "Effects of Alcohol and Cognitive Set on Sexual Arousal to Deviant Stimuli." *Journal of Abnormal Psychology* 87(1978):418-430

Buchman F, *Remaking the World.* London: Blandford Press, 1961

Cohen M, Liebson IA, Faillace LA, and Allen RP, "Moderate Drinking by Chronic Alcoholics: A Schedule-Dependent Phenomenon," *The Journal of Neverous and Mental Disease*, 153(1971):434-443

Davies MA, "Normal Drinking in Recovered Alcohol Addicts." *Quarterly Journal of Studies on Alcohol* 23(1962):94-104

Dembo R, Dertke M, Borders S, Washburn M, and Schmeidler J, "The Relationship Between Physical and Sexual Abuse and Tobacco, Alcohol, and Illicit Drug Use Among Youths in a Juvenile Detention Center." *The International Journal of the Addictions* 23(1988):351-378

Dembo R, Williams L, Wish ED, Dertke M, Berry E, Getreu A, WAshburn M, and Schmeidler J, "The Relationship between Physical and Sexual Abuse and Illicit Drug Use: A Replication among a New Sample of Youths Entering a Juvenile Detention Center." *The International Journal of the Addictions* 23(1988):1101-1123

Ditman KS, Crawford GG, Forgy EW, Moskowitz H, and MacAndrew C, "A Controlled Experiment on the Use of Court Probation for Drunk Arrests." *American Journal of Psychiatry* 124(1967):160-163

Donovan DM, and Marlatt GA, "Assessment of Expectancies and Behaviors Associated with Alcohol Consumption: A Cognitive-Behavioral Approach." *Journal of Studies on Alcohol* 41(1980):1153-85

Driberg T, *The Mystery of Moral Re-Armament: A Study of Frank Buchman and His Movement.* London: Secker & Warburg, 1964

Dukakis K, and Scovall J, *Now You Know*. New York: Simon and Schuster, 1990

Edwards G, Orford J, Egert S, Guthrie S, Hawker A, Hensman C, Mitcheson M, Oppenheimer E, and Taylor C, "Alcoholism: A Controlled Trial of 'Treatment' and 'Advice.'" *Journal of Studies on Alcohol* 38(1977):1004-1031

Emmelkamp PMG, "Drug Addiction and Parental Rearing Style: A Controlled Study." *The International Journal of the Addictions* 23(1988):207-216

Falk JL, and Tang M, "Schedule Induction and Overindulgence." *Alcoholism: Clinical and Experimental Research* 4(1980):266-270

Falk JL, "The Environmental Generation of Excessive Behavior." In *Behavior in Excess*, S.J. Mulé, editor, pp.313-337. New York: Free Press, 1981

Fillmore KM, "Relationships between Specific Drinking Problems in Early Adulthood and Middle Age: An Exploratory 20-Year Follow-up Study." *Journal of Studies on Alcohol* 36(1975):882-907

Gray JA, "Anxiety." *Human Nature* July(1978):38-45

Gustafson R, "Self-Reported Expected Emotional Changes as a Function of Alcohol Intoxication by Alcoholic Men and Women." *Psychological Reports* 65(1989):67-74

Hadaway PF, Alexander BK, Coambs RB, and Beyerstein B, The Effect of "Housing and Gender on Preference for Morphine-Sucrose Solutions in Rats-Sucrose Solutions in Rats." *Psychopharmacology* 66(1979)

Harrison M, *Saints Run Mad*. John Lane the Bodley Head Ltd., London:1934

Higgins RL, and Marlatt GA, "Fear of Interpersonal Evaluation as a Determinant of Alcohol Consumption in Male Social Drinkers." *Journal of Abnormal Psychology* 84(1975):644-651

Jellinek EM, "Phases in the Drinking History of Alcoholics: Analysis of a Survey Conducted by the Official Organ of Alcoholics Anonymous." *Quarterly Journal of Studies on Alcohol* 7(1946):1-88

Jones EE, and Berglas S, "Control of Attributions about the Self Through Self-handicapping Strategies: The Appeal of Alcohol and the Role of Underachievement." *Personality and Social Psychology Bulletin* 4(1978):200-206

Jurich AP, Polson CJ, Jurich JA, and Bates RA, "Family Factors in the Lives of Drug Users and Abusers." *Adolescence* 20(1985):143-159

Kjölstad T, "Notes and Comments: Normal Drinking in Recovered Alcohol Addicts." *Quarterly Journal of Studies on Alcohol* 24(1963):730

Kurtz E, *A.A.: The Story*, San Francisco: Harper & Row, 1987

Lang AR, Goeckner DJ, and Adesso VJ, "Effects of Alcohol on Aggression in Male Social Drinkers." *Journal of Abnormal Psychology* 84(1975):508-518

Lang AR, Searles J, Lauerman R, and Adesso V, "Expectancy, Alcohol and Sex Guilt as Determinants of Interest in and Reaction to Sexual Stimuli." *Journal of Abnormal Psychology* cited from Wilson (1981)

Lean G, *Frank Buchman: A Life*. London: Constable, 1985

Levine HG, "The Discovery of Addiction: Changing Conceptions of Habitual Drunkenness in America." *Journal of Studies on Alcohol* 39(1978):143-174

Lifton RJ, "'Thought Reform' of Western Civilians in Chinese Communist Prisons." *Psychiatry* 19(1956):173-195

Lifton RJ, *Thought Reform and the Psychology of Totalism: A Study of "Brainwashing" in China*. Chapel Hill and London: The University of North Carolina Press, 1961

Light AB, and Torrance EG, "Opiate Addiction VI: The Effects of Abrupt Withdrawal Followed by Readministration of Morphine in Human Addicts, with Special References to the Composition of the Blood, the Circulation and the Metabolism." *Archives of Internal Medicine* 44(1929):1-16. cited from Peele (1985)

Ludwig AM, and Lyle WH, "The Experimental Production of Narcotic Drug Effects and Withdrawal Symptoms Through Hypnosis." *The International Journal of Clinical and Experimental Hypnosis* 12(1964):1-17

MacAndrew C, "The Differentiation of Male Alcoholic Outpatients from Nonalcoholic Psychiatric Outpatients by Means of the MMPI." *Journal of Studies on Alcohol* 26(1965):238-246

MacMillan E, *Seeking and Finding*. New York & London: Harper & Brothers, 1933

Maidman MM, "Notes and Comment: Normal Drinking in Recovered Alcohol Addicts." *Quarterly Journal of Studies on Alcohol* 24(1963):733-735

Marlatt GA, Demming B, and Reid JB, "Loss of Control Drinking in Alcoholics: An Experimental Analogue." *Journal of Abnormal Psychology* 81(1973):233-241

Marlatt GA, Kosturn CF, and Lang AR, "Provocation to Anger and Opportunity for Retaliation as Determinants of Alcohol Consumption in Social Drinkers." *Journal of Abnormal Psychology* 84(1975):652-659

Marlatt GA, and Gordon JR, "Determinants of Relapse: Implications for the Maintance of Behavior Change." in *Behavioral Medicine: Changing Health Lifestyles*, pp. 410-452, New York: Brunner/Mazel, 1980

Marshall M, *Weekend Warriors*, Palo Alto, Ca.: Mayfield, 1979. cited from Marlatt GA, "Alcohol, the Magic Elixir: Stress, Expectancy, and the Transformation of Emotional States," in *Stress and Addiction*, vol. 3, p. 302-322

Minogue SJ, "Alcoholics Anonymous." *The Medical Journal of Australia* May 8(1948):586-587

Nace EP, *The Treatment of Alcoholism*. New York: Brunner/Mazel, 1987

Peele S, *The Meaning of Addiction: Compulsive Experience and Its Interpretation*. Lexington, Mass.: Lexington Books, 1985

Peele S, *The Diseasing of America: Addiction Treatment Out of Control* Lexington, Mass.:Lexington Books, 1989

Pittman B, *AA: The Way it Began* Seattle: Glen Abbey books, 1988

Polich JM, "Patterns of Remission in Alcoholism," pp. 95-112. In *Alcoholism Treatment in Transition*. Edwards SG, and Grant M, editors. London: Croom Helm, 1980

Polich JM, Armor DJ, and Braiker HB, *The Course of Alcoholism: Four Years After Treatment* (Rand Reports four year follow-up). New York: Wiley (1981)

Robins LN, Davis DJ, and Goodwin DW, "Drug Use by U.S. Army Enlisted Men in Vietnam: A Follow-up on their Return Home." *American Journal of Epidemiology* 99(1974):235-249

Rohan WP, Comment on "The N.C.A. Criteria for the Diagnosis of Alcoholism; an Empirical Evaluation Study." *Journal of Studies on Alcohol* 39(1978):211-218

Rozin P, Poritsky S, and Stosky R, "American Children with Reading Problems can Easily Learn to Read English Represented by Chinese Characters." *Science* 171(1971):1264-1267

Russell JA, and Bond CR, "Individual Differences in Beliefs Concerning Emotions Conducive to Alcohol Use." *Journal of Studies on Alcohol* 41(1980)753-759

Sanchez-Craig M, "Random Assignment to Abstinence and Controlled Drinking in a Cognitive-Behavioral Program: Short-Term Effects on Drinking Behavior." *Addictive Behaviors* 5(1980):35-39

Sanchez-Craig M, Annis HM, Bornet AR, and MacDonald KR, "Random Assignment to Abstinence and Controlled Drinking: Evaluation of a Cognitive-Behavioral Program for Problem Drinkers." *Journal of Consulting and Clinical Psychology* 52(1984):390-403

Sanchez-Craig M, and Lei M, "Disadvantages of Imposing the Goal of Abstinence on Problem Drinkers: an empirical study." *British Journal of Addiction.* 81(1986):505-512

Schaeffer HH, "A Cultural Delusion of Alcoholics." *Psychological Reports* 29(1971):587-589

Schweitzer RD, and Lawton PA, "Drug Abusers' Perceptions of their Parents." *British Journal of Addiction* 84(1989):309-314

Seligman MEP, *Helplessness: On Depression, Development, and Death*. New York: W. H. Freeman and Company, 1975

Steele CM, and Josephs RA, "Drinking Your Troubles Away II: An Attention-Allocation Model of Alcohol's Effect on Psychological Stress." *Journal of Abnormal Psychology* 97(1988):196-205

Stewart RM, and Brown RI, "An Outcome Study of Gamblers Anonymous," *British Journal of Psychiatry* 152(1988):284-288

Szasz TS, *The Manufacture of Madness*. New York: Harper & Row, 1977

Tarter RE, "Are There Inherited Behavioral Traits That Predispose to Substance Abuse?" *Journal of Consulting and Clinical Psychology* 56(1988):189-196

Temple MT, and Fillmore KM, "The Variability of Drinking Patterns and Problems among Young Men, Age 16-31: A Longitudinal Study." *The International Journal of the Addictions* 20(1986):1595-1620

Thomsen R, *Bill W.* New York: Harper & Row, 1975

Thornton-Duesbery JP, *The Open Secret of MRA: An examination of Mr. Driberg's 'critical examination' of Moral Re-Armament.* London: Blandford Press, 1964

Vaillant GE, 1983a. *The Natural History of Alcoholism.* Cambridge, London: Harvard University Press, 1983

Vaillant GE, 1983b. "Can Alcoholics Go Back to 'Social' Drinking?" *Harvard Medical School Health Letter* Oct(1983):3-5

Walter HA *Soul-Surgery.* Oxford: The Oxford Group, 1932

White FW and Porter TL, "Self Concept Reports among Hospitalized Alcoholics during Early Periods of Sobriety." *Journal of Counseling Psychology* 13(1966):352-355

Wilson GT, "The Effects of Alcohol on Human Sexual Behavior." *Advances in Substance Abuse* 2(1981):3-40

Wray I, and Dickerson MG, "Cessation of High Frequency Gambling and 'Withdrawal' Symptoms." *British Journal of Addiction* 76(1981):401-405

Zinberg NE, and Robertson JA, *Drugs and the Public.* New York: Simon & Schuster, 1972. Cited from Peele (1985)

Index

Titles of Interest

ADDICTION, CHANGE & CHOICE: THE NEW VIEW OF ALCOHOLISM, by Vince Fox. This ground breaking book covers nearly every important question and controversy in the alcoholism field—what is alcoholism? is it a disease? is it caused by nature or nurture? can "alcoholics" learn to drink socially? how effective is AA? are there better alternatives to AA?
ISBN 0-9613289-7-5 ◆ 256 pp. ◆ $14.95

ALCOHOL: HOW TO GIVE IT UP AND BE GLAD YOU DID (second edition), by Philip Tate. This newly revised, popular cognitive-behavioral self-help book is practical, comprehensive, and easy to use. This book includes chapters on overcoming low self-esteem, depression, and stress, attending self-help groups, and living a better life after quitting.
ISBN 1-884365-10-8 ◆ 224 pp. ◆ $12.95

ALCOHOLICS ANONYMOUS: CULT OR CURE? (second edition), by Charles Bufe. The first critical history/analysis of AA ever published in book form. Well-researched, painstakingly documented. The greatly expanded second edition includes a new chapter on the treatment industry plus new appendixes on coerced AA attendance and the secular alternatives to AA.
ISBN 1-884365-12-4 ◆ 192 pp. ◆ $11.95

THE REAL AA: BEHIND THE MYTH OF 12-STEP RECOVERY, by Ken Ragge. Without doubt the best description/analysis of the AA indoctrination process ever written, and an excellent complement to Charles Bufe's *Alcoholics Anonymous: Cult or Cure?* Where Bufe concentrates on history and ideology, Ragge concentrates on psychology.
ISBN ◆ 1-884365-14-0 232 pp. ◆ $12.95

MAIL ORDERS—PLEASE LIST ITEMS ORDERED. For U.S. and overseas surface, add the amounts for items ordered, add $2.50 S/H (per order—not per item), and send a check or money order to **SEE SHARP PRESS, P.O. Box 1731, Tucson, AZ 85702-1731.** Arizona residents please add 5% sales tax. For credit card orders call **1-800-533-0301, 9 am to 5 pm CST.**

# OF COPIES	TITLE	PRICE
		TOTAL

Print Name _____

Address _____

City_____ State _____ Zip _____